Nature Unbound

Nature Unbound

Conservation, Capitalism and the Future of Protected Areas

Dan Brockington, Rosaleen Duffy and Jim Igoe

publishing for a sustainable future

London • Washington, DC

First published by Earthscan in the UK and USA in 2008
Reprinted 2010

ISBN 978-1-84407-440-2 paperback
      978-1-84407-441-9 hardback

Typeset by Domex e-data Pvt Ltd
Printed and bound in the UK by TJ International Ltd, Padstow
Cover design by Dominic Forbes

For a full list of publications please contact:

Earthscan
Dunstan House
14a St Cross Street
London, EC1N 8XA, UK
Tel: +44 (0)20 7841 1930
Fax: +44 (0)20 7242 1474
Email: earthinfo@earthscan.co.uk
Web: **www.earthscan.co.uk**

Earthscan publishes in association with the International Institute
for Environment and Development

A catalogue record for this book is available from the British Library

Library of Congress Cataloging-in-Publication Data has been applied for.

Contents

List of Figures, Tables and Boxes

Figures

Tables

Boxes

Preface

Writing about conservation is never straightforward. Describing and analysing conservation policies, and particularly the development of protected areas (national parks, game reserves, forest reserves and the like), can lead to intense argument. For some people the story of wildlife and landscape conservation is a story of progress. It is about the fight to persuade societies and governments that it is important to protect nature. This tale makes compelling reading, for while conservation legislation has made significant gains in many parts of the world, its enforcement is weaker and its failures are permanent. There are no more passenger pigeons, dodos or quagga left in the world, and we are currently facing a major extinction spasm. Conservationists are always racing against time, and often doing battle with titanic forces such as population growth or industrial development. Recording this history means following invigorating, compelling, but sometimes tragic struggles.

Some of the greatest literature in conservation is told in this way. In Roderick Nash's classic book *Wilderness and the American Mind* (2001), protected areas are firmly equated with progress. For Nash, the preservation of wilderness in national parks and protected areas is the US's greatest idea and export. Wilderness and its protection in parks is a good thing, and the historian's task is to document the success of humanity in learning about and taking up the model. Nash cheers the successes of the parks movement and decries their failures.[1] He imagines futures where people are concentrated into a relatively few places from where they can travel to vast wilderness areas (if they pass wilderness entrance exams). Similarly Weiner's account of conservation in the Soviet Union emphasizes the bravery of conservation scientists and the perfidy of their opponents. The story of protected areas' demise and revival in the Soviet Union is told as one of courage, death and resurrection (Weiner, 1988, 1999). In both Russia and the US this version of conservation's history is a popular widely received account. Protected areas and the conservation policies that support them are viewed as unquestionably good things. Anything that hinders them is bad, those who defend them are heroes.

But, alternatively, and simultaneously, the story of protected areas could be told as a tragic record of failure, error and underachievement, notwithstanding the extraordinary effort and energy selflessly devoted to it. Bill Adams, in his history of the conservation movement *Against Extinction*, observes that thus far the movement has not done well enough. He notes that the '[t]he 20th century saw conservation's creation, but nature's decline' (Adams, 2004, p231). He argues that unless conservationists can restore people's relationship to the wild then the movement will lose its lifeblood and vigour, such that 'even if the diverse jewels of the earth are "saved", we will still face a gloomy trudge through the new century accompanied by the steady leaching of natural diversity on every hand' (Adams, 2004, p231).

Combine these problems with the protests that parks and protected areas occasion in so many parts of the world and the history of protected areas does not look so good. A strong body of critical literature has arisen, which questions diverse aspects of conservation practice and history. Some authors question conservation's colonial and imperial roots (Mackenzie, 1988; Neumann, 1998). Others portray contemporary conservation practice as a murky political enterprise rather than the struggle of a just cause (Anderson and Grove, 1987; Bonner, 1993; Duffy, 2000; Steinhart, 2006). Else they challenge the marginalization and disempowerment that rural groups experience because of conservation (Jeanrenaud, 2002; Anderson and Berglund, 2003; Walley, 2004; West, 2006) or the transformations it entails (Duffy, 2002; Igoe, 2004b). Some document the material and psychological hardships of eviction from protected areas (West and Brechin, 1991; Brockington, 2002). Many have been particularly concerned with the impact of conservation policies on indigenous peoples (Gray et al, 1998; Colchester and Erni, 1999; Spence, 1999; Jacoby, 2001; Chatty and Colchester, 2002; Colchester, 2003). Finally, some collections compile diverse concerns about all these aspects (Ghimire and Pimbert, 1997; Brechin et al, 2003).

These criticisms have occasionally been met with anger (e.g. Spinage, 1998), but more often bewilderment – how can a good thing like conservation be subject to these criticisms? The conservation movement has often had particular difficulty incorporating criticisms of the negative social consequences of protected areas. One prominent conservationist, after reading a critique that grouped biodiversity conservation together with the extractive industry as 'culture-wrecking institutions', wondered out loud:

> One must ask by what alchemy have the names of those who see themselves as defenders of the planet's biological heritage come to be linked in the same breath with the names of those who are more appropriately seen as its degraders.
>
> (Agrawal and Redford, 2007, p.12)

Equally critics of parks, including ourselves, are often indignant at the wrongs being done in the name of a good cause, and voices quickly become shrill. As we shall see below this often means that the argument about, for example, the effectiveness of parks or community conservation has not asked the right questions. The debate risks getting bogged down in asking whether parks 'work' or not, rather than asking what are the social and ecological gains and losses that result from the changes that parks bring about, who experiences these gains and losses, and in what ways?

We have been among the critical voices above, but our purpose here is not to justify those views, or criticize conservation's defenders. This book is not intended as another brick in the wall dividing two camps. Rather it has been heartening to see in the last five years an increasing rapprochement between conservation advocates and their critics. Old polarizations have broken down. Social scientists have proliferated in conservation meetings, and publish in conservation journals. Amongst conservation's critics there are senior voices calling for constructive engagement with conservationists (Brosius, 2006), just as there are senior conservationists calling for a better engagement with social scientists (Chan et al, 2007).

This book is intended as a contribution to that process. Accordingly we do not take a stand as critics or fans of protected areas here. Rather we ask how they have distributed fortune and misfortune between different groups and we compare the versions of these histories that the winners circulate, and those the losers remember. We ask by what means are conservation goals achieved, the broader processes with which it is intertwined, and the consequences, often unexpected, of these interactions. Addressing these issues will give us a better idea of what a conserved world would look like, and who will enjoy living in it.

Many people have helped us during the course of writing this book; their support, comments and critical engagement with earlier drafts and the ideas therein, has been invaluable: Kathy Homewood, Bill Adams, Sian Sullivan, Jon Hutton, Dilys Roe, Grazia Borrini-Feyerabend, Taghi Favor, Phil Franks, Kai Schmidt-Soltau, Ashish Kothari, Lee Risby, Elinor Ostrom, Tanya Hayes, Kent Redford, Katrina Brandon, Fred Nelson, Paige West, James Carrier, Christo Fabricius, Eric Pawson, Garth Cant, Colin Filer, Kartik Shanker, Mahesh Rangarajan, Meera Oomen, Ravi Chellam, Vasant Saberwal, Barney Dickson, Jo Elliot, Matt Walpole, David Thomas, Bhaskar Vira, Monique Borgerhoff Mulder, Pete Copollilo, David Wilkie, Tim Davenport, Neil Burgess, Libby Lester, Graham Huggan, Richard Ladle, Paul Jepson, Lindsey Gillson, Kathy Willis, Hassan Sachedina, Emmanuel Nuesiri, Timothy Doyle, John Urry, Liz Bondi, Melissa Leach, Christopher Clapham, Feargal Cochrane, Marina Novelli, Will Wolmer, Jeanette Manjengwa, Steven Brechin and Marshall Murphree.

Colleagues and doctoral students at the University of Manchester have proved to be invaluable sounding boards for some of the ideas contained in this book; we would like to thank the Society and Environment Research Group (SERG), especially Noel Castree, Tony Bebbington, Gavin Bridge, Admos Chimhowu and Phillip Woodhouse, John O'Neill and Erik Swyngedouw; we would also like to thank the Environment and Development Reading Group (especially Katie Scholfield, George Holmes, Hilary Gilbert, Lorraine Moore, Lisa Ficklin, Lindsay Stringer, Rupert Frederichsen and Tomas Frederiksen). We must also thank Bharath Sundaram and colleagues at the Ashoka Trust for Research in Ecology and the Environment (ATREE) at whose field station in the Biligiri Rangaswami Temple Wildlife Sanctuary this manuscript was completed.

We are also grateful for the support of funders for our work: Dan Brockington held an Economic and Social Research Council (ESRC) Research Fellowship on the Social Impacts of Protected Areas (RES-000-27-0174). Rosaleen Duffy held three ESRC grants to examine Transfrontier Conservation, illicit mining networks and conservation, and ecotourism and charismatic animals (grant numbers RES-000-22-0342, 00-22-3013 and RES-000-22-2599). Jim Igoe held a Fulbright teaching and research grant for the 2005–2006 academic year, during which time he taught at the College of African Wildlife Management in Mweka, Tanzania, and conducted research in the privatization of conservation.

Note

1   In the fourth edition of his celebrated book Nash writes: 'I will veer away from the hallowed (if always somewhat hollow) traditions of academic objectivity. I have tenure now; in fact I am retired! I don't have to conform to those canons of impartiality that my graduate school mentors valued so highly. So I can come out of the closet. I like wilderness, and although I wrote as a scholar about its history, I'm also a fan and an advocate.' Nash, R. (2001) *Wilderness and the American Mind.* New Haven: Yale University Press. *Nota bene:* hollow indeed, why not declare your stance from the start?

List of Acronyms and Abbreviations

ANGAP	Association Nationale pour la Gestion des Aires Protégées
ANWR	Arctic National Wildlife Refuge
ATREE	Ashoka Trust for Research in Ecology and the Environment
AWF	African Wildlife Fund
BI	Birdlife International
BINGO	big international non-governmental organization
CAMPFIRE	Communal Areas Management Plan for Indigenous Resources
CAR	comprehensive, adequate, representative (protection)
CBD	Convention on Biodiversity
CBNRM	Community Based Natural Resource Management
CBT	community-based tourism
CCAD	Central American Commission on Environment and Development
CC Africa	Conservation Corporation Africa
CI	Conservation International
CITES	Convention on International Trade in Endangered Species of Wild Fauna and Flora
COP	Conference of the Parties
CPR	common pool resource
CPR	common property regime
DDT	dichlorodiphenyl trichloroethane
DRC	Democratic Republic of the Congo
ESRC	Economic and Social Research Council
FSC	Forest Stewardship Council
GCF	Global Conservation Fund
GEF	Global Environment Facility
GIS	geographic information system
ICD	Integrated Conservation with Development
IDCP	Integrated Development with Conservation Projects
IFI	International financial institution
IFRI	International Forestry Resources and Institutions
IMF	International Monetary Fund
IPA	Indigenous Protected Area
IPCC	Inter-Governmental Panel on Climate Change
IPZ	Intensive Protection Zone

IUCN	International Union for Conservation of Nature
MBRS	Mesoamerican Barrier Reef System Project
MNC	multinational corporations
NEAP	National Environmental Action Plan
NES	National Eco-tourism Strategy
NGO	non-governmental organization
PEC	Problem Elephant Control
PEFC	Pan European Forest Certification
SAP	Structural Adjustment Programme
SERG	Society and Environment Research Group
SPWFE	Society for the Preservation of the Wild Fauna of the Empire
TFCA	Transfrontier Conservation Area
TNC	The Nature Conservancy
UNEP	United Nations Environment Programme
UNWTO	United Nations World Tourism Organization
USAID	United States Agency for International Development
VSO	Voluntary Service Overseas
WCMC	World Conservation Monitoring Centre
WCS	Wildlife Conservation Society
WDPA	World Database of Protected Areas
WSSD	World Summit on Sustainable Development
WWF	World Wide Fund for Nature

1

Nature Unbound

A good place to begin a study of wildlife and landscape conservation is to look at trends in the growth of protected areas in the last few years. Protected areas are all the national parks, game reserves, national monuments, forest reserves and the myriad other places and spaces for which states provide special protection from human interference. There is a curious pattern in their recent history, which we have shown in Figure 1.1. The period of most dramatic growth was between 1985 and 1995. While these data have to be treated with caution, the pattern is striking and its timing odd.[1] For that time was also the period when neoliberal economic policies were dominant globally (Peet and Watts, 1996). Neoliberalism is based on the ideas of reducing the power, reach and interference of government (expressed in the catchphrase 'small government') and giving industry greater freedom and less red tape. Neoliberal policies were favoured by the powerful financial institutions, particularly the International Monetary Fund and World Bank, with tremendous influence over the details of many governments' policies through the implementation of economic liberalization in the form of Structural Adjustment Programmes (SAPs) (Clapham, 1996; Harrison, 2004, 2005). Yet it was precisely when pressures to reduce government were greatest that the extent of state control and restriction on land and natural resource use increased more dramatically than any other period.

Could there be a mechanism behind the pattern, or is it mere coincidence? Could there be anything about the nature of modern capitalism that seems to favour the establishment of protected areas? One explanation is that conservationists have collectively responded to the threats and damage of contemporary capitalism by securing lands from development. In the face of increased development pressures they have risen to the challenge, identifying the places that need protection, fighting and winning the political battles required for governments to support their plans. They have created international conventions to further their cause, strengthened conservation and wildlife departments in numerous countries to fight for nature, as well as nurturing and training state actors throughout the world to champion conservation causes in their respective countries (Frank et al, 2000).

There is some truth to this idea, many protected areas were set up explicitly to limit development and had significant success in doing so. Fights to save places such as Jervis Bay near Sydney in Australia, and the West Coast Forests in South Island, New Zealand, resulted in new, or stronger, protected areas. Moreover these fights have been defining moments in the history of environmentalism. The

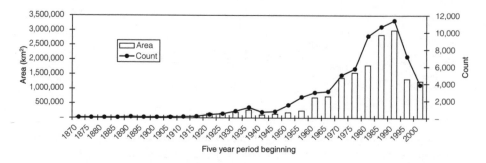

Figure 1.1 *The global growth of protected areas*

Source: The World Database of Protected Areas (2005)

successful campaigns to prevent the construction of the Franklin Dam in Tasmania, and the dams proposed in the Dinosaur National Monument in the US, strengthened and invigorated the movement internationally. Conversely, in India for example, extractive and timber corporations find that protected areas limit their operations and have actively campaigned for their denotification (Saberwal et al, 2001).

Many contemporary battles are also fought on these lines, while expanding to include the question of indigenous land rights. For example current disputes about oil exploration in Alaska and its impact on the Arctic National Wildlife Refuge (ANWR) represent a complex mix of national security, indigenous rights, notions of wilderness and global energy supply (Lovecraft, 2007). The ANWR was established in 1960 to conserve wildlife populations in their natural habitats.[2] Supporters of opening ANWR for oil exploration have claimed that it could reduce dependence on oil supplies from the Middle East and that current oil installations in ANWR have been designed and sited to take account of wildlife populations. Critics are adamant that the area should remain as a 'pristine wilderness', while other interest groups have lobbied for the rights of indigenous groups to maintain their access to fishing grounds.[3] The creation of the Kuna Yala Reserve in Panama united conservationists and indigenous peoples in the protection of indigenous homelands from the environmentally destructive spread of homesteaders and cattle ranchers (Chapin, 2000). Alliances between the Kayapo Indians and international conservationists, beginning in the 1980s and championed by the rock star Sting, have thus far protected Brazil's Xingu National Park from flooding by proposed hydroelectric dams along the Xingu River (Turner, 1993; Nugent, 1994).

But the problem with trying to interpret the spread of conservation in terms of successfully fighting and resisting capitalist development is that it suggests a confrontational stance to capitalism in the conservation movement. Dramatic confrontation against construction projects remains the leitmotif of groups like

Greenpeace. But, in the main, conservation is more conciliatory and accommodating of the needs of capitalism than it once was (Daily and Walker, 2000). Fights to save places have given way to complicated geographic information system (GIS) software models, which distribute protected areas optimally across the landscape according to such priorities as rarity and vulnerability while minimizing cost. The more sophisticated GIS models specifically include human economic and social needs to reduce the potential for dispute (Sarkar et al, 2006; Wilson et al, 2006, 2007). Many conservationists now work to a simple pragmatic mandate: cooperating with the powers that be in order to protect nature. From this perspective, the growth of protected areas under neoliberal regimes is a testimony to their success in working with the system, speaking comfortable truths to power.

But this again is only part of the story. For it suggests a distance between the values and practices of biodiversity conservation and those of neoliberal capitalism. According to this explanation, conservationists compromise with the demands of capitalism, with humanity's hunger for resources and industries' demand for profit, because they have to. But their own values and priorities remain distinct from these dominant forces and values. We do not believe that this is accurate. It is more appropriate to recognize that capitalist policies and values, and often neoliberal policies and values, pervade conservation practice; indeed in some parts of the world they infest it.

If that seems far-fetched, consider the current situation in Laos where the World Bank is currently supporting a US$50 billion dollar project to build a series of dams on the Mekong River. The dams will eventually supply energy to Laos and its neighbours, most notably Thailand, stimulating and sustaining economic growth for years to come. But they come at a huge ecological cost. Thousands of square kilometres of lowland tropical rainforest will be lost, and are indeed now being logged by the Laos military to ensure that as much valuable timber as possible is extracted before the waters rise. But this project has the support of the International Union for Conservation of Nature (IUCN) and the World Wide Fund for Nature (WWF, which was one of the organizations that was instrumental in protests against the Xingu Dams in the 1980s). These organizations are able to support the dams in Laos because the project also involves setting up new protected areas in the highlands, safeguarding both the watersheds and the valuable biodiversity therein. Ironically, amidst all the destruction, this is a project that will vastly increase Laos' protected area network, for it had hardly any prior to this project (Goldman, 2001b).

Situations like the one in Laos are not new. In the 1970s and 1980s the donor-backed Acclerated Mahweli Development Project in Sri Lanka partitioned the landscape into dams, irrigation fields and national parks and moved people around accordingly (Levy, 1989; Stegeborn, 1996; Gamburd, 2000). More recently two new national parks (Campo Maun and Mban et Djerem) have been set up in Cameroon in mitigation for the damage caused by the new

Chad–Cameroon oil pipeline, again funded by the World Bank. It is increasingly expected that large projects that damage the environment in some way should provide some sort of compensation. And where they destroy habitat it is only logical that they should protect another place to make good the wrong done. And it is only logical that the developers should seek the advice of conservation experts in the IUCN or WWF to help them to do this properly. Nevertheless the end result is that conservation and capitalism are allying mutually to reshape the world.

It is even possible for mining to increase the amount of space that conservationists find available to conserve. In many parts of the world mining companies are given concessions by governments – large plots of land that they need to drill for oil or mine for ore or gems. The space required for their operations can often be only a small part of the concession. But the remaining land is restricted to local hunters and farmers and can contain untouched vegetation and wildlife (e.g. Laurance et al, 2006). There are also cases of more fundamental alliances forming in which conservation interests and mining interests are (apparently) united to bring profound change to landscapes and livelihoods. Consider the development of the ilmenite (titanium dioxide) mine in the Fort Dauphin area of Madagascar by Qit Minerals Madagascar (80 per cent owned by Rio Tinto and 20 per cent owned by the Government of Madagascar). Rio Tinto claims that the project will provide the catalyst for 'broader economic development in the country while providing conservation opportunities' and it will provide 'net positive benefits, to biodiversity conservation.[4] The company has set aside zones in the mining project for conservation, which will form part of the national system of protected areas in Madagascar. It also set up an ecotourism project, which has been running since 2000, to allow local communities to benefit from the conservation initiatives established by Rio Tinto.[5]

The titanium mine is a perfect example of the global networks that allow the objectives of conservation and capitalism to go hand in hand. Qit Minerals Madagascar has been working with a range of environmental organizations since 1996 to develop social and environmental projects to mitigate the impact of the mine, including the Royal Botanical Gardens at Kew, Missouri Botanical Gardens, Earthwatch and the Smithsonian Institute.[6] Indeed, other global conservation organizations operating in Madagascar have taken the decision that they need to work with Qit Minerals Madagascar to gain concessions to conservation and speak in terms that the Malagasy government and mining companies will understand. Non-governmental organizations (NGOs) such as Conservation International have argued that the areas set aside for conservation will be more lucrative in the long term through the development of ecotourism (Duffy, 2008b).

On the other hand, the mine has been severely criticized by Friends of the Earth who argue that the project was threatening unique forest resources and leaving local people struggling to survive in the area affected by the mine. Other researchers note that the case for the mine's proposed protected areas was based in part on the belief that forests needed protection from local people who were cutting down too many trees. However, satellite data analysis of these forests suggests that this may be a simplistic rendering of environmental change (Ingram, 2004; Ingram et al, 2005). Local communities have complained that the compensation payments are not sufficient since land prices have risen in that area and promises of employment have not materialized.[7]

These cases are stark examples of conservation and capitalism re-categorizing the landscape together. In many other cases the links and continuities between the two are more subtle – and also more pervasive. They are about changing attitudes to wildlife and landscapes, about introducing markets and commodifying nature, about adapting tourists' expectations, and tourists' hosts, and about modifying the societies and communities that live close to valuable nature, about the role models and inspirations that make us conservationists in the first place.

Sklair (2001) has examined the convergence of environmentalism and capitalism in his analysis of the 'transnational capitalist class'. According to Sklair, this class is composed of corporate executives, bureaucrats and politicians, professionals, merchants and the media who collectively act to promote global economic growth based on the 'cultural-ideology of consumerism'. He argues that this class is effectively in charge of globalization but also has to resolve crises that arise from its global growth strategy. With respect to environmental problems, he argues, following Gramsci, that corporations and what we call 'mainstream conservation' have colluded to form a 'sustainable development historical bloc' (Sklair, 2001, p8). The historical bloc offers solutions to the environmental crises that are inherent to global consumer capitalism, while all the time maintaining and strengthening an accompanying 'consumerist ideology'. Indeed, increased consumption becomes central to the solutions (p216). In this book we extend this perspective to argue that the global proliferation of protected areas and related conservation strategies reflect the emergence of this historical bloc. We argue that although these strategies may limit the growth of industry in some contexts, they simultaneously offer solutions to crises of the global growth strategy that makes the spread of industrial enterprise possible in the first place. Protected areas create new types of value that are essential to the global consumer economy.

In sum, conservation is not merely about resisting capitalism, or about reaching necessary compromises with it. Conservation and capitalism are shaping nature and society, and often in partnership. In the name of conservation, rural communities will reorganize themselves, and change their use and management of wildlife and landscapes. They ally with safari hunters and tourist companies to sell the experience of new tourist products on the international market. In the name of conservation, mining companies, governments, international financial institutions and some conservation organizations work together to achieve common goals that suit the interests of conservation and capitalism. This set of relationships can be counter-intuitive, yet it is clear that they are forming powerful alliances, and can overcome local objections and protest.

As these types of interventions spread and become more sophisticated, it becomes increasingly difficult to determine if we are describing conservation with capitalism as its instrument or capitalism with conservation as its instrument. The lines between conservation and capitalism blur. While it is debatable whether this alliance of conservation and capitalism is capable of saving the world, there is no doubt that it is most capable of remaking and recreating it. One of the central premises of this book, therefore, is that dealing with the types of problems conservationists face will become easier if we recognize the dynamics of capitalism of which they are part. Similarly, understanding the problems conservation causes, how protected areas distribute fortune and misfortune, requires an analysis of the bigger picture of how they are incorporated into the broader economy.

In this book we will be describing, analysing and documenting these changes. We will be considering who wins and who loses from these processes, and what their consequences are for conservationists' own goals. The book is based on two questions, and structured by two tasks. The questions are:

1   In what ways do conservation policies and conservation interventions make wild nature more valuable to capitalist economies?
2   With what consequences is this value realized?

The tasks are first, to examine existing knowledge that social scientists have been creating in recent years about conservation policy and practice. A great deal has been written, and an overview is important. Our substantive chapters address the role of conservation NGOs and the international apparatus of conservation, indigenous people and local knowledge, fortress conservation, community conservation, ecotourism, and market-based conservation. We examine the different debates in each, summarizing existing knowledge and outlining unanswered questions. Second, at the end of the book, we integrate these into a broader argument, exploring the connections between these disparate processes, their contradictions and their future implications.

Conservation and conservation strategies

Can we talk about *all* forms of conservation thus, and *all* conservation strategies? The movement is diverse and referring to 'conservationists' or 'the conservation community' implies a unity of thought, values and practice that is simply not found. Conservation is an incredibly broad church and one that is riven with conflict. Within journals and meetings and in individual campaigns there are sharp disagreements about ethics, morals, practices and compromises.

There are conservationists who find solace in wild places without human presence, and those who love peopled landscapes. There are conservationists for whom landscape is irrelevant and only species matter, and conservationists whose concern is strictly their love of particular places and for whom global considerations are not particularly relevant. There are ardent conservationists whose experience of conservation needs and conserved places is virtual and vicarious, enjoyed through books, films, the internet and the celebrities who endorse them, there are those who live for their fieldwork, those who protest and campaign, those who educate and those who push policy. There are conservation bureaucrats who sacrifice family and field time to trawl a circuit of international meetings, and those who flourish in such environments.

There are particularly deep divisions about some issues. Consider for example the debate about trade in live animals or their products. The World Parrot Trust insists that the trade in wild birds is repugnant, resulting in many deaths for each live animal moved, and fuels the loss of species (Gilardi, 2006). Others suggest that it can raise funds for conservation, and bans merely drive illegal trades underground where it is harder to monitor (Cooney and Jepson, 2006; Roe, 2006). The fight about the ivory trade causes deep divisions in the conservation movement. The proliferation of elephants in southern Africa has resulted in over-crowding in some reserves and culls in others. There are powerful calls to make ivory trade legal in order to raise more money for conservation. Whereas in East Africa, especially Kenya, a strong stance against the ivory trade has itself been a powerful fund-raising tool.

There is also disagreement about the use of violence or compromise for conservation causes. The Sea Shepherds are most effective in their use of limpet mines to combat whaling. They and Greenpeace fight regular battles with whalers on the high seas. Earth First! produced a field guide to monkey-wrenching (named after Edward Abbey's book *The Monkey Wrench Gang*) with instructions on salting dirt air strips (to attract wildlife to stir up the ground and make the strip unusable) and spiking trees with lumps of metal to injure, or deter lumberjacks. Major conservation organizations are cooperating with many large corporations to generate revenues, else win control over lands that, for example, extractive industries control from their concessions but which they do not require for the purposes of their mining. They are opposed by a radical fringe who insist that they have sold out and that true conservation should be about resisting resource use and high-consumption lifestyles.

It is important to distinguish conservation causes from concern for animal rights and individual animals. For example, animal rights campaigners will insist that killing animals for their skins or food is wrong, regardless of the funds any business can generate. Hence researchers combating the bushmeat trade in West Africa who recognize that people will need to eat wild meat and wish to control its supply and production more effectively are at odds with animal rights activists who wish to stop the trade entirely. In Kenya safari hunting has been banned, whereas in the rest of East Africa and in southern Africa it sustains a multi-million dollar business (Lindsey et al, 2007), with much opportunity for revenues to reach local communities (Novelli et al, 2006). The fox hunting ban in the UK is condemned by many country residents as an imposition by urbanites who do not understand how they relate to nature. Animal rights campaigners have also prevented the eradication of a grey squirrel population that had established itself in northern Italy. The grey squirrel is native to North America, but is larger and more competitive than the European red squirrel and tends to replace it where the two come into contact. It is the dominant species of squirrel in most of the UK. The resultant spread of the grey squirrel from their foothold in Italy will cause suffering to red squirrels on the continent, and other species on which the grey squirrels feed (Perry, 2004).

For conservationists combating the extinction crisis, the resources and political clout these causes enjoy can be frustrating. If scarce resources are directed at species that are relatively secure, or worse still, at individuals rather than species, the broader cause can suffer. The most recent case that best captures the feelings, and expense, at work arose in 2003 on South Uist, an island off the west coast of Scotland. The island is the home to breeding colonies of endangered birds, such as snipe, redshank, lapwing, dunlin and ringer plover which were threatened by a hedgehog population introduced in the 1970s by an individual seeking to control garden slugs. With no natural predators and light vehicle traffic, the hedgehog population grew to approximately 5000 by 2003.[8] Scottish Natural Heritage took the decision that hedgehogs had to be removed from the island, so they ordered a cull. However, the decision was highly unpopular with some sections of the community who formed Uist Hedgehog Rescue, which argued that the hedgehogs had a right to exist and that the cull was cruel. Their campaign attracted donations of over £30,000 from the public and attention from the *New York Times* and a Toronto radio station.[9] 'Operation Tiggywinkle' was launched, encouraging local residents to hand in hedgehogs for £5 per animal so that they could be flown to mainland Scotland and released in the wild there. (Representatives of Operation Tiggywinkle had negotiated a special 50 pence airfare for each animal with Highland Airways.) It is not at all clear how the moved animals, or the hedgehogs already resident in the recipient areas, fared as a result of the move.

It is also important to recognize the difference between conservation causes and broader environmental issues. Dowie (1996) observes that early conservation organizations and conservationists (who would have called themselves preservationists) were not concerned with 'environmental issues'. These come to the fore in the US in the latter half of the 20th century when concern about pollution, pesticides and energy become prominent, particularly after Rachel Carson published *Silent Spring* (Dowie, 1996, pp23–28). In practice there is often a good deal of overlap between broader environmental issues and more specific concerns about wildlife conservation. Chemicals like DDT concentrate up the food chain and damage the eggs of raptors, dirty rivers are lifeless, and carbon offset policies have profound implications for tropical forest conservation. Dowie notes that the major conservation organizations in the US have become environmental organizations too. Nonetheless it is important not to conflate conservation issues with more general environmental concerns.

We realize therefore that we are generalizing horribly when we talk about 'conservation' and 'conservationists'. We are especially concerned in this book with a particular historical and institutional strain of western conservation, not because we believe that it represents the full diversity of people who call themselves conservationists, but because it dominates the field of conservation in terms of ideology, practice and resources brought to bear in conservation interventions. The ideas and values of this dominant strain of conservation are perhaps most clearly represented in the larger conservation organizations which dominate conservation funding. Because of its powerful position, we refer to this historical/institutional strain as 'mainstream conservation'.

Mainstream conservation is best recognized by its distinctive collaborative legacy: cooperation and network building between specific groups and interests that became strengthened and institutionalized over time. The collaborative legacy of mainstream conservation has its roots in the American conservation movement and the creation of national parks in the American West at the end of the 19th century. As Tsing (2004, p100) explains, early American conservationists, like John Muir, pursued strategies that revolved around the enrolment of urban elites in nature conservation and corporate sponsorship. This was easier and more effective than gaining the support of local people, who often saw exclusionary approaches to conservation as inimical to their interests, and who tended to be viewed as culturally backwards despoilers of nature (see also Bonner, 1993; Neumann, 1998; Burnham, 2000; Jacoby, 2001; Igoe, 2004b). The global network of conservation institutions that emerged from this process, and in the context of European colonialism, bore much stronger affinity to the views and interests of a narrow group of western elites than to those of people living in or near to the places conserved. This situation is starkly visible in two ways: 1) the displacement of people by protected areas globally; and 2) the oft decried cultural/political divide between predominantly urban-based conservation organizations and rural communities (Saberwal et al, 2001).

Another important element of mainstream conservation's collaborative legacy is the continuous presence of business interests (the exploration that led to the creation of Yellowstone National Park was sponsored by a railroad company) and the consistent intertwining of states, private enterprise and philanthropy. This can be seen in the early involvement of Laurence Rockefeller in buying up land for the creation of national parks in Wyoming (Muchnick, 2007) and the US Virgin Islands (Fortwangler, 2007), and the continued involvement of Ted Turner in buying up land for national forests in the American West (Mutchler, 2007). In fact, protected areas and other types of conservation interventions in many parts of the world could not exist without private support (Fortwangler, 2007; Igoe and Brockington, 2007). From this perspective, it is not surprising that mainstream conservation, and all that it influences and implies, has allied with capitalism. It stands to reason, therefore, that the recent proliferation of protected areas described above is directly linked to an intensification of this collaborative legacy.

But notwithstanding the power of mainstream conservation there is still a wide diversity of conservation activity, strategy and intervention. One of the better mappings of the varieties of activities available is found in Nick Salafasky and colleague's work (2002), a modified version of which we show in Table 1. These authors divide conservation activities into protection and management, law and policy, education and incentives. Note that the divisions within the conservation movement do not map easily onto particular strategies. There are sharp divisions within the mainstream as to which strategy might work best in different situations. In this book we will write least in the coming pages about education and most about protection in parks, and the diverse alternatives to protection in parks generally called 'community conservation'. Salafsky and colleagues' typology is helpful, but note that economic aspects and incentives are restricted to the last column only. We, however, see all forms of conservation policy and intervention as changing the relationships between people and nature and people and each other in similar ways to these 'incentivizing' behaviours. Moreover in the laws, policies, educational ideas and mechanisms of protection there will be countless interactions with the economy and markets. Neoliberal conservation is not restricted to raw market forces alone.

Monique Borgerhoff Mulder and Pete Coppolillo (2005) have also offered a useful typology of conservation strategies (Figure 1.2). They find two axes differentiating most conservation projects. First there are projects which differentiate between use and preservation, second those which distinguish between centralized state control and devolved local control. They map many of the conservation strategies Salafsky and others describe onto this matrix.

Both typologies are helpful because they emphasise that parks and protected areas, while being an important part of conservation strategies, are but one aspect of them. Likewise community conservation measures are but one part of conservation strategies. There are many others and a conserved world will be increasingly transformed in all its aspects. We think protected areas are important because of the area of land that they cover and because of the consistencies in protected area policy that exist internationally. They deserve special attention. Similarly, diverse forms of community-based conservation will be geographically important simply because of the sheer number of people living in rural areas where natural resource management will be important and an important part of their livelihoods. More than 50 per cent of the world's population is rural and most of these people are found in the developing world. These also deserve special attention. But they are just two of many possible conservation initiatives.

Table 1.1 *A taxonomy of biodiversity conservation approaches and strategies*

Protection & Management	Law & Policy	Education & Awareness	Changing Incentives
Strictly Protected Areas *reserves & parks* *private parks*	**Legislation & Treaties** *developing international treaties* *lobbying governments*	**Formal Education** *developing school curricula* *teaching graduate students*	**Conservation Enterprises** *linked: e.g. ecotourism* *unlinked: e.g. jobs for poachers*
Managed Landscapes *conservation easements* *community-based management*	**Compliance & Watchdog** *developing legal standards* *monitoring compliance w/standards*	**Non-Formal Education** *media training for scientists* *public outreach via museums*	**Using Market Pressure** *certification: positive incentives* *boycotts: negative incentives*
Protected & Managed Species *bans on killing specific species* *management of habitat for species*	**Litigation** *criminal prosecution* *civil suits*	**Informal Education** *media campaigns* *community awareness raising*	**Economic Alternatives** *sustainable agriculture/ aquaculture promoting alternative products*
Species & Habitat Restoration *reintroducing predators* *recreating wetlands*	**Policy Development & Reform** *research on policy options* *devolution of control*	**Moral Confrontation** *civil disobedience* *monkeywrenching/ ecoterrorism*	**Conservation Payments** *quid-pro-quo performance payments* *debt-for-nature swaps*
Ex-Situ Protection *captive breeding* *gene banking*			**Non-Monetary Values** *spiritual, cultural, existence values links to human health*

Source: Adapted from Salafsky et al (2002). This table categorizes the types of tools available to conservation practitioners. Columns contain broad categories of tools. Each cell contains a broad *approach* (bold font) and then two examples of more specific *strategies* (italic font) under this approach. Reproduced with permission

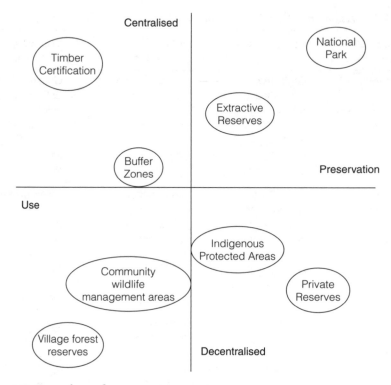

Figure 1.2 *A typology of conservation practice*

Source: Borgerhoff Mulder and Coppolillo (2005). Reproduced with permission

But just as important as the types of conservation strategy presented by these typologies are the processes and dynamics that produce the different strategies. Consider for example the relationships between conservation organizations and rural groups. There are many instances where conservation organizations provide valuable funds sought after by local groups (e.g. Murphree, 2005), which were well used and congruent with local objectives. There are other cases where they have fought with local groups against unjust regimes in defence of threatened environments (Hafild, 2005). Conversely Chapin (2004) and Dowie (2005, 2006) have alleged that large conservation NGOs are combining with corporate interests to the detriment of local landholders. Romero and Andrade (2004) have also criticized deals between conservation NGOs and timber companies, in which logging concessions are turned into conservation lands after timber extraction, because both land uses can deny resource use and exclude local groups.

To understand these alliances, conflicts and outcomes we must recognize that quite different conditions of government and civil society operate now compared to those that drove protected area formation in a pre-neoliberal era. Instead of discreet government departments, private enterprises, NGOs and communities, there are global networks that interpenetrate and elide these categories (Sklair, 2001; Igoe and Fortwangler, 2007). Such networks include people from the community level to the global headquarters of major corporations, multilateral agencies, and transnational conservation NGOs. Sunseri (2005) and Dzingirai (2003) have shown how these networks facilitate the exclusion and eviction of people from new conservation areas in Tanzania and Zimbabwe respectively.

Mbembe (2001) has argued that these networks are forged in conditions of fragmented state control. They are effectively bargains in which outsiders, such as conservation NGOs, bring money and other external resources, on which officials from impoverished states are highly dependent. The officials in turn bring the legitimacy and power of sovereignty – the means of coercion that make it possible to gain advantage in struggles over resources traditionally the exclusive purview of the state (Mbembe, 2001, p78). Mbembe called these arrangements 'private indirect government'.

Private indirect government is particularly significant to our argument because the data in Figure 1.1 may well be a substantial *underestimate* of the extent of conservation's territorial gains. These data omit private and community-based protected areas. Yet these are precisely the means by which the reach of conservation is extended in neoliberal regimes. Where conservation's neoliberalism is rolled out, new types of 'territorialization' emerge – demarcation of spaces within states for the purposes of controlling people and resources (Vandergeest and Peluso, 1995). This may be achieved through privatization (such as the extensive private protected areas in South Africa, Scotland and Patagonia). It may also be achieved by presenting collective legal titles to rural communities, allowing them to enter into business ventures with outside investors (Lemos and Agrawal, 2006, p310). Finally, it may be achieved through state-controlled territories that are made available to investors through rents and concessions. In all these processes elite global networks of government agents, NGOs, communities and their representatives and private enterprises can be strongly involved and profit from their involvement.

Finally a note about terminology and some things we will not be considering in such detail. Whole books have been written about trade and conservation, and the role of conservation conventions and international agreements, including for example Sara Oldfield (2002) *The Trade in Wildlife: Regulation for Conservation* and Jon Hutton and Barnabas Dickson (eds) (2000) *Endangered Species, Threatened Convention: The past, present and future of CITES*. We will be examining these, but not in as much detail as other sources. Attempts to reconcile conservation concerns with the development needs of the poorest are sometimes called Integrated Development with Conservation Projects (IDCPs) or Integrated Conservation with Development (ICD) (Wells et al, 1992; Barrett and Arcese, 1995; Wells et al, 1999). However, this terminology can be used in a confusing way. It can refer to donor-driven projects that try and support both the conservation sector and related development concerns in that geographical area.

These have experienced ample and justified criticism for being insufficiently integrated and failing to deliver on conservation (and often development objectives) (Wells et al, 1992; Wells et al, 1999). Sometimes the same terminology can refer to any scheme that advances both development and conservation objectives, be they donor driven or not. We eschew the term below. We prefer 'community conservation' referring to conservation initiatives that place some power in the hands of rural groups who live close to the resources in question – but can include all sorts of donor input into policy and its application.

The outline of the book

We will be covering a number of key issues in this book affecting conservation debates. Here we summarize chapter by chapter what they are and what we will be examining in each case.

We turn first to an account of the growth of protected areas historically and geographically, describing the main patterns in different regions of the world. Here we examine the power of the *idea* of protected areas. We note that there are historical and conceptual limitations of current notions of protected areas, and the difficulties of listing them in databases and categorizing them. But, with these limitations firmly in mind, we then offer a short history of the spread and growth of protected areas since the creation of Yellowstone in the USA and draw out a number of common themes from recent developments.

In Chapter 3 we consider the changing prerogatives for conservation, considering the desire to conserve wilderness and the crisis of biodiversity decline – 'nature's end' – afflicting diverse ecosystems and species. We argue that the value of wilderness in defining conservation goals is limited, but that there is clear evidence of a substantial increase in extinction and endangerment rates. We also discuss the limits of science to give conservation a mandate to act.

Chapter 4 examines the effectiveness and consequence of parks. Here we have found a confused literature that has often failed to ask the right questions, else involved debates that have talked across each other. We examine how well parks have conserved vegetation and wildlife and find that they generally do work well, but that it is much harder to tell if or where they are better strategies than more community-based initiatives. We then examine the consequences of protected areas noting that they can distribute diverse forms of good and ill fortune to different sectors of society. We consider two confused debates that have arisen with respect to the role of conservation in causing and reducing poverty and the role of local people in supporting conservation.

Chapter 5 looks at the operation of community conservation initiatives in more detail. We look at four things: the complexities of 'community' and how to understand what might be hidden by the term; the politics of devolution; the operations and requirements of common property resource management; and a detailed discussion on the complexities of co-management. The chapter is predicated on our insistence that community conservation will, like 'fortress conservation', necessarily distribute fortune and misfortune to different groups. We argue that it is helpful to interpret these changes as part of the ways in which rural groups become more legible and accessible to capitalism.

Chapter 6 takes a careful look at the nature and politics of collaborations between indigenous people and conservation causes. We note the ways in which indigenous groups have been disadvantaged by protected areas, we consider how they and conservationists have found common cause. These alliances are often built on built on paradoxes and ironies as indigenous leaders and groups negotiate the structured institutions of neoliberal capitalism. We examine at the end of the chapter some of the problems and exclusions that arise.

In Chapter 7 we examine one of the key debates in conservation: the role of tourism. Tourism has become a major argument in justifying the maintenance of protected areas; and in particular conservation organizations, national governments and the private sector amongst others have argued that through the development of tourism protected areas can become major revenue earners, especially for developing countries. In this chapter we analyse how tourism is one mechanism through which the twin objectives of conservation and capitalist development can be pursued.

Chapter 8 considers in more detail a number themes that have frequently surfaced in the preceding chapters – namely the role of the international conservation apparatus. We focus on international agreements governing trade, conservation NGOs and Transfrontier Conservation Areas. These are some of the arenas where the cutting edge of conservation practice is most clearly visible and the interconnections between conservation and capitalism can be most clearly seen.

In Chapter 9 we explore a number of developments in conservation practice that well illustrate our thesis that conservation and capitalism are remaking the world in partnership. We look at conservation and carbon markets, the work of certification and the growth of private parks. We end with a detailed discussion on spectacles of consumption as one of the key means by which conservation imagines what it would like the world to be like and one of the key mechanisms by which it attempts to achieve that vision. Finally we draw these arguments together by considering how our ideas about conservation and capitalism fit with broader analyses of the power and transformations of capitalism. Here we draw on the work of Marx, Debord and Baudrillard to discuss what the changes we see in conservation might portend for capitalism more generally.

Notes

1   Caution is required because of the gaps in, and incompleteness of, the data on which see Chapter 2, also Chape, S. et al (2005) 'Measuring the extent and effectiveness of protected areas as an indicator for meeting global biodiversity

targets'. *Philosophical Transactions of the Royal Society B* 360: 443–455; Lemos, M. C. and Agrawal, A. (2006) 'Environmental governance'. *Annual Review of Environment and Resources* 31: 297–325; West, P., Igoe J. and Brockington, D. (2006) 'Parks and people: The social impacts of protected areas. *Annual Review of Anthropology* 35: 251–277.

2   http://arctic.fws.gov/purposes.htm (accessed 12 November 2007).

3   www.anwr.org/ (accessed 12 November 2007).

4   www.riotintomadagascar.com/ (accessed 10 November 2007).

5   www.riotintomadagascar.com/development/ecotourism/index.html (accessed 10 November 2007).

6   www.riotintomadagascar.com/overview/impact/index.html (accessed 10 November 2007).

7   www.foe.co.uk/resource/press_releases/rio_tintos_madagascar_mini_22102007.html (accessed 10 November 2007).

8   'Operation Tiggywinkle', *The Guardian* (UK) 7 April 2003, at www.guardian.co.uk/uk_news/story/0, 3604, 931040, 00.html#article_continue (accessed 12 November 2007); for more information on the Scottish Natural Heritage Uist Waders Project see www.snh.org.uk/scottish/wisles/waders/ (accessed 12 November 2007).

9   'In for the Quill', *The Scotsman* (UK) 3 April 2003, at news.scotsman.com/topics.cfm?tid=372&id=393372003 (accessed 12 November 2007).

2
Histories and Geographies of Protected Areas

Until the lions have their praise singers, the tales of the hunt will
always glorify the hunter

(African proverb)

Strong protected areas have been a rallying cry for the conservation movement for
a long time. John Terborgh, in *Requiem for Nature* (1999), insisted that strong
parks are fundamental for the future of conservation. He argued they need
defending with an international conservation fund and policing force, with the
authority to carry arms (and presumably use them) and make arrests. For
Terborgh parks provide a final defence, a bottom line, some last vestiges of the
world before people damaged it, a denial that people should, through 'sustainable
use', continue to modify the planet. They are 'a line in the sand' (p199) drawn
against the incoming tide of humanity.

Adams, in *Against Extinction* (2004), criticized this view as 'ecofascism', a recipe
for unjust violence meted out by people who do not understand the ways
environments are socially constructed, or the political and economic forces
driving the destruction of nature. Such strategies are akin to hiding your head in
the ground, perversely refusing to face up to realities. 'Juggernauts [such as the
world economy]' says Adams 'do not respect lines in the sand' (p224). Lines will
not stop the ever-growing demand for natural resources, land and wealth. If
parks' boundaries are to be effective they will require a far more effective
engagement with the forces threatening their destruction. Moreover, insistence
on strong parks has been accompanied by a pervasive dismissal of the ecological
value of nature outside parks, which can lead to its neglect for conservation
purposes. As Cronon has argued (1995), and others have shown, neglect of
unprotected lands is profoundly harmful to conservations interests (Proctor and
Pincetl, 1996; Rosenweig, 2003).

An excessive emphasis on strong parks may facilitate, perversely, the creation
of polarized landscapes that are predominantly hostile to the sort of nature
Terborgh and others wish to preserve. Adams (1996) has argued elsewhere that
there is a tension between what is considered 'wild' and what is defined as
'human-made' that forms a fundamental dynamic of conservation. For Adams,
conservation of 'nature' cannot be carried out in a vacuum, such that
conservation becomes about protecting nature in specific places while destroying

it in others (Adams, 1996, pp4–5). Instead he suggests that conservation should be developed to embrace the whole landscape because of the problems associated with fragmentation of nature represented by isolated protected areas (Adams, 1996, p170).

But in other respects a line in the sand, or on the map, or just in someone's head, is all that is required. We need to think carefully about the nature of the world economic juggernaut, and the lines it threatens. The juggernaut is not just a consumer and transformer of resources. It is the latest stage of modernity, and modernity is a line-drawing machine. It separates, categorizes, divides and encloses. There will be many occasions when the lines parks provide are precisely those that can be easily incorporated into the plans and requirements of advanced capitalism. In some contexts parks have become shot through with the very forces from which they seek to protect the landscapes they enclose. In the current world economy parks often become synonymous with consumptive and touristic experiences that are of questionable conservation value. As Anderson points out in Siberia: 'Parks do not protect what exist but instead create new barriers to which people must adapt' (Anderson, 2001, p21). Protected areas are spaces – virtual or real – that offer opportunities to the extension of capitalist and state interests as well as opportunities for resistance to this extension (cf. Tsing, 2004, ch 1).

This chapter examines the power of the *idea* of protected areas and their geographic spread. This is not quite the same thing as examining the power of protected areas proper. What they actually do is the subject of Chapter 4. But the idea of what something is can be more important than its actual consequences. Redford and colleagues (2006) have observed that conflicting ideas about parks are producing a brittle, confrontational debate with conflicting versions of what parks were being deployed unconstructively by their critics and defenders.

In this chapter we explore some of the manifestations of the power of the idea of protected areas. We examine how protected areas as a way of categorizing and viewing the world has developed and flourished as part of the growth of mainstream conservation. We then look at some of the actual details of their growth and spread, which is a more complicated pattern than might first appear. Finally, we draw out some general themes that emerge from these histories.

The idea of protected areas

One of the ways of exploring the power of an idea is to examine the myths that persist around it. These myths can be false, else have only a weak historical basis, but they serve to reinforce the ideas they are associated with, despite these flaws. Protected areas, for example, have an origin myth. Traditionally histories of protected areas begin with Yellowstone, the first national park in the USA, established in 1872.[1] According to this story the origins of national parks are popularly traced to an early vision of the painter George Catlin who travelled through the American West in the 1830s, visiting over 50 tribes, and inspiring the first use of the term 'national park'. Catlin advocated that:

> ...some great protecting policy of government preserve a large expanse of land in all its pristine beauty and wildness ... where the world could see for ages to come, the native Indian in his classic attire, galloping his horse ... amid the fleeting herds of elks and buffalos [this could become a] nation's Park containing man and beast, in all the wild freshness of their nature's beauty. (Spence, 1999, p10)

Later visionaries put Catlin's plan into action, setting aside tracts of land that were fitting monuments to America's growing greatness. Subsequently this policy, the USA's greatest idea according to Nash (2001), has been applied by an increasingly enlightened world.

Accounts of protected areas must pay careful attention to Yellowstone because this is the place and date when the protected area movement imagines itself to begin, and because the influence of this movement's 'Yellowstone model' for protecting nature has had such a profound influence all over the world. The World Database of Protected Areas (WDPA) takes Yellowstone as its starting point.

But this story is problematic for three reasons. First, as we shall examine in Chapter 6, the people that Catlin imagined would be part of the landscape were systematically purged from the newly created national parks. Moreover, the fact of their removal was then forgotten until only recently (Spence, 1999; Burnham, 2000; Jacoby, 2001).[2]

Second, although Yellowstone may be the start of US national parks, the history of protected areas simply does not begin there. Mongolia established an earlier national park, setting aside the sacred Bogd Khan Mountain in 1778 (Milner-Gulland, 2004), with evidence of further protection dating back to 1294 (Verschuuren et al, 2007). Indian princes established personal game reserves and massive personal tallies on shoots. They replenished diminishing stock, even importing lions from Africa for the purpose (Rangarajan, 2001). Earlier than that Indian elephants were protected after their domestication in the 4th to 3rd century BC (Rangarajan, 2001) and the Emperor Ashoka (268–233 BC) is now celebrated for his environmental edicts. In England in the 11th century the invading King William I declared, much to the resentment of his new subjects, hunting reserves over 30 per cent of his new domain in which he alone, or those whom he permitted, could hunt royal game (deer, boar and hares) and in which cultivation was restricted. The first nature reserve in Indonesia was established in 684 AD by the king of Srivijaya (Mishra, 1994). The Qin Dynasty in China set up imperial hunting reserves in mountainous areas in the 3rd century BC (Xu and Melick, 2007). The Roman Empire established a system of forest protection and set aside areas for wildlife. The Emperor Hadrian set aside half of

Mt Lebanon to protect its cedars in the 2nd century AD (Sulayem et al, 1994). The ancient empires of Babylon, Assyria and Persia also set up hunting reserves. There have long been powerful and wealthy rulers with the means to set aside lands, wildlife or forests they wanted protected.

Third, the official history of protected areas is only a record of what large powerful societies (states) have done, and only a memory of those that have left written records. There are many examples of smaller scale societies conserving places or resources in order to ensure their food supplies, else as sacred sites (Berkes, 1999). Pastoral groups in East Africa establish grazing reserves to conserve fodder in the dry season close to water in order that small stock, calves and sick animals can survive the long dry season (de Souza and de Leeuw, 1984; Peacock, 1987; Potkanski, 1997; Brockington, 2002). The Huna Tinglit in Alaska regulated their harvest of seabird eggs in accordance with clutch size (Hunn et al, 2003), caribou hunters controlled their killings, insisting on respect for prey (Berkes, 1999). Indigenous fishing communities in the western USA and sub-arctic controlled their fish takes (Gomez-Pompa and Kaus, 1992; Berkes, 1999; Sarkar, 1999). Maori practise sustainable mutton bird harvesting in New Zealand (Kitson, 2002) as part of a broader array of *kaitiakitangi* (roughly meaning guardianship) over natural resource use (Roberts et al, 1995; Taiepa et al, 1997). In diverse African societies sacred groves, often valued as burial sites, have high biodiversity, comparing favourably with protected forests (Mgumia and Oba, 2003; Sheridan and Nyamweru, 2008). The vegetation of temple groves in many villages in India is left completely untouched, and there are many cases of individual villages and groups protecting particular species (Saberwal et al, 2001). Mountain farmers in Switzerland have monitored use of their land and resources for centuries (Netting, 1981), and in the Himalaya farmers have been known to trigger landslides on farmed slopes, and then re-terrace them to improve the quality of the soil (Ives and Messerli, 1989). Ashish Kothari, Neema Pathak and their colleagues have devoted much time and resources to providing careful and rigorous assessments of the potential and extent of such locally based conservation initiatives (Kothari et al, 1998; Kothari et al, 2000; Pathak et al, 2004).

We cannot tell the long-term history of these practices in this book. However, Berkes (1999) insists that these are learned behaviours, often built on periods of misuse and over exploitation. Conservation ethics result from people learning from their mistakes (although as Berkes points out, they may fail to learn and have to suffer the consequences). It is thus reasonable to assume that forms of resource management will have been practised for a long time, and that their histories will be troubled. There will be cases of management practices cracking under stress and conflict, of sacred values and sites waning, of cultivated landscapes going wild, of local forms of protection causing inequality and inequity. But the larger point is that the history of protecting places from human influence has a far longer history than can be appreciated by perusing official state records. The present geography of protection too is far greater and more complex than these same records suggest.

Clearly histories of protected areas that begin at Yellowstone are flawed. But when mistakes of this kind are made the flaws are not the most interesting thing. It is more important to consider how and why this mistake was made, why it persists, and what interests it serves (Ferguson, 1990). We see the dominance of the Yellowstone creation myth as reflecting the power of mainstream conservation, and particularly the northern, and particularly US-based conservation organizations and conservation thinking. Mainstream conservation has long promoted national parks similar to the Yellowstone model all over the world. A history of parks that begins with Yellowstone fits this model of progress.

But it is also interesting to explore the tensions and disagreements within powerful positions. Just as Yellowstone is a powerful model, it is also a disputed one by many conservationists and, increasingly, many within the mainstream. In some respects the conservation movement recognized the limitations of equating protected areas with national parks a long time ago. The International Union for Conservation of Nature (IUCN) set up a system of categories that recognized the diversity of protected areas as early as the mid-1970s, and has adapted them since then (Box 2.1). The vision is broadening. When the World Parks Congress set itself the goal of setting aside 10 per cent of the land surface of the planet in 1992 it included all categories of protection in that goal. Nonetheless, strictly protected areas remain the principal goal for a substantial community of conservationists (Locke and Dearden, 2005). For these thinkers the category system just allows some types of protected areas to be discounted.

Box 2.1 Classifying protected areas: The evolution of the IUCN categorization system

The number of protected areas have grown dramatically in number and diversity. They contain a myriad objectives, from protecting places, landscapes and features, to saving species, habitat and ecosystems, to conserving wilderness and anthropogenic landscapes, and almost as many management goals, from touching nothing but restricting access, to intensive and active restoration including the eradication of unwanted life to the importing of lost or endangered species. To facilitate comparison of achievements and planning the IUCN has sought to categorize protected areas with increasing rigour. Initially the IUCN, conflating protection with pristineness, was principally concerned with areas where people were limited (Kalamandeen and Gillson, 2007). Its 1966 list divided protected areas into into three categories – national parks, scientific reserves and national monuments. In the early 1970s expanded categories were proposed, which recognized the role of people in the landscape and in conservation goals (Kalamandeen and Gillson, 2007). These categories were formalized in 1978 into ten groups (see below), with the top five becoming part of the UN list of protected areas. These formed the basis for the 1994 categorization, which added a sixth category of area for places managed mainly for sustainable resource use.

Table 2.1 *The protected area category system*

1978			1994	
Group	**Category**	**Definition**	**Category**	**Definition**
A	I	Scientific Reserve	Ia	Strict Nature Reserve: Protected area managed mainly for science.
			Ib	Wilderness Area: Protected area managed mainly for wilderness protection.
	II	National Park	II	National Park: Protected area managed mainly for ecosystem protection and recreation.
	III	Natural Monument/ National Landmark	III	National Monument: Protected area managed mainly for conservation of specific natural features.
	IV	Nature Conservation Reserve	IV	Habitat/Species Management Area: Protected area managed mainly for conservation through management intervention.
	V	Protected Landscape	V	Protected Landscape/ Seascape: Protected area managed mainly for landscape/seascape conservation and recreation.
B	VI	Resource Reserve	VI	Managed Resource Protected Area: Protected area managed mainly for the sustainable use of natural resources.
	VII	Anthropological Reserve		
	VIII	Multiple Use Management Area		
C	IX	Biosphere Reserve		
	X	World Heritage Site		

There are problems in applying these categories to real life situations. What exactly, for example, does category 4 (management for conservation through management intervention) exclude? Surely the management of the most famous category 2 protected area, Yellowstone National Park, intervenes to control tourists for conservation purposes. It is also difficult to tell the precise difference between categories 5 and 6.

In general the categories are thought to protect a gradation in human influence with the first most protected and showing least human influence. But they cannot be taken to be accurate predictors of human presence. Eighty-five per cent of national parks in Latin America are occupied by people, as are 52 per cent of Indian national parks. Conversely in Australia the national park designation has been used to justify calls to exclude human resource use on the grounds that 'Cattle grazing is not compatible with the national and international standards for a national park' (Taskforce, 2005, p71). In fact the debates over the categorization system neatly capture the deeply ambivalent and divided feelings within the conservation community to the role and presence of people in valued nature, with some groups wanting the role of people recognized and affirmed, and others recognized but restricted with primary objectives being restricted to biodiversity conservation objectives. There are cogent calls not to recognize the categories 5 and 6 as being too weak or general to contribute to biodiversity conservation (Locke and Dearden, 2005).

Before the 2003 World Parks Congress the IUCN initiated the 'Speaking a Common Language' Project to examine how the categories were being applied. This found that the system was facilitating some planning, advocacy and data collection work but that confusions still existed as to the application of the categories in some instances. They also noted new and unexpected use of the categories. In some instances they were being used to determine the appropriateness of proposed or existing human activities in some areas, and in others they were being used to evaluate management effectiveness.

More importantly for our argument here, the category system's success in expanding perceptions of what 'parks' and protection mean has just added to the power of the idea of protected areas. An expanded idea of what protected areas are just becomes another aspect of the power of mainstream conservation to define what constitutes protection. It is a totalizing vision, meaning that it is all-encompassing in ambition, internally coherent and consistent. But it remains an imperfect one.

This point is most easily understood by considering the growth and development of the WDPA, housed and maintained by the World Conservation Monitoring Centre (WCMC) in Cambridge, in conjunction with the United Nations Environment Programme (UNEP), and informed by a coalition of powerful conservation NGOs. It was first formed in 1962 (as a list of 'National Parks and Equivalent Reserves' (Adams, 2004, p97)); it has been gradually revised and updated since. It can now include information on the size and establishment date of each protected area, whether it is a terrestrial or marine, GIS shape-files of its boundaries and a variety of other information. Often the updating has taken place in bursts of activity.

There are many gaps in the WDPA – there are parks and reserves that are missing entirely, or others missing data (such as their establishment date, area or GIS files of their boundaries). The updating process has involved filling in these gaps: the 2005 version records over 4 million km^2 of protected areas that existed in 1990 but which the 1992 version of the WDPA did not report. But there have been some remarkably large holes. For example, in 2005 72 per cent of entries for the USA lack any establishment date, and 20 per cent have no size data. There is also a problem with the simple terrestrial/marine classification system. Many marine protected areas include substantial amounts of land, leading to an exaggeration of conserved marine areas (which are already woefully small) and an underestimate of terrestrial protected areas by about 2 million km^2 (West and Brockington, 2006). Rather amusingly when we used some simple extrapolations to fill in the missing size and date data for different regions it seemed *highly likely that the 10 per cent target which the World Parks Congress set itself in 1992 had in fact already been achieved in the late 1980s.* The conservation community was already doing rather well, at least by its own standards; it just did not know about it.

Even if the database was a perfect tool on its own terms, it would still be blind to the existence of all sorts of other types of protected areas that it cannot recognize. The WDPA is only a list of official state activities. It omits private protected areas, even if they contribute a substantial amount to the conservation estate. For example, South Africa conserves about 6 per cent of its land mass in government parks and reserves, but 13 per cent in private game reserves (Cook, 2002). That figure is growing as more land owners try to profit from the growing hunting and game capture markets that private game reserves can provide for, with varied and sometimes problematic consequences for the farm labourers who lose their livelihoods (Luck, 2003; Connor, 2006; Langholz and Kerley, 2006). Other nations with an extensive area of private wildlife estate, also accompanied by similar, if more distant, histories of displacement and exclusions are Scotland and, to a lesser extent, the USA. The WDPA also omits community conserved areas – the sacred groves, community woodlots, grazing areas or local nature reserves that are recognized and enforced locally, but are not part of the official state portfolio (Pathak et al, 2004). Yet one estimate suggests that unofficial community conservation conserves about 3.7 million km^2 of forests and forested landscapes (how well is not clear) in Asia, Africa and Latin and North America, as much as set aside in formal protected areas (Molnar et al, 2004a; 2004b).

There are also all sorts of vital information not included in the database. For example, the presence of a park on a statute book does not mean that it exists on the ground. All these statistics about increased conservation estate cannot be assumed to be gains for conservation goals unless we also know that these protected areas are being effectively managed. Conversely, if you are interested

Box 2.2 Setting global conservation priorities

Conservation priority models try to determine the best way to allocate funding given to global conservation NGOs, which are free to spend their resources anywhere around the world. There are three broad types: prioritizing vulnerable biodiversity (where current human transformations are greatest), irreplaceable biodiversity (where rarity and endemism are greatest) and regions least influenced by people (Brooks et al, 2006). The table below summarizes nine global models and their degree of overlap.

To the extent that they prioritize different goals these models are meant to be complementary. The fact that they identify different areas is not so important. But these models are not just means of prioritizing expenditure, they are also fund-raising tools. There can therefore be considerable competition between rival NGOs to come up with the neatest, sexiest plan that best fires donors' imagination. The clear winner in terms of its catchiness and fund-raising power is Norman Myers' idea of 'biodiversity hotspots', which identifies the regions with the most endemism and habitat loss (for variations, see Myers et al, 2000; Brummitt and Lughadha, 2003; Myers and Mittermeier, 2003; Ovadia, 2003; Shi et al, 2005). When hotspots were criticized Myers defended them for their fund-raising power. He noted that E. O. Wilson has called hotspots 'the most important contribution to conservation biology of the last century' (quoted in Myers, 2003, p917) and it has generated about $750 million in funding (Myers, 2003).

When the hotspots idea was published in the prestigious journal *Nature* there was an instant response from a large number of concerned conservationists who noted with alarm the duplication of efforts and waste of resources by competing global conservation organizations in their rival attempts to come up with the best prioritizing model (Mace et al, 2000). Redford and colleagues found 21 different approaches at work among 13 different conservation organizations and, while noting the fundamental importance of systematic collaboration, noted that this far it was 'sporadic at best' (Redford et al, 2003, p127).

One way of reconciling the different models is to examine the costs and difficulties of implementing them. Conservation plans have, in the real world, to cope with the fact that they cannot be implemented instantly, and that implementing them gradually may mean different plans are more appropriate (Meir et al, 2004). Perhaps most importantly they have explicitly to recognize the costs of implementing them (Balmford et al, 2003b). Globally the costs of conservation strategies vary by at least an order of magnitude more than measures of biodiversity and threat. When implementation costs are incorporated explicitly into conservation planning quite different conservation plans result that can bring much more effective returns on investment (Meir et al, 2004; Wilson et al, 2006; Murdoch et al, 2007; Wilson et al, 2007). This work can equate conservation investment to mean purchasing land for protected areas but current research emphasizes the importance of considering a diversity of strategies that include, but are not limited to protected areas (Meir et al, 2004; Murdoch et al, 2007).

Table 2.2 *The different prioritizing mechanisms*

Priority	Name	Definition	No of sites	% of planet's land surface identified	Overlap with similar models, expressed as a % of planet's land surface	Source
High vulnerability	Crisis ecoregions	≥ 20% habitat conversion where conversion rate is ≥ 2 times proportion of protected area coverage	305	30	10%	(Hoekstra et al, 2005)
High vulnerability and irreplaceability	Biodiversity hotspots	≥ 0.5% of world's endemic plants where ≥ 70% of primary habitat is already lost.	34	16	10% (High Vuln) 0–12% (Irrep)	(Myers et al, 2000)
Irreplaceability	Endemic bird areas	≥ bird species with ranges of < 50,000km² and with more of these endemic than shared with adjacent regions	218	10	0.7–6.8%	(Stattersfield et al, 1998)
Irreplaceability	Centres of plant diversity	> 1000 plants of which ≥ 10% are endemic to the site or region; else islands with ≥ 50 endemic species or ≥ flora endemic	234	9	2–6%	(WWF and IUCN, 1997)
Irreplaceability	Megadiversity countries	Countries with ≥ 1% of world's plants endemic	17	35	4–19%	(Mittermeier et al, 1997)

Table 2.2 *The different prioritizing mechanisms* (cont'd)

Priority	Name	Definition	No of sites	% of planet's land surface identified	Overlap with similar models, expressed as a % of planet's land surface	Source
Irreplaceability	Global 200 ecoregions	Biomes characterized by high species richness, endemism, taxonomic uniqueness, unusual phenomena or global habitat type rarity	142	37	6–18%	(Olson and Dinerstein, 2002)
Irreplaceability and low vulnerability	High-biodiversity wilderness areas	≥ 0.5% of world's plants endemic, ≥ 70% of primary habitat remaining and 5 people per km^2	5	8	0–6% (Irrep) 3–4% (Low Vuln)	(Mittermeier et al, 2003)
Low vulnerability	Frontier forests	Forested regions large enough to support viable populations of all native species, dominated by native species and with structure and composition driven by natural events	NA	9	3–7%	(Bryant et al, 1997)
Low vulnerability	Last of the wild	10% of wildest $1km^2$ grid cells per biome	NA	24	4–7%	(Sanderson et al, 2002)

Source: Adapted from Table S1 (Brooks et al, 2006).

in the impact of parks on people then the WDPA will not tell you whether a park is occupied, or whether it was occupied, or what forms of resource use are allowed within it.

Finally, the WDPA is no mere list of things that exist; it actually changes how conservation is practised. Its publication 'demanded standardisation of increasingly diverse practices of governments around the world' (Adams, 2004, p97). This is particularly true with respect to the application of the IUCN category system, which is being used to rewrite and modify protected area legislation in an increasing number of countries (Bishop et al, 2004). The WDPA, then, is no simple tool. As we wrote elsewhere, it 'is not just a record of practice, it is also a way of seeing the world with blind spots and blurred vision not easily perceived by its operators, but these blindspots become darker and fuzzier as the machine becomes better' (West et al, 2006, p254). It is not just a way of seeing the world; it is also a vehicle for remaking it.

This then is the final aspect of the power of the idea of protected areas, they provide a means of categorizing and surveilling the work of conservation, for documenting progress and defining new challenges and tasks. Protected area networks and databases, combined with geographical information systems and remote sensing data, which map habitat, threats, species ranges and human activities, make the world legible to the powerful regimes of mainstream conservation as never before. These efforts have been lead by the larger NGOs, which attempt to prioritize their spending, and fund-raising, using different means of assessing conservation need (Box 2.2). The specific areas identified as high priority vary according to the exact criteria chosen to establish them, and although collectively they 'target' an astonishing 79 per cent of the world's land surface, there is more overlap within some criteria (Brooks et al, 2006). These GIS models are one of the main driving forces behind the further expansion of the protected area estate globally. Other more specific models identify where the protected area network fails to cover areas of endemism (Rodrigues et al, 2004), or where particularly threatened and limit-range species require protection (Ricketts et al, 2005).

A short global history of protected areas

While it is a problematic starting point, it is still useful to consider how protected areas spread after Yellowstone. The US national parks inspired others abroad (Adams, 2004). Canada, Australia and New Zealand set up national parks in the late 1800s, the latter following a gift of land from the Maori leader Te Heu Heu to Queen Victoria in order to protect sacred mountains. New Zealand rapidly became one of the most protected countries in the world, in terms of area set aside, once it had set aside the massive and dramatic Fjordland in South Island. But it retained a strongly productivist outlook, and as in Canada and the US, much of its protected land was worthless for farming, and valuable only for tourism (Runte, 1979). Only in recent decades has New Zealand's green movement set aside significant areas of more lowland ecosystems. Notably it ceased state timber operations in the west coast and established national parks there, much to the resentment of local groups who resented the interference of urban electorates (Scott, 1989; Pawson, 2002; Norton, 2004; Wilson and Memon, 2005).

In the Soviet Union a different story unfolded. Here the initial effort, supported by the Bolshevik state, focused on the establishment of *zapodevniki* – pristine strict nature reserves without tourism or resource use, which were set aside as reference ecosystems for the purposes of scientific research. Russian scientists, grappling with massive social and ecological change, were the first to propose setting aside land to study whole ecological communities, and the Russian government at first heeded their calls (Weiner, 1988). It is not known how many people were moved when creating these places, but it would be surprising if none were; population movements under Stalin were massive and brutal enough for development purposes. Weiner notes that the *zapodevniki* became precious exceptions to the wholesale transformation of Soviet nature, 'an archipelago of freedom' (Weiner, 1988, p38) that biologists fought to defend. But after World War II many *zapodevniki* were liquidated to make way for the demands of the Soviet Union's grand plans, and because their presence and advocates facilitated opposition to the state's decisions (Weiner, 1999). On 29 August 1951, 88 out of 128 reserves were abolished, and those that survived were reduced in area. 1.26 million km^2 of protected land (0.06 per cent of the country's area) was reduced to just $13,840km^2$ (Weiner, 1999, p129).

But the repression did not mean that *zapodevniki* lost their appeal or supporters, despite the obvious dangers of opposing the state in the USSR. They revived under later regimes, growing rapidly in area and extent in the 1970s (Nikol'skii, 1994); in 1983 there were 145. At the same time scientists were realizing the difficulty of identifying discrete pristine portions of nature that comprised *zapodevniki*, and other forms of protection grew in importance, with the first national parks in Russia gazetted in 1983. Protected areas of diverse kinds now account for 8 per cent of the land in the former Soviet Union. Since its recent economic reforms new space for protected areas has been opened up as state-run farms have collapsed, removing people and resource use. Anderson reports an ironic situation developing in the far north where feral reindeer from abandoned state reindeer farms have joined herds of wild reindeer in large scale migrations. This has led to efforts by the World Wide Fund for Nature (WWF) to save 'Europe's last great wild reindeer herd', which will involve establishing new national parks in the far north (Anderson, 2001).

Formal protected areas may have begun in the New World, but they did not initially prosper there (aside from New Zealand). For the briefest glance at the distribution of protected areas in 1960 shows that they had been most liberally established in sub-Saharan Africa (Figure 2.1).

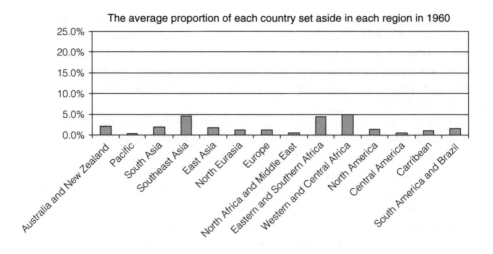

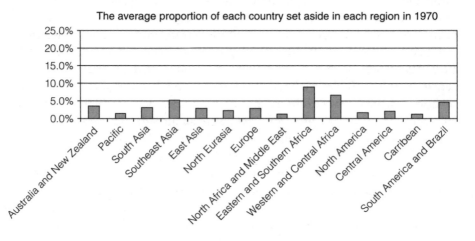

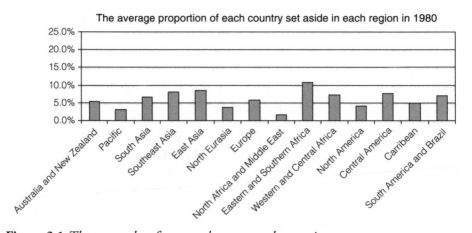

Figure 2.1 *The geography of protected area growth over time*

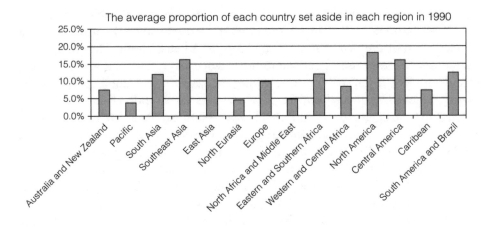

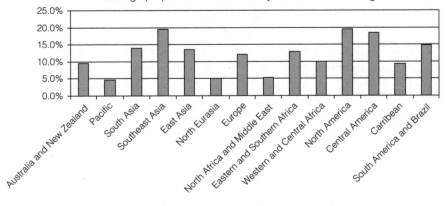

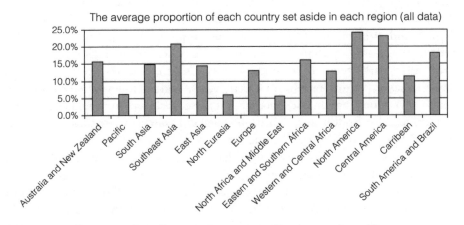

Figure 2.1 *The geography of protected area growth over time* (cont'd)

Note: The final graph includes protected areas for which no establishment dates have been given.

Again the movement there was inspired by the US model, which influenced powerful hunters in Britain who were part of the aristocratic Society for the Preservation of the Wild Fauna of the Empire (Adams, 2004). They lobbied for game reserves to ensure good hunting specimens but also national parks that would be free from any use (and additional reservoirs of good specimens for nearby hunting runs). Their first success was to support James Stevenson-Hamilton's struggles to set up the Kruger National Park, so named after a popular, but false, idea that Paul Kruger (the President of the Transvaal Republic in what was to become South Africa) was a strong conservation supporter (Carruthers, 1989; 1995).[3] But the myth served it well and it became popular for visitors and an icon of conservation on the continent. The rapid growth of protected areas prior to 1960 owes something to the anxiety of colonial rulers to set aside land before they lost power. But the emphasis on conservation has been maintained since. Not until the 1980s did the global distribution become more equal.

In India, British rule continued the previous rulers' traditions of hunting reserves in places, but its main impact was to place a large part of the country under the control of the Forest Department. In the 1920s hunting was restricted in some forest reserves, and in 1936 the first national park was established. But the first real boost for protected areas and wildlife sanctuaries came with Indira Gandhi's support for Project Tiger, which saw national parks and wildlife sanctuaries grow in the 1970s and 1980s. It remains one of the few countries that have rigorously surveyed the number of people living in its protected areas: over 70 per cent of wildlife sanctuaries and 50 per cent of national parks were occupied (Kothari et al, 1989). It is also the only country rigorously to survey eviction from protected areas (Rangarajan and Shahabuddin, 2006).

In Indonesia the Netherlands Indies government established the Ujung Kulon nature reserve to protect the Javan rhino in 1921 as part of a complicated system of game reserves, wildlife sanctuaries, national parks and strict nature reserves (Jepson and Whittaker, 2002). Many now support diverse forms of human settlement and activity (Jepson et al, 2002). Elsewhere in the region Korean and Cambodian parks tend to be in the lower IUCN categories. In Thailand the network has expanded rapidly in recent years, and includes strictly protected areas. A vigorous national debate and diverse local environmentalisms, and environmentalist Buddhisms, flourish in Thailand as lowland irrigators insist that highland farmers are threatening the integrity of their watersheds (Darlington, 1998; Laungaramsri, 1999). Calls for eviction from parks here are locally driven (Ghimire, 1994; Buergin and Kessler, 2000; Sato, 2000, 2002; Buergin, 2003). China long had virtually no strictly protected areas, the 2006 WDPA lists just two category 4 protected areas. Otherwise its nature reserves are category V. These reserves are now expanding rapidly, increasing by 50 per cent since 1999, although actual levels of protection vary considerably (Xu and Melick, 2007). Protection is further reinforced by a blanket ban on timber extraction in many forests, which has served massively to increase demand for wood from the wider region.

North of the Sahara, and in the Middle East, protected area coverage has long been patchy and thin (Sulayem et al, 1994). Protected area establishment tends to come in bursts of intense activity. Egypt, Kuwait, Lebanon, Oman and Saudi Arabia all effectively began their current protected area systems in the 1980s. Others (Morocco, Yemen, Iraq) are yet to begin.

In Central America and the Caribbean the growth of national parks and protected areas has been most prominent in the 1980s. One of the popular success stories is Costa Rica. Boza (1993) has enthusiastically described the history of the country's gradual growth in environmental awareness and activism, from minimal levels in the 1970s, to sustain protected areas over 25 per cent of its landmass. Sarkar, however, offers a warning note, reporting that there was a concomitant increase in deforestation in the country as land clearance intensified outside protected areas (Sarkar, 1999). It is not clear whether protected areas saved forests from destruction or augmented the rate of clearance beyond their borders.

Protected areas were first set up in South America in Chile and Argentina at the beginning of the last century. They have flourished particularly since 1980 (they doubled in size between 1980 and 1994). Their expansion was partly in reaction to the new agricultural frontiers created by national development plans and land hunger (especially in the Amazon) (Pardo, 1994). The region has also come under increasingly close attention from all four of the major international NGOs (WWF, Conservation International (CI), Wildlife Conservation Society (WCS) and The Nature Conservancy (TNC)). NGO expansion was facilitated by the opening up of the region's many military governments to more democratic rule and by donors' investment in strengthening civil society. There have been several protests about the actions of conservation NGOs in the region, some quite polemical (Chapin, 2004; Romero and Andrade, 2004; Rodriguez et al, 2007). But the region is remarkable for the high proportion of national parks that contain people (85 per cent; see Amend and Amend, 1995), and the general lack of cases of eviction due to conservation in the area, although there is discontent about other forms of marginalization and insecurity (Gray et al, 1998). There appears to be more eviction cases in Central America (Brockington and Igoe, 2006).

Britain, despite its admiration for the Yellowstone model in its colonies, used a different sort of national parks model (Adams, 1986; Adams, 2004). In England they were established from 1951, all in hilly districts popular among walkers and holiday goers. Scotland did not establish national parks proper until 2002. In both nations these national parks are an oddity compared to others internationally. Land on them is privately owned, and access for many years restricted to footpaths and rights of way. 'Access lands' on which the 'right to roam' has been granted date from only 2000. Their landscapes are heavily influenced by people, with heather moors deforested in Neolithic times and now managed for grouse shooting and (in Scotland) deer; one of the main land uses is sheep farming. They also contain significant industrial developments including quarries and sizeable towns. The role of the park boards governing them is to control and restrict development to maintain the character of their landscapes. In England, parallel to the national parks is the system of National Nature Reserves and Sites of Special Scientific Interest. Growing from a suggested list of 73, there are now over 200 National Nature Reserves, some owned by the government, others leased else managed in agreement with the land owners. Sites of Special Scientific Interest are more numerous, numbering over 6500 and covering over 26,000km^2. Their creation does not bring in restrictions on land use; rather owners are expected voluntarily to consult the relevant conservation bodies over appropriate management.

Britain generally reflects to some extent broader European trends. Most protected areas (as a proportion of the size of the protected area estate) were set aside for their scenic value, and often for the benefits of urban populations. Many of these parks rarely provide strict protection, and are mainly found in mountains. More recently there has been a trend to set up protected areas in lowlands, even, given that the region has a surfeit of agricultural land, to re-wild landscapes, flooding fens and reintroducing herbivore guilds into the Netherlands (Taylor, 2005). Within Europe, Scandanavia has particularly exemplary systematic conservation planning but significant gaps and weaknesses remain in the most biodiverse environments, particularly in the Mediterranean (Pardo, 1994).

Finally there is the special case of Antarctica. As a continent over which no state presides it has no protected areas, although there are a few on outlying islands owned by individual states. Instead the continent is protected by its climate, its isolation, and by the agreement of all the states who have signed up to the Antarctic Treaty (signed in 1959). The Madrid Protocol to this treaty (adopted in 1991) concerns specific environmental matters, and notably bans mineral extraction. The protocol made provision for states to police their own activities and impacts in an environment where human impacts endure for many years. Each party to the treaty assesses the impacts of their proposed activities and provides guidance as to how to minimize impact. If the party decides that activities that it is proposing are deemed to have more than a 'minor or transitory impact' then they are reviewed by an international Committee for Environmental Protection. The protection then is as strong as the vigilance of each country that is party to the treaty. In general it has worked well with research activities being moderated and bases being cleaned up and rubbish better handled. However, the USA recently began building a 'traverse' – an ice highway – to the South Pole in order to experiment with supplying its base there overland rather than by air.

Box 2.3: Famous and less famous protected areas from around the world

There is an incredible variety of protected areas on the planet. We list here some of the more well known, and less well known in different parts of the world.

The Better Known...

1. Bogd Khan Mountain National Park
In Mongolia and possbly the world's oldest. A 2122m mountain first officially protected in 1778.

2. North East Greenland National Park
The world's largest national park at 972,000km². Officially a marine protected area, but contains almost half of Greenland.

3. Tassili N'Ajjer National Park
The world's largest terrestrial park at 720,000km², occupying a large portion of the Sahara Desert in Algeria.

4. Kruger National Park
In South Africa and probably one of the most famous in the continent. Significant portions are claimed back by former (evicted) residents.

5. Uluru National Park
Once known as Ayers Rock, this is one of the iconic Australian tourist destinations and one of the first national parks in the world given back to indigenous groups to manage in cooperation with the state.

6. Tongariro National Park
New Zealand's first, and gifted to the Crown by the Maori leader Te Heu Heu. Whether it was his to give is disputed and the focus of current co-management negotiations.

7. Manu National Park
Over 15,000km², in Peru, and one of the most significant in South America. Favoured habitat of John Terborgh, author of *Requiem for Nature.*

8. Wolong Nature Reserve
Focal point of China's Giant Panda populations. Populations have expanded to over 1500 following breeding success and improved counting techniques.

9. Samriska Tiger Reserve
Despite being a flagship of India's campaign to Save the Tiger all tigers were lost from Samriska by 2005, fuelling demands for stronger protection.

10. Serengeti National Park
With Kruger, one of the most renowned on the continent. It was set up in the 1950s in Tanzania and is one of the better studied, and better filmed.

11. Virunga National Park
In the troubled Democratic Republic of Congo this park conserves nearly 8000km^2 of land on the border with Uganda and Rwanda and contiguous with other protected areas. Famous for the rare mountain gorillas, it has recently been the scene of a number of gorilla massacres.

12. Yellowstone National Park (USA)
Popularly revered as the world's first national park. Contains spectacular scenery, wildlife and geothermal formations in about 9000km^2.

13. Yosemite National Park (USA)
Once home to John Muir Yosemite; receives millions of visitors each year and boast spectacular glaciated scenery. Just over 3000km^2.

14. The Mesoamerican Biological Corridor
This is not strictly a protected area but it deserves attention. The corridor is an ambitious plan to link protected habitats from Mexico to Panama with controlled land use and conservation with development projects. Many projects are part of its framework; a key donor is the Global Environmental Facility of the World Bank.

15. The Great Barrier Reef
Covers over 344,000km^2 and is the largest protected area in Australia. It comprises many different zones, of which 33 per cent are 'no-take' zones.

16. Peak District National Park
Established in 1951 in the UK it protects 1400km^2 of farms and grouse moors and also contains the odd quarry. Surrounded by urban areas, criss-crossed with roads, and is one of the most visited parks in the world. Before the park was established its highest peak was the scene of a famous mass trespass by socialist ramblers protesting their exclusion in 1932.

17. The Galapagos National Park
A 7700km^2 marine park, belonging to Ecuador, and found 1000km off the South American coast in the Pacific Ocean. It protects islands whose endemics are famous for inspiring Charles Darwin's theory of evolution. The park covers 97 per cent of the islands and has to cope with discontented neighbours and many tourists.

18. Sagarmatha National Park
Established in 1976 in Nepal and contains Mt Everest. Initially locally unpopular with Sherpa villagers but more recent moves to empower traditional resource management has improved relations.

19. Angkor Wat National Park
Cambodia's first, set up in 1925 to protect the astonishing remains of the 12th century city and Hindu temple.

Some less well known and surprising cases ...

20. Cayman Brac East Grouper Spawning Site
Covers over 17km²; established in 2002 to protect the Nassau grouper from over-exploitation at its spawning sites.

21. Dr Carlos Spegazzini Mycological Reserve
A 60-hectare site preserving rare fungi and named after a great South American fungi explorer and discoverer.

22. St Katherine National Park
In the Sinai peninsula in Egypt this park houses an ancient monastery, marginalized Bedouin herders and the world's smallest butterfly, the Sinai Baton Blue, whose habitat comprises a single species of thyme found only at high altitude.

23. Lapiosuon-Ison Äijönsuon soidensuojelualue Protected Mire
One of four in Finland. Set up in 1988 and covers 26,000 hectares.

24. Fort Ross Underwater Park
An extension of the Fort Ross Historic State Park in California, the underwater park includes shipwrecks and relicts of the shipping industry.

25. Tyrendarra Indigenous Protected Area
Owned and managed by the Winda-Mara Aboriginal Corporation this site protects a portion of an ancient lava flow and unusual sites of permanent Aboriginal settlement including stone houses and eel aquaculture.

26. Kanevskiy Nature Zapodevnik
One of the earliest of the Soviet Regime, set up in 1923. A 2000-hectare site preserving broad-leafed forest in the middle of the Ukraine.

27. Altmatt – Biberbrugg
One of 512 'Raised and Protected Bogs of National Importance' designated in Switzerland in 1991.

28. Waikaka Willow Bank Stewardship Area
One of the smallest protected areas in the WDPA, this along with a few other stewardship areas in New Zealand is reported to be just 0.05ha in size.

29. Dryodasos Mongostou Korinthias Aesthetic Forest Protects
520 hectares of evergreen sclerophyllous forest on the Greek mainland.

30. Lyapinskaya Ethnic Territory
Found in eastern Russia, of unknown size and establishment date.

31. Chico Mendes Extractive Reserve
Covers nearly 10,000km² in the far west of Brazil. It is named for Chico Mendes who defended rubber tappers against cattle barons. Mendes was killed but extractive reserves continue for rubber tappers to pursue their livelihoods, although some now are escaping the poverty that had rendered their impact on the forests slight.

32. Monteverde Cloud Forest Reserve
This 100km² private reserve in Costa Rica was once home to the endemic golden toad, which had a range of just 4km². This species is emblematic of the collapse of amphibian populations. It was present in normal numbers in 1987, but only eight were found in 1988, with one male seen in 1989. None have been found since.

33. Al-Haram al-Makki Inviolable Sanctuary
Located in Saudi Arabia; sometimes called Mecca by English speakers. The sanctuary contains the holiest site in Islam.

34. Twentynine Palms Marine Corp Military Reservation
Found in California, USA, this is the world's largest marine corp base and the corp's premier live fire exercise site. Overlaps with the Amboy Crater Wilderness Study Area and close to the Joshua Tree National Park, which receives nearly a million visitors a year.

35. Monocacy National Battlefield
The site of the 'battle that saved Washington' between Confederates and the Union in the American Civil War in 1864. This protected area was established in 1934.

36. Rota Commonwealth Forest Primeval Reserve
One of eight Primeval Reserves in the Pacific US Dependency of Northern Mariana Island, this reserve protects 500ha of forest.

37. Tsurugisan Quasi National Park
One of 55 such parks in Japan. National parks are controlled by central government, quasi national parks by regional governments. Tsurugisan is a popular destination for mountain climbers.

38. El Palmar y Alfredo Rural Development Area
1437km² in size and found in Venezuela where seven rural development areas were established in the 1970s and 1980s.

39. Isla de la Estados Touristic, Historic, Ecological Provincial Reserve
Conserves 100,000 hectares of Patagonian forest in Argentina.

40. Port Meadow with Wolvercote Common and Green
The largest piece of common land in England, Port Meadow is a large open space near the river Thames in north Oxford, which floods seasonally. Select houses nearby still carry stints (grazing rights for specified numbers of stock).

Themes

The result of this remarkable expansion is a tremendous variety in places enjoying some form of state protection, which can be called protected areas. There are more than 100,000 and they cover nearly 12 per cent of the world's land surface. That total continues to grow (Table 2.3). The spread of protection is highly uneven, the largest ten parks collectively account for more than 10 per cent of the protected area estate. Each of these larger protected areas is individually bigger than the 65,000 smallest protected areas put together. It is also important to note the relative proportions of land set aside in IUCN categories 1–4, which are generally more strictly protected, and categories 5–6, which are often not. Finally, observe the sheer diversity in protected areas across the world and the extraordinary variety of their pasts and politics. The diverse forces that promote the establishment of protected areas in different countries have produced an odd constellation of places, each set aside for different causes. Sometimes protected area estate can resemble a street in an old town, filled with buildings from a kaleidoscope of styles and different architectural eras. The diversity is so great that the current difficulty of the conservation movement is how to provide some order and commensurability to a roll call of protected areas. We have compiled a sample of well known and less well known protected areas in Box 2.3 to provide a flavour.

There are several important trends visible in the expansions of recent years. First, there are a growing number of cases where large additions to the protected area network are made all in one go in one country. Noticeable examples include Gabon, which recently announced the establishment of 13 new national parks, comprising 11 per cent of the area of the country in 2002. As we saw above, the Peoples Democratic Republic of Laos has a programme to set up a large number of new reserves in association with the damming of the Mekong River. Madagascar has also made a commitment to triple the amount of land under protected areas through the Durban Vision Initiative, which is discussed in greater detail in Chapter 8 (Horning, 2005; Duffy, 2006a). In these cases the growth was facilitated by the influence of powerful NGOs – the WCS in Gabon and the WWF and IUCN in Laos. CI and TNC have been powerfully influential in the Americas. Elsewhere in Africa, the Peace Parks Foundation is promoting the spread of Transfrontier Conservation Areas involving large tracts of land in sub-Saharan Africa (Van-Amerom and Büscher, 2005; Duffy, 2006b; Ramutsindela, 2007).

Second, most protected areas were established before any of the current concerns about extinction and habitat loss were well formulated. Many conservation lobbies are now playing catch up, trying to identify the areas most needed for effective protection, using the GIS models we identified earlier. These types of analysis can be extremely effective. Where data, funds and political will are available, complex GIS models can now determine where different sorts of protected areas are most needed (Margules and Pressey, 2000; Sarkar et al, 2006; Wilson et al, 2007). Australia and South Africa lead the work in systematic planning (Mace, 2004). In Australia all the different habitat types in the country have been mapped, and the country is now endeavouring to ensure comprehensive, adequate, representative (CAR) protection. Tasmania was the first place to use and apply systematic planning to identify protected area development (Sarkar et al, 2006).

Table 2.3 *Distribution of marine and terrestrial protected areas in different IUCN regions*

IUCN Region[1]	Terrestrial		Marine		Total		Proportion of land protected[2]			
	Count	Area km²	Count	Area km²	Count	Area km²	Cat[3] 1–4	Cat[3] 5–6	Uncat'd	Total
Antarctica	67	2265	59	68,054	126	70,318	0.00%	0.00%	0.01%	0.02%
A'lia and N. Z'd	9085	798,684	467	702,165	9552	1,500,849	6.88%	3.11%	0.04%	10.04%
Pacific	199	55,311	288	33,451	487	88,762	0.80%	1.23%	7.98%	10.01%
South Asia	1076	327,247	184	28,832	1260	356,079	5.41%	0.30%	1.59%	7.30%
Southeast Asia	2238	656,193	420	213,546	2658	869,740	5.11%	4.50%	4.99%	14.60%
East Asia	2986	1,921,762	295	64,675	3281	1,986,437	1.92%	14.12%	0.26%	16.30%
North Eurasia	17,642	1,610,320	82	430,708	17,724	2,041,027	5.24%	0.48%	1.56%	7.29%
Europe	43,159	662,995	745	162,969	43,904	825,964	3.13%	6.30%	3.28%	12.70%
N. Af. and M. East	1230	1,204,928	141	161,356	1371	1,366,284	2.11%	6.85%	0.41%	9.37%
E'n and S'n Africa	3924	1,789,578	152	116,942	4076	1,906,520	5.92%	4.63%	4.90%	15.46%
W'n and Cen. Africa	2554	1,290,420	43	60,908	2597	1,351,328	5.46%	0.77%	3.86%	10.09%
North America	12,863	3,147,172	760	2,189,346	13,623	5,336,519	6.07%	5.09%	3.08%	14.23%
Central America	548	117,954	129	38,317	677	156,271	6.90%	8.01%	7.64%	22.55%
Caribbean	494	18,836	473	69,309	967	88,145	5.22%	1.55%	1.25%	8.02%
S. Am. And Brazil	2500	3,206,623	202	369,987	2702	3,576,609	4.65%	4.48%	8.87%	18.01%
Total	100,565	16,810,289	4,440	4,710,564	105,005	21,520,853	4.35%	4.09%	2.91%	11.34%

Table 2.3 *Distribution of marine and terrestrial protected areas in different IUCN regions* (cont'd)

				Count of all protected areas in each size class			
	< 1 km²	≥ 1 km² < 10 km²	≥ 10 km² < 100 km²	≥ 100 km² < 1000 km²	≥ 1000 km² < 10,000 km²	≥ 10k km² < 100k km²	≥ 100k km² < 1000k km²
Antarctica	40	40	14	8	2	1	0
A'lia and N. Z'd	5242	2559	1165	425	123	20	2
Pacific	83	101	93	43	23	1	0
South Asia	161	236	370	384	63	5	0
Southeast Asia	230	509	831	786	166	12	0
East Asia	259	413	1542	812	181	20	2
North Eurasia	7166	3083	1507	1158	289	33	1
Europe	26,885	7678	2908	1137	141	2	0
N. Af. and M. East	223	217	303	239	57	13	2
E'n and S'n Africa	527	926	1,290	831	300	31	0
W'n and Cen. Africa	90	629	875	643	179	28	0
North America	3118	3568	3069	1553	525	69	2
Central America	66	157	225	162	32	1	0
Caribbean	373	236	140	55	14	1	0
S. Am. And Brazil	285	418	716	623	410	82	1

Table 2.3 *Distribution of marine and terrestrial protected areas in different IUCN regions* (cont'd)

		Count of all protected areas in each size class					
	< 1 km²	≥ 1 km² < 10 km²	≥ 10 km² < 100 km²	≥ 100 km² < 1000 km²	≥ 1000 km² < 10,000 km²	≥ 10k km² < 100k km²	≥ 100k km² < 1000k km²
Total	44,748	20,770	15,048	8859	2505	319	10
Area (km²)	10,612	75,767	539,300	2,895,756	7,591,812	6,960,583	3,447,024

[1] The countries that make up each region are available at http://sea.unep-wcmc.org/wdbpa/ (accessed 23 September 2005). We have modified these categories slightly in the following ways. The IUCN classify Comoros, Djibouti, Madagascar and Mauritius as part of as Western and Central Africa. We have assigned them to Eastern and Southern Africa. Brazil forms an entire IUCN region on its own, but we have grouped it with South America. Sao Tome and Principe, Anguilla and the British Indian Ocean Territories have not been allotted regions by the IUCN and we placed them in Western and Central Africa, the Caribbean and South Asia respectively.

[2] Only terrestrial protected areas are included as we only have data for the size of land areas within each country, and therefore cannot express marine protected areas as a proportion of country size.

[3] The IUCN Protected Area Categories are explained in Box 2.1.

Third, while much effort in systematic conservation planning goes into identifying new protected areas and prioritizing investment in existing protection, it is important to note that the most complete plans now extend far beyond traditional models of saving places by setting them aside in state-governed protected areas. The driving force here is to search for conservation arrangements at the large landscape level that will allow broader ecosystems to persist, not just the smaller protected parts of it. The classic study that contributed to this was in East Africa where the large migrations of wildlife following rainfall are simply not contained within national parks (Western, 1994). The wildlife depended on rural people's lands, prompting conservationists to find ways of making wildlife valuable to these people's decision making. In general the results have not been satisfying, with wildlife numbers of most species declining outside and inside protected areas as their effective space contracts. Some observers are pessimistic as to the outcome. Tim Caro and Paul Scholte recently advised African conservationists that:

> We may have to get used to faunal relaxation [i.e. fewer animals] in Africa's network of famous reserves ... leaving a continent containing isolated pockets of large mammal diversity living at low population sizes. Just like Europe.
>
> (Caro and Scholte, 2007, p234)

We are not convinced that it is reasonable to argue that if Africa cannot be as conservationists hoped that therefore it will be like Europe. But nevertheless, even if the success of sustaining wildlife in the larger landscape has been unsatisfactory thus far, the imperative remains. Studies of primates in Kenya have found that a matrix of agricultural land and natural woodland can both be important for sustaining primate populations (Anderson et al, 2007). Many species of birds in Central America do better in shade-grown coffee plantations than where modern sun-tolerant coffee is found, although unfarmed forest is better still (Greenberg et al, 1997; Rappole et al, 2002a, 2002b; Philpott and Dietsch, 2003). Models of tigers in India suggest that a few reserves (21) could sustain 'stand-alone' populations, but that 129 would depend upon the surrounding matrix of land use, and that conservation policies accordingly have to engage with the unprotected lands and their occupants (Ranganathan et al, 2008). In the UK brownfield sites (wastelands and derelict ground) are recognized as being important habitat for biodiversity, often free of the pressures of agricultural intensification or inappropriate land management that plagues the British countryside (Benton, 2006). Studies of forestry in both the US and the UK have argued that more effective protection for more biodiversity will be achieved by working at the landscape scale and by including privately owned, as well as public forests (Proctor and Pincetl, 1996; McAlpine et al, 2007).

Some observers insist that there are tremendous opportunities for saving wildlife in niches outside protected areas. Rozenweig advocates 'reconciliation ecology' – land use compatible with wildlife (Rosenweig, 2003). Leader-Williams and Hutton observe that much more space for nature, and by implication species, could be found beyond protected area boundaries. Instead of preserving 10–30 per cent of tropical biodiversity in 1–2 per cent of its land they want to preserve 80–90 per cent on 5–15 per cent of the land (Hutton and Leader-Williams, 2003). There is a powerful truth in these arguments – few of us would want to live in a world where all the interesting nature was only found inside special protected areas. Part of the purpose of this book explores how these ideas might become real, and what happens when they do.

But Balmford, Green and colleagues have sounded a note of caution (Balmford et al, 2005b; Green et al, 2005a, 2005b). They note that, overall, we are more likely to conserve more species in undisturbed habitat, and therefore that intensive agriculture, which minimizes the area impact on the land, is potentially better than extensive agriculture, which sprawls over the landscape. Therefore there may be circumstances where it is preferable to minimize human influence by concentrating its effects, rather than by diluting it as reconciliation ecology proposes. No one way (intensive or extensive) will always be preferable. Answers will depend on the ecologies at work. Donald's review of the consequences of intensification of important agricultural systems found, not surprisingly, that we needed to understand the consequences of the expansion and intensification of the production of these commodities better (Donald, 2004).

Finally we should note that, in addition to setting up new protected areas and integrating land use outside them with objectives within, conservationists are also actively seeking to restore degraded ecosystems to their former glory. This is perhaps more common in the developed parts of the world, which enjoys surplus agricultural capacity. They vary in their scale. Agricultural land of 265ha near Wicken Fen in Cambridgeshire, UK, has been purchased since 2000 and its drainage removed to restore the fenland (Taylor, 2005). More ambitious is the recreation of extensive new 'primordial landscapes' in the Osstvaardersplassen, a 5400ha site in Holland. This seeks to restore entire communities of free-ranging herbivores that once roamed Europe in the Neolithic period. They have introduced ancient species of horse and cattle ('reconstituted aurochs'). Wild boars will follow once they can find a means of reducing the risk of swine fever, which might threaten the country's piggeries. Unfortunately predators able to take on the larger herbivores have yet to be introduced and as a result herds have multiplied freely, lost condition and suffered high mortality. The proliferating carcasses, however, saw the spontaneous reappearance of the Black Vulture (*Aegyptus monachus*) in the region for the first time in 200 years (Onneweer, 2005). In South Africa, where private game ranches are one of the fastest growing forms of land use, recreating wildlands is a routine business and there is a vibrant trade in wildlife and continual transformation of former grazing land into wildlife rich hunting grounds or national parks. Davies (2000) describes the process in the Madikwe Game Reserve in South Africa, which saw in the introduction of 23 new species (over 8000 individuals) in the mid-1990s at the cost of $3 million.[4] The more enterprising South African wildlife farmers make money rounding up their stock for sale by selling the right to participate in game capture safaris. Perhaps the grandest of all is in the USA where the Wildlands Project seeks to set aside 50 per cent of the North American continent in new networks of protected areas over the next 100 years or more (Mann, 1993).[5]

Conclusion

In this chapter we have shown that the power of parks is derived not only from their ability to protect specific landscapes, but the ideals and ideas that define and inform this protection. These ideas and ideals have value beyond the actual effects of protected areas. Ideals of pristine wilderness are used in NGO fund-raising appeals, to sell products from Disney Vacations to gas guzzling SUVs. Parks also provide a green public enhancement to countries with poor human rights records, like Gabon and Bolivia, to large-scale economic interventions, and to companies who claim to care about people and the environment. Parks embody these ideals and seek to impose them on specific landscapes. Sometimes they succeed and sometimes they fail, but this does not change the fact that they are at the centre of the ways in which most westerners imagine nature. Whether they ever visit Yellowstone or Serengeti, many westerners are aware of the ideas and ideals that they represent and experience an emotional response to these ideas and ideals.

But these ideas and ideals, especially as they are promoted by parks, conceal a great deal. In fact, part of their value is that they may conceal the types of social and ecological change that parks create or contribute to. It also conceals the diversity of landscapes and practices that fall under the rubric of parks. The data that we have presented in this chapter represents a small fragment of this diversity. In subsequent chapters we explore how the idea and ideals of parks intersect with the imperatives of mainstream conservation in different times and places, how they interact with the cultures, values and livelihood practices of indigenous peoples, and how they become free floating commodities of significant value in a globalized world economy that revolves increasingly around ideas and images and the marketing of specific types of experiences through digitized media. But our first task, in the next chapter, is to examine more closely the imperatives that have driven the conservation trends whose history we have briefly described.

Notes

1   Yosemite was the first state park, established in California, USA in 1864. For good histories see Adams, W. M. (2004) *Against Extinction: The Story of Conservation*.

London: Earthscan; Jepson, P, and R. J. Whittaker, R. J. (2002) 'Histories of protected areas: Internationalisation of conservationist values and their adoption in the Netherlands Indies (Indonesia)'. *Environment and History* 8: 129–172; Kalamandeen, M., and Gillson, L. (2007) 'Demything "wilderness": Implications for protected area designation and management'. *Biodiversity and Conservation* 16: 165–182.

2　Not all early conservationists thought like that. Sarkar notes that John Muir himself recognized that Indians trod lightly on the landscape and that their burning played an important role in it. Sarkar, S. (1999) 'Wilderness preservation and biodiversity conservation: keeping divergent goals distinct'. *Bioscience* 49(5): 405–412. But a report written by anthropologists for the Service in the 1990s was suppressed by the Superintendent of Yellowstone for its title: *Restoring a Presence* (Nabakov and Lawrence, 2004).

3　Stevenson-Hamilton was nick-named 'Skukuza' meaning the one who drives out because he insisted that African residents would have to leave the national park. One of the most popular camps in the park is named Skukuza after him.

4　One game ranch in South Africa even houses three species of South China Tiger sent there to breed and learn hunting skills while waiting for their own habitat to be conserved.

5　www.wildlandsprojectrevealed.org/htm/summary.htm (accessed 22 August 2007).

3

The Imperatives for Conservation

Conservation is not a scientific activity

Lawton, 1997

Before we explore the consequences of different types of conservation strategies it is well to dwell on the different imperatives under which conservation measures have been advanced. These have varied over the years. Whereas protected areas were once set up in unusable lands, now they are established in fertile lowlands to conserve representative habitat therein. In this chapter we explore the different imperatives that have justified conservation, we focus in particular on two – the wilderness lobby and the extinction crisis. Both have been critiqued in recent years and it is important to clarify our position on them. We argue below that justifications based on ideals of wilderness are problematic but that it is foolish to ignore the dramatic changes in rarity and extinction that people have caused.

Wilderness and the wild

The reasons for establishing protected areas have been diverse, but there have been a number of persistent concerns driving their establishment. One of the oldest imperatives for conservation has been to preserve animals for hunting. Conservation has long been advocated and led by the rich and powerful in order that they might enjoy good hunting. The birth of the international conservation movement as we recognize it today was due to the influence of powerful aristocratic hunters who wished to preserve suitable specimens for their sport from the alleged depredations of Africans (Mackenzie, 1988). The international hunting fraternity remains a powerful force behind conservation today. Countries that prohibit hunting (Kenya and India) are unusual for doing so.

Landscape preservation has been another powerful force. The scenery, wildlife and people of the American West provoked the first idea of a 'national park' by the painter Caitlin. The majesty of landscapes also inspired John Muir. Note that these ideas have political power not just because of the landscapes themselves, but also because they intersected with powerful nation-building forces within America, and that country's own search for features adequate to portray its greatness (Runte, 1979). Britain's first national parks set aside highly anthropogenic hilly pastoral landscapes such as the Lake District made popular by Romantic poets such as Wordsworth.

But one of the most powerful forces behind protected area establishment has been the desire to protect wilderness from encroachment and human interference.

The drive to ensure that there is a 'Big Out There' other to ourselves inspires some of the most radical conservation thinkers and activists. It is a particularly strong component of the conservation movements in Australia, New Zealand and the US. Its advocates insist that wilderness heals society and people; that we need these places to provide a counterpoint to the destruction and management of the rest of our lives; that here, where the human touch is weak, and nature's voice strong, we can get a more measured sense of our place in the world. They draw inspiration from Thoreau's words on wildness (Box 3.1).

Box 3.1 Extracts from 'Walking' by Henry David Thoreau

I wish to speak a word for Nature, for absolute freedom and wildness, as contrasted with a freedom and culture merely civil – to regard man as an inhabitant, or a part and parcel of Nature, rather than a member of society ... When I go out of the house for a walk, uncertain as yet whither I will bend my steps, and submit myself to my instinct to decide for me, I find, strange and whimsical as it may seem, that I finally and inevitably settle southwest, toward some particular wood or meadow or deserted pasture or hill in that direction ... Eastward I go only by force; but westward I go free. Thither no business leads me. It is hard for me to believe that I shall find fair landscapes or sufficient wildness and freedom behind the eastern horizon. I am not excited by the prospect of a walk thither; but I believe that the forest which I see in the western horizon stretches uninterruptedly toward the setting sun, and there are no towns nor cities in it of enough consequence to disturb me ... The West of which I speak is but another name for the Wild; and what I have been preparing to say is, that in Wildness is the preservation of the World. Every tree sends its fibers forth in search of the Wild. The cities import it at any price. Men plow and sail for it. From the forest and wilderness come the tonics and barks which brace mankind ... I believe in the forest, and in the meadow, and in the night in which the corn grows. We require an infusion of hemlock, spruce or arbor vitae in our tea ... Life consists with wildness. The most alive is the wildest. Not yet subdued to man, its presence refreshes him. One who pressed forward incessantly and never rested from his labors, who grew fast and made infinite demands on life, would always find himself in a new country or wilderness, and surrounded by the raw material of life. He would be climbing over the prostrate stems of primitive forest-trees ... Here is this vast, savage, hovering mother of ours, Nature, lying all around, with such beauty, and such affection for her children, as the leopard; and yet we are so early weaned from her breast to society, to that culture which is exclusively an interaction of man on man – a sort of breeding in and in, which produces at most a merely English nobility, a civilization destined to have a speedy limit.

However, the power and suitability of wilderness as a guiding light for conservation has come under scrutiny in the last 15 years (Sarkar, 1999; Kalamandeen and Gillson, 2007). Wilderness alone is inadequate for nature's conservation. Some of the largest wildernesses identified as conservation priorities are not speciose (Mittermeier et al, 2003). Most protected areas are too small, individually and collectively, to preserve species that have large ranges, or migration routes. These depend upon lands inhabited by people outside protected areas to survive (Homewood and Rodgers, 1991; Western, 1994). Many of the thorny problems of conservation practice revolve around how to cope with areas where high biodiversity and people's numbers coincide (Luck et al, 2004; Myers et al, 2000).

Pursuit of wilderness has often brought conservation into conflict with people that may not have been necessary for conservation goals (other than wilderness creation) to be achieved. Ideas, and practice, of wilderness can often negate long histories of association between people and places and thus also excludes them historically (Adams and McShane, 1992; Denevan, 1992; Gomez-Pompa and Kaus, 1992; Rose, 1996; Saberwal et al, 2001). Indeed it may be positively counter productive in that human disturbance and land use may be instrumental in preserving biodiversity (Sarkar, 1999; Willis et al, 2004; Igoe, 2004b; Willis and Birks, 2006; Kalamandeen and Gillson, 2007). The classic cases here are the Keoladeo National Park (Bharatpur) in India and the swallowtail butterfly in the UK. At the Keoladeo National Park grazing was banned to protect wetland bird habitat, but the grazing checked vegetation succession that was essential for the birds and the Park suffered substantial habitat degradation after the livestock were removed (Middleton, 2003). Early attempts to set up reserves for the swallowtail butterfly excluded the reed and sedge cutters whose work allowed milk parsley to grow, on which swallowtail caterpillars feed.

Most fundamentally wilderness limits conservation's theatre of operations. As William Cronon famously observed, the trouble with wilderness is that it gives no room for people in nature (Cronon, 1995). They have to be excluded, both physically and conceptually. The pursuit of wilderness makes all that is beautiful and wild in anthropogenic landscapes somehow tainted, spoilt and less worth fighting for. Undue attention to wilderness risks blinding people to the value of used and modified lands. It also promotes an ethic in which the only landscapes worth saving are those that are distant and exotic, while landscapes that are proximate and mundane appear unworthy of our concern. In such a context it becomes increasingly difficult for people to reflect on the economic impacts of their daily lives. From this perspective it appears clear that wilderness and efforts to create and save it can impede conservation's vision.

A practical illustration of that problem is provided by a fascinating analysis of the spotted owl debate in California (Proctor and Pincetl, 1996). These authors noted that while the nesting habitat of the owl was restricted to old growth forest, younger growth, which had been logged, could provide useful feeding habitat and corridors between nesting sites. The value of these logged sites was greater since they tended to be at lower altitude with more productive ecosystems than the higher, colder old growth stands. However, the campaign to save the old growth habitat from the loggers paid little attention to these timber concession areas, even though modifications to their harvesting strategy could have improved their management to enhance spotted owl populations.

A number of authors observe that it is not so much wilderness that is important but *wildness* and people's relationship with it (Adams, 2004). This means looking for it in the mundane and ordinary and everyday nature most people encounter. It also means that conservationists will have to wrestle with the pigeon paradox (Dunn et al, 2006). That is, as most people will live in cities, they are more likely personally to come into contact with nature through interacting with unremarkable biodiversity (pigeons) than they are with the species most conservationists value. The task therefore is to value and celebrate these interactions the better to inculcate conservationist sentiment (Adams, 1996).

Ironically, celebrating wildness has been central in the foundations of the mythology of wilderness in the US. Simon Schama's close reading of Thoreau's work suggests that while he remained a lifelong advocate of wilderness, he was thoroughly excited by wildness. His love for the former derived from the latter. It was Thoreau's ability to find wildness in the small scale and intimate that enabled him to 'travel widely in Concorde' (Schama, 1996, pp571–578). He famously said that 'in wildness is the preservation of the world' (and this is often misquoted as 'wilderness') but he also recognized that 'It is in vain to dream of a wildness distant from ourselves. There is none such. It is the bog in our brain and bowels, the primitive vigour of Nature in us, that inspires that dream' (quoted in Schama, 1996, p578). If wilderness celebration requires a way of imagining and categorizing the world it just needs a slightly broader mind to celebrate wildness. Moreover doing so is hardly inimical to the conservation movement. The logic of our argument is that conservation's remit will grow, not diminish, if the importance of wilderness lessens.

The extinction crisis

By far the most urgent imperative voiced by conservationists is the need to preserve biodiversity and combat the extinction crisis.[1] Extinction is an uncertain science. Counting the number of species that have gone extinct is hard. While we can be sure that extinction is the destiny of every species, proving it has happened recently is difficult. We have to prove that an organism is not there any more. This is hard if the species is small, or its habitat hard to search, and many years (usually 50) have to elapse before it can be declared extinct. The sighting or resurrection of apparently lost species, such the Ivory Billed Wood Pecker, or the Black-footed Ferret, demonstrates the problem.

It is even more difficult to state extinction rates as a proportion of existing species, simply because we do not know how many species there are in the world. We currently know of 1.5–1.75 million, but estimates for the total number vary between 7 and 15 million (Stork, 1997; Dirzo and Raven, 2003; Mace, 2004), with upper limits of 30 million still repeated (Baillie et al, 2004).[2] This makes it an exciting time to be a taxonomist, with 15–20,000 new species being described annually, as two reviewers recently enthused – 'we live in an age of discovery' (Dirzo and Raven, 2003, p148). But it is important to know the total number of species because a high rate of loss (the normal rate is about one species lost per million species per year; see Pimm et al, 1995) represents an extinction event, or mass extinction. There have been five such events in geological history, the most recent of which resulted in the demise of the dinosaurs (Pimm and Brooks, 1997). Rates of loss are now so high that most conservationists believe that we are beginning a sixth extinction spasm, caused by human activity.

The current high rates of extinction began about 40,000 years ago with the loss of large mammals from the Americas, Europe and Australia (there is evidence of losses of smaller species in other habitat elsewhere – Balmford, 1996). This was due to a mixture of the effects of human hunting combining with climate change (Barnosky et al, 2004; Koch and Barnosky, 2006), although the relative importance of each is hotly disputed (Grayson and Meltzer, 2003, 2004; Fiedel and Haynes, 2004; Wroe and Field, 2006, 2007; Brook et al, 2007). The impact of human hunting, habitat clearance and introduction of predators in Pacific islands over the last 12,000 years is more severe and less debated: each of the 800 islands has lost an average of ten species or populations of birds. An estimated 2000 species of rail alone are thought to have gone extinct due to human activity (Steadman, 1995).

Since 1500 the rate of extinction globally has increased, driven in part by the wave of losses of vulnerable endemics, particularly birds, on islands following European colonization (Balmford, 1996). The dodo is the most famous victim but perhaps the most drastic case is New Zealand. These islands used to be entirely populated by birds with no mammals (save bats). Polynesians hunted eight species of moa, then the world's largest bird, to extinction a few hundred years after their arrival in ca 1000–1200 AD and introduced dogs and Pacific rats. Pakeha (European) immigrants killed off and thoroughly endangered many other species of birds through hunting, habitat change and especially the introduction of aggressive Norwegian rats, as well as cats, deer, tar (a mountain sheep), rabbits, mice, wasps, possums and mustelids (Young, 2004).

Much of the more recent concern is driven by 'ecology's oldest generalisation' (Simberloff, 1986, p166): the species–area relationship. Since larger areas support more species, as habitat is lost so the number of species declines (Rosenweig, 2003). The general rule of thumb is that a loss of 90 per cent of habitat will reduce species by 50 per cent (Heywood et al, 1994). The influence of habitat loss in recent extinctions and the occurrence of threatened species is clear. Habitat clearance in many biomes is closely correlated with threats to species, except where introduced predators and hunting increase the dangers (Pimm and Askins, 1995; Brooks and Balmford, 1996; Brooks et al, 1997; Pimm and Raven, 2000; Brooks et al, 2002). Many biomes carry an 'extinction debt' – that is, they have lost habitat but not yet all the species that one would expect to find in these smaller areas (Tilman et al, 1994; Cowlishaw, 1999).

The magnitude and scale of humanity's impact on the world then presents conservation biologists with three pressing questions:

1 Which species have gone and which are most threatened?
2 How long have the remainder got?
3 What is the current rate of extinction?

The first question is most authoritatively dealt with in the IUCN *Red List*. It records that altogether 360 vertebrates, 373 invertebrates (of which 303 are mollusks) and 110 plants are listed as having gone extinct or extinct in the wild since 1500 (Baillie et al, 2004). It also assesses the status of living species, on the basis of assessments produced by panels of experts who examine the numbers and viability of as many of the world's organisms as they can, categorizing them using the criteria in Table 3.1.[3] Species classified as Critically Endangered, Endangered or Vulnerable are collectively grouped as threatened species. Table 3.2 shows that, while some taxa are yet to be well evaluated, a high proportion of known groups are threatened. But this is clearly also only a first approximation. Some of the most numerous groups (especially insects) are poorly known, others are virtually untouched. At current rates it will take another 600 years to list the planet's life (Woodruff, 2001, p5474, and cf. Stork, 1997).

It is important to note that there is not a simple relationship between population numbers and level of threat. Mace notes that more details of population characteristic are required than simple numbers accurately to predict extinction risk (Mace, 1994). Many species have been able to persist for millennia, and we can expect their populations to go into periods of decline as part of normal variations (Simberloff, 1998). Conversely, apparently secure species can disappear rapidly (Pimm et al, 1995). Pimm (1991, pp340–341) reports the example of at least seven species of birds on Guam following the introduction of the brown tree snake. (Now, 12 species are reported lost, with declines of over 90 per cent in all species; see Wiles et al (2003)). There are other examples: when rats invaded Big South Cape Island off New Zealand they rapidly eradicated two bird and one bat species. (One of the bird species was saved from extinction by removing it from the island (Young, 2004, pp156–157). Simberloff reports the loss of five bird species from Hawaii in 1992 when Hurricane Iniki struck the island of Kauai (Simberloff, 1998, p119). Brown (1995) reports eight small but persistent species and 14 once abundant but now extinct or endangered in North America (p212).

The fate of small populations has generated two responses from conservation biologists. Caughley (1994) calls these the 'small population paradigm', and the 'declining population paradigm' respectively. The former examines population and extinction dynamics of small, capped groups. It is generally concerned with persistence in the absence of disturbance and determining what is a minimum viable population. It provides much more specific predictions about the fate of particular species whose numbers are low than the generalities of species – area relationships, but on its own it is of limited use to conservationists because 'it treats an effect (smallness) as if it were a cause' (p215). More relevant for our purposes is the declining population paradigm, which tackles the causes of decline, and for whom a minimum viable population is one pregnant female. But Caughley notes that this paradigm is weak on theory, and this is visible when we tackle the second question – how long have we got before more species go extinct as species reduce in proportion to the habitat available?

Some findings from studies of plants suggest that even after habitat is lost species can persist for many decades (Turner et al, 1994), but the common assumption in the literature is that species decline decreases exponentially. Ecologists then calculate the extinction half-life, which is the time taken for half the species destined for extinction to go extinct. Half-life lengths vary according to the taxa examined and the means of habitat loss and nature of isolation resulting. Current estimates can be divided into two sets that differ by two orders of magnitude. Terborgh (1972) predicted that Barro Colorado Island in Panama (formed in 1914) would lose 20 per cent of its species in 100 years, but estimated that rates of loss had been much slower on Trinidad, which he estimated had lost 0.6 per cent of its birds in the first 100 years and 6.6 per cent in the first 1000. Diamond (1972) calculated a half-life of 10,000 years for Pacific Islands. Cowlishaw (1999) calculated extinction half-lives of about 5000 years for primates on Bioko Island, Equatorial Guinea (off West Africa), which he noted was similar to the 10,000 years calculated for terrestrial mammals by Heaney's (1986) study in Malaysia. Brooks and colleagues (1999), examining bird declines in forest fragments in and around Kakamega in Kenya, calculated that it would take about 50 years (with a range of 23–80) for half the species destined for extinction to disappear, and 100 years for 75 per cent to go. Pimm and Brooks (1997) noted these differences in reported half-life and suggested that on larger islands the relaxation effects (i.e. species loss) may be scale dependent, and that they may have experienced fewer disruptive processes than the Kenyan forest fragments. The longer relaxation times were also on islands caused by processes of sea-level rise not anthropogenic change. The shorter half-lives are most commonly used when estimating extinction rates of threatened species.

Estimates of species numbers, half-lives and probabilities of extinction are used to estimate the current rate of loss per year. Given the levels of ignorance surrounding precisely how many species there actually are, it is widely feared that far more species have disappeared, or are threatened than we actually know about. Estimates of species lost per year have varied by several orders of magnitude according to how many unknown species they consider. The extreme initial estimates are less commonly repeated but estimates remain three orders of magnitude above background rates. The highest is E. O. Wilson's who is reported to have said that we are losing hundreds of thousands of species a year (Mann, 1991). His own written estimate was lower – in the same year Ehrlich and Wilson suggested that the loss of tropical forests alone was removing 4000 species a year, as a very conservative estimate, and possibly 40,000 (Ehrlich and Wilson, 1991). A decade later, Dirzo and

Table 3.1 *The IUCN Red List categories from Baillie et al 2004*

Extinct	Species for which extensive surveys show there is no reasonable doubt that the last individual has died
Extinct in the wild	Species that survive only in cultivation, in captivity or as a naturalised population(s) well outside the past range
Critically endangered	Species that are facing an extremely high risk of extinction in the wild according to any one of the criteria below

A1: Population Reduction	A2–4: Population reduction	B1: Small Range
≥ 90% decline population size in 10 years/3 generations where causes are reversible, understood and ceased.	≥ 80% decline in population size 10 years/3 generations in past present or future where causes are less well understood.	< 100km² extent of occurrence, plus two of severe fragmentation (1 locality); continuing decline or extreme fluctuations in occurrence, habitat or mature individuals.

Endangered	Species that are facing a very high risk of extinction in the wild according to any one of the criteria below

A1: Population Reduction	A2–4: Population reduction	B1: Small Range
≥ 70% decline population size in 10 years/3 generations where causes are reversible, understood and ceased.	≥ 50% decline in population size 10 years/3 generations in past present or future where causes are less well understood.	< 5000km² extent of occurrence, plus two of severe fragmentation (≤ 5 localities); continuing decline or extreme fluctuations in occurrence, habitat or mature individuals.

Vulnerable	Species that are facing a high risk of extinction in the wild according to any one of the criteria below

A1: Population Reduction	A2–4: Population reduction	B1: Small Range
≥ 50% decline population size in 10 years/3 generations where causes are reversible, understood and ceased.	≥ 30% decline in population size 10 years/3 generations in past present or future where causes are less well understood.	< 20,000km² extent of occurrence, plus two of severe fragmentation (≤ 10 localities); continuing decline or extreme fluctuations in occurrence, habitat or mature individuals.

Near Threatened	Species that do not qualify for Critically Endangered, Endangered or Vulnerable, but are close to qualifying, else likely to qualify in the near future.
Least Concern	Species that do not qualify as extinct, threatened or near threatened. Widespread and abundant species are included in this category
Data Deficient	Species for which there is inadequate information to make a direct or indirect assessment of extinction risk
Not evaluated	Not assessed.

B2: Small Range
< 10km² area of occupancy, plus two of severe fragmentation (1 locality), continuing decline or extreme fluctuations in occurrence, habitat or mature individuals.

C: Small and declining population
< 250 mature individuals and estimated continuing decline of 25% in 3 years /1 generation and either 90% of mature individuals in one subpopulation or ≤ 50 mature individuals in each subpopulation.

D1: Small Population and Range
< 50 mature individuals (no extra range criterion).

E: Probability of extinction
≥ 50% in 10 years or 3 generations

B2: Small Range
< 500km² area of occupancy, plus two of severe fragmentation (≤ 5 localities), continuing decline or extreme fluctuations in occurrence, habitat or mature individuals.

C: Small and declining population
< 2,500 mature individuals and estimated continuing decline of 20% in 5 years /2 generations and either 95% of mature individuals in one subpopulation or ≤ 250 mature individuals in each subpopulation.

D1: Small Population and Range
< 250 mature individuals (no extra range criterion).

E: Probability of extinction
≥ 20% in 20 years or 5 generations

B2: Small Range
< 2000km² area of occupancy, plus two of severe fragmentation (≤ 10 localities), continuing decline or extreme fluctuations in occurrence, habitat or mature individuals.

C: Small and declining population
< 10,000 mature individuals and estimated continuing decline of 10% in 10 years/3 generations and either 100% of mature individuals in one subpopulation or ≤ 1000 mature individuals in each subpopulation.

D1: Small Population and Range
< 1000 mature individuals and/or area of occupancy, 20km² or number of locations ≤ 5.

E: Probability of extinction
≥ 10% in 100 years

Table 3.2 *The IUCN Red List*

Grouping	Class	No. of sp.	No. sp. eval. 2006	% sp. eval	No. of sp. threatened	Sp. threat'd as % of sp. described	No. of. crit end. sp.	No. of. end. sp.	No. of vuln. sp.
Vertebrates	Mammals	5416	4856	89.7	1093	20.18	162	348	583
	Birds	9934	9934	100.0	1206	12.14	181	351	674
	Reptiles	8240	664	8.1	341	4.14	73	101	167
	Amphibians	5918	5918	100.0	1811	30.60	442	738	631
	Fishes	29,300	2914	9.9	1173	4.00	253	238	682
	Subtotal	**58,808**	**24,284**	**41.3**	**5624**	**9.56**	**1111**	**1776**	**2737**
Invertebrates	Insects	950,000	1192	0.1	623	0.07	68	129	426
	Molluscs	70,000	2163	3.1	975	1.39	265	222	488
	Crustaceans	40,000	537	1.3	459	1.15	78	87	294
	Others	130,200	86	0.1	44	0.03	6	9	29
	Subtotal	**1,190,200**	**3978**	**0.3**	**2101**	**0.18**	**417**	**447**	**1237**

Plants	Mosses	15,000	93	0.6	80	0.53	22	32	26
	Ferns and allies	13,025	212	1.6	139	1.07	32	39	68
	Gymnosperms	980	908	92.7	306	31.22	63	85	158
	Dicotyledons	199,350	9538	4.8	7086	3.55	1277	1836	3973
	Monocotyledons	59,300	1150	1.9	779	1.31	147	266	366
	Subtotal	287,655	11,901	4.1	8390	2.92	1541	2258	4591
Others	Lichens	10,000	2	0.0	2	0.02	1	1	0
	Mushrooms	16,000	1	0.0	1	0.01	1	0	0
	Subtotal	26,000	3		3		2	1	0
Total		1,562,663	40,166		16,118	10.3	3071	4482	8565

Raven, following Pimm and Brooks (1997) and using half-lives of 50 years, predicted that 500 of the threatened birds and 565 the 1130 threatened animals will go extinct in the next 50 years (Dirzo and Raven, 2003, p162). This gives a figure of well over 1000 extinctions per million species per year, over a 1000 times the background rate. Alternatively, using the actual predicted probability of species in each category going extinct (Criteria E of Table 3.1), we calculate that the extinction rate is just over 200 species per year, which is about 130 species per million species per year. This assumes that all small populations are subject to the same levels of threat and includes none of the species that have not been evaluated. Finally Myers and Lanting (1999) predicted that between 50 and 150 species a year are going extinct.

These high predicted yearly losses, however, are yet to begin. If we just use known species listed as threatened in 1996 (animals) and 1998 (plants), and predict yearly extinction rates based on the probability of extinction estimated for each category, and assuming that each species in each category is subject to the same likelihood of going extinct, we should have seen over 1000 extinctions by 2006 (Table 3.3). Actual known extinctions from 1990s to the present were 11 (Baillie et al, 2004, pp47–48), plus the Yangtze River Dolphin (lost since Baillie et al went to press), although up to 122 further species of amphibian are listed as possibly extinct with the decline occurring since 1980 (Stuart et al, 2004, 2005; Pimenta et al, 2005; Mendelson et al, 2006).

The relative lack of actual extinction has prompted some observers to criticize the validity of extinction concerns (Lomborg, 2001). That is not our position (Brockington, 2003). For us the discrepancy illustrates the widely recognized difficulties of using extinction rates as a measure of human impact (Balmford et al, 2003a; Heywood et al, 1994). Some commentators believe that it is best to consider the more threatened species to be 'committed to extinction' (Heywood et al, 1994). That means that there is no longer the habitat to sustain them and they will die out in the normal course of events without constant interventions to maintain them. The discrepancies have also helped to fuel a debate on the utility of red lists of themselves, in part because of the instability of the definition of species on which the list depends (Cuaron, 1993; Smith et al, 1993; Burgman, 2002; Possingham et al, 2002; Lamoreux et al, 2003; Mace, 2004). Mace, observing that the number of primate species has virtually doubled to over 350 in two decades, largely due to taxonomic revisions, concluded that:

> Because we know that the rules for delimiting species have changed over time, we cannot judge the real severity of the recent increase in the number of endangered primates nor ... can we compare this trend with other taxa within and outside the mammals.
>
> (Mace, 2004, p714)

Others warn against using high extinction rates for known taxa as a basis for predicting other losses. Balmford and colleagues insist that:

Table 3.3 *Comparing predicted and actual extinctions*

Group	Crit. End. 1996/98	End. 1996/98	Vuln. 1996/98	Crit. End. Sp. lost per decade assuming 50% loss in 10 years	End. Sp. lost per decade assuming 20% loss in 20 years	Vuln. Sp. lost per decade assuming 10% loss in 100 years	Predicted extinctions 1996/8 to 2006/08	Actual extinctions and extinctions in the wild
Mammals	169	315	612	85	32	6	123	1
Birds	168	235	704	84	24	7	115	1
Reptiles	41	59	153	21	6	2	29	0
Amphibians	18	31	75	9	3	1	13	1
Fishes	157	134	443	78	13	4	95	0
Insects	44	116	377	22	12	4	38	0
Molluscs	257	212	451	129	21	5	155	0
Plants	909	1197	3222	364	96	26	486	8
Total	1763	2299	6037	791	206	54	1051	11

2004 IUCN Red List of Threatened Species. <www.iucnredlist.org>. Downloaded 31 July 2007 (Baillie et al, 2004, p47)

...any extrapolation from extinction rates for well-known groups to estimates of the total number of extinctions per year across all groups is impossible.

(Bamford et al, 2003a, p326)

They observe that there are plenty of other estimates of habitat decline and population loss, and other indices of deleterious human influence on diverse ecosystems need to be examined, and could be expanded (Balmford et al, 2003a; Jenkins et al, 2003; Balmford et al, 2005a). Nevertheless the continued efforts to refine the red lists now allow for measures of trends in the threat status of birds (the best known taxon), which only consider in status based on real changes to bird numbers (Butchart et al, 2004, 2005, 2006a). These deal with many previous criticisms and show a persistent decline (Figure 3.1).

Whether or not threatened species are going extinct now, the decline in their abundance poses considerable costs to conservation, both in terms of determining where to invest resources and in trying to protect marginal populations and habitats. Occasionally (expensive) species rescue can be dramatically successful (Butchart et al, 2006b). Following intensive efforts the Chatham Island Black Robin recovered from one breeding pair, the Mauritius kestrel from four

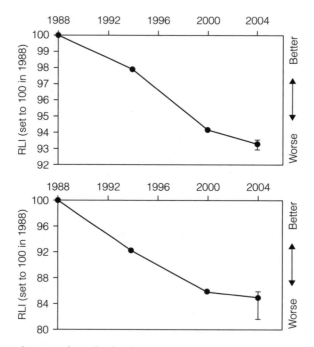

Figure 3.1 *Red List indices for birds*

Source: Butchart et al, 2004. Reproduced with permission

individuals (Butchart et al, 2006b; Rodrigues, 2006). But it is often expensive to breed and 're-wild/release'. A number of conservation NGOs have questioned whether the money would not be better spent on in-situ conservation. Note this cautionary tale of captive breeding. Caughley (1994) reports that a meeting of experts decided that the only way to save the Sumatran rhinoceros was through captive breeding. But they did not adequately consider the expense of capturing the animals, the dangers of doing so, or the breeding success in captivity. Caughley reports Leader-William's analysis of the programme did not make happy reading. He found that nine animals died during or after capture, that only one was born in captivity, and that to a female pregnant when caught and that the expense of doing this to the species was US$2.5 million. The same funds could have been used to protect 700km² of rhino habitat (holding 70 adults) for 20 years. This is a critical debate between zoos and other forms of conservation organizations: that the amount of money spent on maintaining the species ex-situ and building/sustaining enclosures in zoos could be more effectively used to protect the species in their natural habitats. Even if captive breeding can save species from extinction it is expensive for the conservation movement to have to mount such rescue missions.

Conclusion

What are the implications for conservation of these declines in abundance and increase in extinction? The simple take home message is that more and stronger conservation measures are required, including protected areas. There are two complications.

First, while the impending extinction crisis is real, it is used by scientists to gain political leverage. Myers himself admitted to providing high estimates of extinction in order to put them onto 'scientific and political agendas'.[4] Mace notes that one of the factors driving taxonomic revision is the kudos and bargaining power that new, threatened species provide scientists (Mace, 2004). She warns that the listing of species as threatened should prompt local action sensitive to local circumstances, and that some species not listed may also deserve attention.

An aspect of this lobbying is the practice of conservation biologists to frequently speak of imminent extinction, or commitments to extinction, but not always define their timescales. For example the Alliance for Zero Extinction has produced a list of endangered and critically endangered species with restricted ranges that are highly likely to disappear if their habitat goes (Ricketts et al, 2005). The extinction of each is thought to be 'imminent'. But the meaning of imminent is undefined. Which for example might last ten years unaided, and which 20? Is the probability of extinction the same for all these species?

Second, as our understanding of the causes of extinction has grown so has recognition of the importance of a diversity of strategies. There have been some remarkable cases of species snatched from extinction. But these require far more than mere setting aside land in protected areas. Intensive management is required, including vigorous poisoning and trapping campaigns of introduced predators, and removal of introduced vegetation (Saunders and Norton, 2001; Gillies et al, 2003). Managing these areas is more akin to gardening than traditional notions of protected area management. Caughley (1994) notes the importance of pragmatically uniting the knowledge of the small population paradigm and the declining population paradigm in order that the ultimate and proximate causes of extinction can be adequately dealt with. He cites the recovery of the Lord Howe Woodhen as a successful instance of this cooperation and the attempt to save the Californian Condor as a failure.

Finally we should note that conservation cannot claim a scientific mandate from species loss for its work. The crisis is real, but the mandate is not scientific. It is much stronger than that. The science of biodiversity can tell us what is happening, but not why we should want to conserve things in the first place, how and where and with what consequences. These questions are the product of social and political debates. As Lawton observed, in the statement with which we began this chapter:

> Science may help inform the process of (protected area)
> establishment, but the decisions are ultimately political, ethical,
> aesthetic, even religious, and embrace much more than just scientific
> information. At its heart conservation is not a scientific activity.
>
> (Lawton, 1997, p4)

Notes

1   Biodiversity refers to diversity at all scales – genes, species, habitat and ecosystems – but is often equated with species numbers.
2   These figures are for eukaryotic species, which exclude bacteria.
3   This is not always an easy process. The disagreements that have arisen over the state of Brazilian amphibians make it clear that when evaluators insist on a 'strongly evidentiary viewpoint' 95 fewer species were identified as threatened compared to evaluators who use a 'precautionary but realistic approach' (Stuart, et al, 2005). Reading between the lines we infer that there are strong reasons for experts to expect these species are in trouble, but inadequate field evidence for one group of empirically driven scientists to declare them so (Pimenta, et al, 2005).
4   www.gristmagazine.com/grist/books/myers121201.asp (accessed 20 January 2003).

4

The Power of Parks

The scientific mind does not so much provide the
right answers as ask the right questions.

Claude Levi-Strauss (1969 (1964), p7)

The last two decades have seen the crystallization of fears by conservationists that
there is a substantial extinction crisis looming, if not already unfolding. They
have witnessed the growth of a substantial network of protected areas whose
development is becoming increasingly driven by, and responsive to, the
geography of rarity, endemism and land-use change. But the same period has also
seen substantial critiques of conservation practice, both in terms of its impact on
nature, and its consequences for society. The result has been a vigorous
examination of protected areas (often euphemized as 'parks'). The discussion has
often been confusing according to the questions that different protagonists were
asking. We attempt to provide some clarity here.

First, we consider how well parks work. More precisely, we ask: is strong
protection from human influence by states the best way to protect valuable
nature, or would conservation objectives be advanced by encouraging other
mechanisms that allowed more human use, development objectives or local
control? We argue that there are good data demonstrating that parks protect
vegetation and wildlife well from human transformation, but poor data as to their
relative performance against other conservation mechanisms such as community
conservation or village governed forest reserves, or other such schemes. In other
words we do not understand the circumstances that might make formal protected
areas the best means of achieving conservation objectives.

Second we examine the impacts of parks on people. We consider how they have
distributed different types of fortune and misfortune to their neighbours and
stakeholders at different spatial scales. We examine the state of knowledge about
eviction from protected areas. We argue that there are clear, sometimes
widespread benefits arising from parks, many of which are hard to value in dismal
economic terms, and that these have often been accompanied by varying degrees
of local disempowerment, dispossession and marginalization. We argue that
enquiries into eviction alone can risk displacing more important issues. We note
that it is difficult to gain any comprehensive idea of the general social impacts of
parks for want of any systematic data collection.

In recent years these questions have become embroiled in two other confusing
conflicts. First, there is the poverty and conservation debate, which concerns

conservation's role in causing and reducing poverty. Second there is the principle of local support, which states that parks without local support are bound to fail. We examine both, arguing that each is often founded on misunderstandings or confusions and that there is much more room for agreement between each side than is first apparent.

This chapter does not develop the central thesis of the book about how conservation and capitalism are combining. But the issues we examine here have dominated discussions in conservation circles for many years and it is important that we outline our position and thinking on them. This chapter does review in detail how protected areas change nature and society. Given that our argument is that conservation and capitalism are combining to reshape the world we need to consider more carefully precisely what changes protected areas, the central conservation strategy, bring.

How well do protected areas work?

Protected areas play a vital role in conservation strategies and have been vigorously defended (Kramer et al, 1997; Brandon et al, 1998; Oates, 1999; Terborgh, 1999). These arguments are partly based on the obvious successes of the more strictly protected areas, generally termed 'parks' in protecting nature, and partly on diverse failures and uncertainties associated with alternative strategies.

With respect to protecting vegetation, there are strong debates in Canada, New Zealand and Australia about the place of grazing on public lands and the best way of protecting grasslands from unwanted change, but these are not debates about the effectiveness of parks per se. On the contrary, opponents of parks know that they will be effective in excluding grazing if established; that is why they oppose them. The disputes here are about the ecological necessity of protecting the land from livestock, with farmers disputing the findings of ecologists and the ability of the latter to know the land as they do. In New Zealand and Australia any land protected from livestock has also to be protected from introduced herbivores, carnivores and plant species (Mark, 1989; Gillies et al, 2003).

There is much more dispute about the most effective means of conserving tropical forest. With respect to tropical forests' protection, the importance of parks is strongly supported by a number of studies. Bruner and colleagues (2001a) found, on the basis of questionnaire evidence of managers and experts of a sample of 93 tropical parks in populated areas, that 40 per cent had experienced improvement of vegetation cover, 43 per cent had shown no further forest clearance since establishment. Naughton-Treves and colleagues (2005) compared 36 deforestation rates inside and outside protected areas. In 32 cases the deforestation rate was between 0.1 and 14 per cent faster outside protected areas' boundaries. DeFries and colleagues (2005) examined the increasing isolation of 198 highly protected tropical forests using coarse resolution satellite data and found that two thirds experienced significant deforestation within 50km of their borders, but only a quarter had such within their boundaries.

There are problems with these studies. For example, it is not normally appropriate to use questionnaire data to assess vegetation change. It is simply not accurate, and prone to bias. In the case of Bruner and colleagues' work many of the respondents had a vested interest in showing that the parks were working because they were on the staff. Naughton-Treves et al are handicapped by the methodological problems of quantitatively comparing the rates of deforestation across different studies. They also do not say what proportion of the deforestation rates were 0.1 per cent and which 14 per cent lower. Nor do they, or DeFries and her colleagues, mention the possibility that in some cases gazettement may hasten land-use change beyond protected area boundaries. Nevertheless the trend in these findings is clear. There are clear suggestions that in some, if not many, circumstances, protecting a place by designating it as a park can much reduce unwanted vegetation change.

But does this mean that parks are better than other forms of protection? If we wish to protect a coastal forest in Madagascar, or a rainforest in New Zealand, is it necessary to impose state enforced regulations? Government conservation departments can be far removed from local realities, else simply absent and unable to enforce their rules. There are all sorts of situations where some form of local control may be better than distant state controls. None of the studies above, however, address that question (Bruner et al, 2001b; Vanclay, 2002). They are only concerned with how parks do compared to their surroundings, not with how they perform compared with other means of protection. Ostrom and Nagendra's review of this literature concluded that the 'debate over the effectiveness of strictly protected areas needs to be extended to a much larger landscape of tenure regimes' (2006, p19225).

This is an important issue, but has been tackled with surprisingly few rigorous studies. There are some relatively small-scale studies based on satellite data and aerial photographs. Nepstad and colleagues have compared the relative efficiency of large uninhabited parks and inhabited extractive and indigenous reserves in preventing fire and deforestation in the Brazilian Amazon using satellite data between 1997 and 2000 (for deforestation), and 1998 (for fires). They found that both forms were effective against preventing fire and deforestation, with no significant differences between either. They noted that the good performance of occupied reserves was achieved despite their being at the frontier of deforestation pressure, whereas parks benefited from their relative lack of proximate habitat change (Nepstad et al, 2006). Ostrom and Nagendra report poor performance of selected parks in South Asia that excluded local management, and better performance of community managed forests nearby (Ostrom and Nagendra, 2006).

The most ambitious attempt to test the relative efficacy of protected areas is work by Tanya Hayes and Elinor Ostrom, who have considered the relative

Table 4.1 *A comparison of the distribution of parks in Hayes' sample and others*

Country	Hayes, 2006; Hayes and Ostrom, 2005			Naughton-Treves et al, 2005	DeFries et al, 2005	Bruner et al, 2001a
	Non-parks	Parks not in WDPA	Parks in WDPA			
Argentina	–	–	–	–	5	–
Bolivia	3	6	–	–	2	–
Brazil	2	1	–	–	32	7
Columbia	–	–	–	–	9	8
Equador	1	–	–	4	2	7
Paraguay	–	–	–	3	3	1
Peru	–	–	–	5	4	6
Venezuela	–	–	–	–	11	–
Belize	–	–	–	–	2	1
Costa Rica	–	–	–	12	2	–
Guatemala	6	1	–	2	4	–
Honduras	1	–	–	1	2	4
Mexico	2	4	–	2	–	1
Nicaragua	–	–	–	–	1	–
Panama	–	–	–	–	2	–
USA	7	–	–	–	1	–
Jamaica	–	–	–	1	–	–
Cambodia	–	–	–	–	4	1
China	–	–	–	1	3	–
India	28	11	1	–	10	–
Indonesia	–	–	–	3	29	8
Japan	–	–	–	–	1	–
Laos	–	–	–	–	–	10
Malaysia	–	–	–	–	3	–

Table 4.1 *A comparison of the distribution of parks in Hayes' sample and others* (cont'd)

Country	Hayes, 2006; Hayes and Ostrom, 2005			Naughton-Treves et al, 2005	DeFries et al, 2005	Bruner et al, 2001
	Non-parks	Parks not in WDPA	Parks in WDPA			
Myanmar	–	–	–	–	1	–
Nepal	22	23	2	–	1	–
Philippines	–	–	–	–	1	7
Sri Lanka	–	–	–	–	4	–
Taiwan	–	–	–	–	4	–
Thailand	–	–	–	–	29	3
Vietnam	–	–	–	1	2	3
Brunei D'm	–	–	–	–	1	–
CAR	–	–	–	–	1	–
Congo	–	–	–	–	2	–
Cote d'Ivoire	–	–	–	–	2	4
DRC	–	–	–	–	4	–
Ghana	–	–	–	–	–	10
Kenya	–	1	4	1	1	–
Liberia	–	–	–	–	1	1
Madagascar	4	4	–	–	5	5
Malawi	–	–	–	–	1	–
Senegal	–	–	–	–	–	2
Tanzania	1	1	1	–	–	6
Togo	–	–	–	–	–	2
Uganda	10	3	13	8	–	6
Australia	–	–	–	–	2	–
Total	87	55	21	44	198	93

effectiveness of parks compared to community controls in two recent papers (Hayes and Ostrom, 2005; Hayes, 2006). They looked at data collected by the International Forestry Resources and Institutions (IFRI) network on 163 forests, of which 76 were 'parks' and 87 'non-parks', where park was defined as falling in one of the six IUCN categories (Table 4.1). All forests in the IFRI database provide relatively standardized data about institutions governing their use, ownership, user communities and forest products used. To compare forest condition Hayes and Ostrom used assessments of vegetation density made by independent professional foresters who compared the vegetation density of IFRI forests to other forests in the same ecological zone.

Hayes and Ostrom report no difference in the vegetation density of parks and non-parks. But they found evidence that might make parks imposed and policed by government a less robust form of conservation than protection rooted in local institutions. For instance, they found that density of vegetation was higher where more forest products had rules governing use, and lower where there were no rules. They found vegetation density was more abundant where more user groups could define the rules and sparser where fewer could. Thus what makes for more effective protection (denser vegetation relative to similar forests) is not the official designation, but rather the role of residents in defining rules for forest products.

But there are several problems with this analysis. There were no data about the size of these forests, and so it is impossible to assess the relative significance of the contribution of parks and non-parks to protected area networks. There are also problems with how the term 'park' was defined. Few of the parks in the analysis were included in the World Database of Protected Areas (WDPA) (Table 4.1). This could reflect its incompletenesses, but it could also mean that there is simply inadequate overlap between this sample of parks and those other authors have used. The WDPA lists nearly 4700 other protected areas in the countries Hayes and Ostrom examined, including nearly 1700 forest reserves, which are not part of their analyses. The WDPA is not the ultimate authority as to what constitutes a park. But it has formed the basis for other studies (Rodrigues et al, 2004; DeFries et al, 2005; Naughton-Treves et al, 2005). Rigorous methodologies need not be based on the WDPA, but it would be useful for comparative purposes to know how samples of parks relate to the WDPA.

It is perhaps unfortunate that Hayes and Ostrom tied their work so tightly to parks. The term is a shibboleth (Redford et al, 2006, p1); it is widely used, but in ways that reinforce prejudice, obscuring more than it reveals. One could argue that parks are in fact irrelevant to their argument. They are in fact concerned with the importance for conservation of locally derived rules of resource-use control. There is a risk that the value of their findings will be lost by the confusion over the term 'park'.

But this work also shows us that Hayes' question, 'Are parks effective?', is just a little too blunt. Effective for whom, for what nature? And if Bruner and his colleagues show that 40 per cent of (large tropical forest) parks 'have seen an improvement in vegetation cover', they also show that 17 per cent were not 'holding their borders' against agricultural expansion and a further 43 per cent merely had no further net clearing (cf. Roe et al, 2003). The question to ask in these circumstances is not whether they are failing or succeeding, but rather under what circumstances were they strong, and when were they weak? As we will argue later, it is not adequate simply to assert that they will be weak without local support.

With respect to wildlife the value of parks is again clear, but the relative effectiveness of parks compared to other strategies, and the impact of different levels of hunting on conservation objectives is less so. We know that the answer to the question 'Do parks reduce mortality from hunting?' is 'Yes', but given that, several other questions become important:

- Precisely what impacts does hunting have on animal populations?
- How many and how large do parks need to be to protect wildlife?
- How will the impact of parks vary for different taxa according to their size and distribution across the landscape?
- What mosaic of parks and other strategies are required to advance conservation objectives?
- What hunting or other types of resource use could be allowed in parks?

We can sketch some broad geographical patterns dividing the world into temperate and tropical regions and the latter into forests and grassland. In temperate countries strong well-organized local sports hunting lobbies have campaigned vigorously and effectively for good hunting habitat. This form of hunting is often highly compatible with conservation objectives, as it means more land where wildlife can thrive. Parks are routinely hunted in the UK, and in many other countries that forbid hunting in protected areas, wildlife habitat extends far beyond park boundaries on private lands because of the lucrative revenues hunting on them can command.

There are some important exceptions to this rule. In Australia hunters want sustained populations of Sambar deer, and Brumbie runners want wild horses, both of which are large introduced species with problematic impacts on the ecosystem. In New Zealand large populations of deer, chamois, thar, goat and pig cause severe damage to vegetation (Mark, 1989). Hunting of these species is freely allowed in national parks, and again hunting lobbies desire sustained populations that other conservationists wish removed. Nor is this just a New World problem. In Scotland large deer populations inhibit the regrowth of forest (Toogood, 2003).

Hunting by indigenous people of indigenous fauna in temperate areas can be viewed with suspicion by some conservationists. Use within or near protected areas is often resented. In New Zealand Maori harvesting of mutton birds is a bone of contention with conservationists (Taiepa et al, 1997), as are Maori desires to hunt wildlife, such as the rare *kereru* (native pigeon) for traditional purposes (Galbreath, 2002; Young, 2004). Similar disputes are visible in Australia over hunting dugong (albeit not temperate) and the harvest of marine resources inside national parks, and in North America over indigenous whaling and seal kills.

In the tropics, the importance of parks for protecting wildlife is not disputed, but again the relative importance of parks to other strategies is not clear. In grasslands and open habitat, especially in Africa, parks are often inadequate to support many large species that migrate long distances and which depend on land outside their borders (Borner, 1985; Western, 1994). There are many attempts to sustain wildlife populations beyond park borders, which we will review in the next chapter. Improvements in village forest management have seen improvements in populations of many species, including large, slow breeding ones (Monela et al, 2004; Blomely and Ramadhani, 2006).

Commercial hunting operations outside national parks, and sometimes of village land can provide substantial sources of revenue, which if well distributed locally can make wildlife valuable (Novelli et al, 2006). In Africa it is a valuable industry and estimated to generate about $200 million a year, with half of that spent in South Africa (Lindsey et al, 2007). Sport and trophy hunting has increasingly become part of conservation argument and policies, and is promoted as a low-impact sustainable use approach, adding value to natural resources (Hofer, 2002; Novelli and Humavindu, 2005; Novelli et al, 2006). The studies show the central importance of sport hunting for wildlife to Namibian tourism economy. The ecological impact varies with the quality of control exerted over adherence to trophy quotas (Loveridge et al, 2007). Interestingly Novelli and colleagues argue that sport hunting should be defined as a form of ecotourism because although it depends on killing individual animals it has a lower overall impact on the environment and brings in a greater level of revenue than regular photographic tourism. Sport hunters do not require the levels of infrastructure in the form of hotels, restaurants, bars and roads that non-consumptive tourism depends on (Smith and Duffy, 2003; Novelli et al, 2006).

Such 'consumptive' forms of wildlife tourism are highly controversial, either because they can kill charismatic animals such as elephants (Fortmann, 2005), or because they can restrict local access to valued resources (Dzingirai, 2003; Robbins and Luginbuhl, 2005). As a result community-based conservation and tourism programmes that are reliant on sport hunting have also been criticized; for example, Communal Areas Management Plan for Indigenous Resources (CAMPFIRE) in Zimbabwe was highly dependent on trophy hunting as a source of revenue and as such attracted criticism from the Humane Society of the US and International Fund for Animal Welfare, amongst others (Smith and Duffy, 2003, pp145–158).

As to the relative importance of parks and commercial hunting operations for conservation, it is in fact often not realistic to compare the two. For viable commercial hunting often depends on nearby parks as a source of wildlife. Both are seen as complementary but the mosaics of land use resulting tend to reflect the willpower of governments, locals and donors rather than much systematic planning.

Hunting in tropical forests is particularly worrying for conservationists. Productivity of wild meat is an order of magnitude less than more open habitats (Milner-Gulland et al, 2003), and there is also often fewer domestic livestock to provide local needs for meat. Demands for protein (Brashares et al, 2004) and an urban preference for wild meat is driving substantial hunting. The impacts of changing animal abundance cascade through the ecosystem (affecting animal-dispersed seeds) and society (affecting income and diet, Stoner et al, 2007). Again there are clear geographical patterns in the consequences driven by population density (figures below are from Milner-Gulland et al, 2003). In Asia, where high population densities in forest (522/km²) combine with strong demands from prosperous urban areas, the effects are considerable, with numerous local and regional extirpations. One review suggested that 'commercially important species have disappeared or exist at low densities (Corlett, 2007). Bennett (2002) notes that diets have changed in order to cope with the lack of wild meat due to the combined effects of habitat loss and hunting.

In West Africa (population density 99/km²) substantial defaunation has already taken place with only resilient fast-breeding species remaining (Bennett et al, 2007) and offtake rates of many species are unsustainable in many parts of Central Africa. Wilkie and Carpenter (1999) report that hunting reduced species density by 43–100 per cent, with the greatest effects on large slow-breeding animals. Oates documents empty forests in Ghana with hunters reduced to killing birds (Oates, 1999). Hunting combined with disease has resulted in the catastrophic decline of apes in western equatorial Africa (Walsh et al, 2003).

These problems are present but less severe in Latin American forests (population density 46/km²). Hunting has a noticeable impact on population abundances and structure (Bodmer et al, 1997; Bodmer and Lozano, 2001). Kent Redford coined the term 'empty forest' to describe hunted forests in the neotropics (Redford, 1992). Indigenous hunters in the Amazon do not appear to hunt in order to conserve their prey populations, instead taking animals opportunistically, regardless of their gender and attempting to maximize return for effort rather than the long-term viability of prey populations (Alvard, 1993, 1995; Alvard et al, 1997). But people's impact is relatively slight because their numbers are few (Smith and Wishnie, 2000). In the Amazon there are large areas of land that are largely unhunted (Fa et al, 2002). These authors suggest that 60 per cent of taxa in the Congo are exploited unsustainably but none in the Amazon.

What are the consequences of these patterns for the parks debate? In the Amazon, as in Australia and New Zealand, conservation concerns reflect desires to preserve fauna that do not reflect the presence of people. Wildlife is not generally threatened by hunting, but inhabited forest is simply less interesting to conservationists. Conservationists also fear repeating patterns of wildlife loss seen in Asia and Africa. As Redford and Sanderson observed of forest peoples and their representatives:

> They may speak for their version of a forest, but they do not speak for the forest we want to conserve.
>
> (Redford and Sanderson, 2000 p1364)

In West and Central Africa large areas free from hunting (parks) are indispensable to conservation objectives. But observers also recognize that a cornucopia of strategies to reduce hunting generally (more protein from other sources), changing the species taken (education campaigns, taxes, enforcement), and local conservation initiatives (no-take areas) will be necessary (Milner-Gulland et al, 2003; Bennett et al, 2007). The latter is particularly important for rural prosperity also. The decline in bushmeat availability due to sales to urban markets presents many problems to rural residents who then lose an important source of income and protein, especially in lean seasons (de Merode et al, 2004; Nielsen, 2006). Research by de Merode has shown that village chiefs have actively prevented the sale in local markets of slow-breeding species taken with heavy weaponry in the Democratic Republic of the Congo (DRC) even during the civil war. Urban markets in contrast showed a massive increase in wild meat availability in that period as controls broke down and hunting and weapons proliferated (de Merode and Cowlishaw, 2006).

The constant call in the literature is for a broader vision of a mosaic of land management – parks, no-take areas and diverse community-based strategies that will allow for larger healthier wildlife populations. What we lack are the data on the distribution and density of many hunted species that would allow us to predict the consequences for wildlife of different mosaics (Milner-Gulland et al, 2003). Beyond securing a basic minimum of sites that might prevent extinction the appropriate configuration of parks and other strategies for effective wildlife conservation is far from clear.

What do parks do to people?

It is not as easy as it might seem to catalogue the way that parks distribute fortune and misfortune among different groups in society. In many cases a benefit to one group is a disadvantage to another. The loss of grazing for transhumant pastoralists and their removal elsewhere might result fewer cattle thefts for more sedentary neighbours. Lost income for women selling traditional medicines gathered in protected areas may be achieved through employment opportunities given to young men to act as forest guards. Prohibitions on hunting by elderly skilled hunters may be accompanied by distributions of cash or payments for local services by hunting revenues from wealthy tourists. Healthy forests on watersheds may benefit lowland irrigators, but could be accompanied by restrictions to the livelihoods of forest dwellers. When the Mkomazi Game Reserve in Tanzania was cleared of its pastoral occupants the cattle keepers lost prime grazing land, and a local cattle market collapsed. Nearby farmers in one village, however, benefited from new investments into schools and other infrastructure, which pastoralists were less able to enjoy because some had moved away and others were now earning less money and so could not send their children to school so easily (Brockington, 2002).

In spite of the difficulties in measuring the costs and benefits of conservation, and the lack of good data about them, debates about parks' impact on people are still often cast in terms of their costs and benefits. Studies have tended to focus either on simply the benefits, or on just the costs. Balanced evaluations of individual protected areas are rare, and on networks of protected areas even fewer. We will discuss each separately.

The benefits that advocates of parks list are legion. Parks safeguard ecosystem services. They act as water catchments, providing vegetation cover that aids infiltration of water into the ground and preventing soil erosion that would otherwise fill dams. They are sources of genetic diversity for food crops. They could house species that could be useful to medical science in its search for cures to human disease. Parks provide recreation and release for tired city dwellers; more than that, they focus tourists into a relatively few places, creating more space elsewhere. The tourist industries they sustain can make valuable contributions to the economy. They provide aesthetic pleasure, both to actual visitors, and through the industries of image making (film, painting, pictures and poetry), which they house. Parks are a focus of research activities, either on species only found easily within them, or because researchers wish to explore dynamics in ecosystems with relatively little human impact. Parks have become a focus of nation building and a focal point of development strategies. By providing people with the types of contact with nature that they lack in their daily lives they inspire them to become conservationists.

But the costs, which critics of parks decry, are also many. They cause eviction and physical displacement; they cause economic displacement, denying people access to fuelwood, thatching grass, water, lumber, meat and diverse other resources. The fact that they often do this to poor and weak rural groups, the better to create relaxing holidays and pleasing vistas for the world's wealthy is unpleasant, and often unjust. Parks also displace people symbolically. They write them out of landscape's history, proclaiming that they do not belong. Parks are a means by which states extend their bureaucratic powers over land use and lives. They can marginalize and disempower local resource management and fundamentally alter the livelihoods from which people derive their identities.

Parks rarely, if ever, do only one of these things, however. Instead they distribute fortune and misfortune at the same time. It is rarely meaningful to speak of benefits offsetting costs, or vice versa. In many cases the groups benefiting and those suffering are different. The benefits to one are a cost to another. 'Net' gain or loss is experienced only at the broad scale and rarely within the lives of those affected. Where individuals do experience both gains and costs they are often not particularly commensurable – it is simply a change, a new set of circumstances in which they now live. Quite often, however, costs are experienced in terms of access to natural resources, while benefits usually come in the form of training, technical development projects, and opportunities in the market economy (Igoe, 2006b). This basic pattern has two important implications for people living in and around protected areas: 1) technical development projects and trainings may indeed be benefits but they are not usually as direct and immediate as benefits from the environment – an especially important distinction in communities where many people are poor and food insecure; and 2) because the concept of development is premised on the idea that people will move to market-based livelihoods. In many cases, however, people displaced are not well absorbed by the market economy. This can be a common outcome whenever natural resources are appropriated from local people at the behest of more distant interests and agendas, whether this appropriation is for a park, a mine or a hydroelectric dam.

As we observed in the Preface, criticisms of parks, however well founded, can still cause resentment among conservationists. One of us (Brockington) has attended high-level meetings to consider the social impacts of protected areas in which senior conservationists have said that conservationists simply need to communicate better the fact that parks are good things and win the argument again. But a more reasonable position is that there is a basic lack of data to make the assertion that parks are good. We have no comprehensive surveys of the social impacts of protected areas. There is still a considerable reluctance on behalf of some conservationists to collect basic data on, for example, evictions from protected areas or tourist revenues generated by them. Calls for systematic studies of the social impacts of protected areas (Brockington and Schmidt-Soltau, 2004) have largely gone unanswered (but see Wilkie et al, 2006 for an exception).

One of the more fundamental gaps in our current knowledge is that we do not even know how many people live in different types of protected area. The WDPA does not record whether not people are found inside protected areas, or whether they would be allowed to live in them. We have to consult individual country case studies to examine this, and the best work is becoming increasingly dated. Work in India in the late 1980s found that 56 per cent of national parks and 72 per cent of sanctuaries had resident peoples (Kothari et al, 1989).[1] A survey of 70 per cent of national parks in South America in 1991 found that 85 per cent had people living inside them (Amend and Amend, 1995).[2] More recent studies also suggest that protected areas are characterized by high rates of occupancy. A study of 91 protected areas in well populated tropical areas found that 70 per cent were occupied by people (Bruner et al, 2001a). Individual studies in Mongolia, East Kalimantan, Myanmar and the Central African Sub-region indicate use rates of 70–100 per cent (Jepson et al, 2002; Rao et al, 2002; Bedunah and Schmidt, 2004; Cernea and Schmidt-Soltau, 2006).

Analyses of satellite data of agricultural activity within protected areas provide little extra guidance. The only global survey concluded that it is practised in 29 per cent of the known area of protected areas (McNeely and Scherr, 2003; Molnar et al, 2004a). Unfortunately this research used an old version of the WDPA in which only 44,000 protected areas with adequate geographical information systems (GIS) data were available (Sebastian, pers. comm. 2005). Polygons or centre points are now available for more than 75,000 sites (Chape et al, 2005). However, there are also problems with the quality of the data. First, it is unable to detect agro-forestry, such as shade-grown coffee. It could also not distinguish between fallowed land growing trees, and unused land. Moreover since agricultural activity was defined as areas with at least 30 per cent of land under crops it thus omits less intensive cultivation. It gives no indication of pastoral use of rangelands (present in 100 per cent of Mongolia's protected areas). Finally the global 29 per cent is a bald statistic. We do not have a breakdown of the extent of agricultural activity by geographic region, category of protected area or ecological potential.[3] It is difficult to say, therefore, how many protected areas are not cultivated because they are cold and inhospitable, or how much of the cultivation is an integral part of the conserved landscape (as in many British protected areas).

It is worth dwelling on one of the most contentious aspects of protected areas: their role in causing eviction of people (Brockington and Igoe, 2006; Redford and Fearn, 2007). Opinions about the natures and scale of this problem are divided. Borgerhoff Mulder and Coppolillo stated that the literature on evictions from protected areas offers 'a massive cataloguing of past, recent and ongoing abuses' (Borgerhoff Mulder and Coppolillo, 2005, p36). David Wilkie and his colleagues asserted, that 'to date little empirical evidence exists to substantiate the contention that parks are bad for local people' (Wilkie et al, 2006, p247). We believe that the truth lies somewhere between these two positions. There are many cases of displacement that Wilkie and colleagues are ignoring. But Borgerhoff Mulder and Coppolillo are exaggerating the quality, extent and order of knowledge. Our grasp of the subject is simply not as good as they claim.

Brockington and Igoe (2006) carried out a global review of protected area evictions. The reports collected covered only 184 protected areas with many giving no details as to their actual impacts. It is highly likely that much has gone unreported. But we can get some inkling of the geography of evictions from these studies. Evictions have been most common in Africa, South and Southeast Asia and North America; relatively few are reported in this literature from South and Central America, Australia, Europe, the former Soviet Union and most of the Caribbean and Pacific.

We also learnt something of the history of eviction. Most protected areas from which evictions have been reported were set up before 1980 (Table 4.2). This is not a global trend, but the consequence of the strong patterns in North America and sub-Saharan Africa that are well represented in the cases we have studied. In

Table 4.2 *Establishment decades of protected area for which evictions have been reported*

	Pre-1940	1940	1950	1960	1970	1980	1990	2000
S.E. Asia	–	–	–	1	3	3	3	–
South Asia	1	–	–	1	6	7	2	–
W. & C. Africa	2	–	4	6	2	2	3	7
E. & S. Africa	6	5	8	17	19	4	3	–
North Amer.	6	1	–	–	8	2	1	–
Cen. Amer.	–	–	–	–	5	3	2	–

some regions (Central America, South and Southeast Asia) the opposite trend is apparent, with more protected areas for which evictions are reported established after 1980. Regardless of the trends in establishment, we should not infer the timing of evictions from the date of establishment. In many cases laws providing for the removal of people from a protected area were not established until long after it was set up.

But there are remarkably few studies published on eviction before 1990, and a surge of publications thereafter (Table 4.3). The surge does not appear to have been driven by a spate of recent evictions. Rather they were mainly the result of a spate of historical investigations (Table 4.4). This has characterized research on protected areas in southern African (Carruthers, 1995; Koch, 1997; Ranger, 1999; Palmer et al, 2002; Bolaane, 2004a, b, 2005; Brooks, 2005) and eastern Africa (Neumann, 1998; Brockington, 2002). It has been a particularly strong feature of scholarship emerging from North America (Catton, 1997; Keller and Turek, 1998; Spence, 1999; Burnham, 2000; Jacoby, 2001; Igoe, 2004b; Nabakov and Lawrence, 2004). In other regions (such as South America) the relative lack of historical re-examination and the general paucity of eviction cases suggest that the practice has been relatively rare of late.

Where eviction is still prevalent it is often bound up with other debates about environmental change or degradation (Tanzania – Usangu Game Reserve), ecosystem services (Thailand – the Karen people in the highlands)

Table 4.3 *The history of publication of eviction*

Decade beginning	1970	1980	1990	2000
Number of studies	8	24	109	104

Table 4.4 *Timing of removals reported in papers published after 1990*

	Protected area established		
Timing of removals	Up to 1990	1990 to present	Total
Pre-1990	97	–	97
Post-1990	14	24	38
Unspec'd	16	1	17

(Laungaramsri, 1999; Buergin and Kessler, 2000; Sato, 2000, 2002; Buergin, 2003), or the appropriate development strategy for undeveloped people who live in parks and who need to be moved out so that they can become proper citizens (Botswana) (Ikeya, 2001). Eviction is one of the techniques conservation requires to achieve its goals. The issue is how it is carried out, and with what consequences to local people (Schmidt-Soltau and Brockington, 2007). Unfortunately many of the important players in conservation circles are yet to come up with a coherent response over how to handle evictions (Winer et al, 2007). There are cases of relocation for conservation both increasing and intensifying inequality (McLean and Straede, 2003), and redressing it, providing once landless evictees with good land (Karanth, 2007).

But more importantly our review also showed that there were far more important things going on than just eviction. It remains the most dramatic and devastating impact, the most violent thing a state can do to its law-abiding citizens. But it is not the most prevalent problem that many people face and there is a real danger that a focus on eviction will divert attention away from more pressing issues.

One such pressing issue is the problem of empowerment and marginalization (which we examine in the following chapters). Another is the impacts of anti-poaching policies. Wildlife poaching is often identified as a key threat to the survival of some of the most high-profile species, including tigers, rhinos and elephants (Neumann, 2004). Poaching can range from subsistence hunting with snares and traps (for antelope, birds etc. for food) and commercial scale hunting for lucrative wildlife products (birds eggs, ivory and rhino horn etc.). But what is poaching exactly? In sub-Saharan Africa, the arrival of colonial rule was also accompanied by new stipulations on hunting. As Mackenzie's (1988) detailed study points out, 'hunting for the pot' by Africans was criminalized through laws banning the use of traps and snares. However, the newly declared reserves and parks were opened up for recreational hunting by Europeans. The colonial legal framework set the boundaries for defining poaching versus acceptable hunting, and also legitimated the ways that colonial authorities often used hunting for game to underpin and subsidize the costs of imperial expansion across Africa (Mackenzie, 1988; Mutwira, 1989).

In a sense this way of thinking about poachers versus hunters is present in current NGO campaigns about the need to prevent poaching. The view of commercial poachers in Africa that has been presented by NGOs and governments is that they are black, poverty-stricken and usually cross international borders to engage in commercial poaching. In the late 1980s the high-profile international campaigns about ivory poaching blamed illegal hunting in Kenya on Somali *shifta* crossing the border to hunt and then sell ivory on the lucrative international black market. However, later analyses of poaching in East and southern Africa pointed the finger at government-level corruption and the role of national armies such as the South African Defence Force, which indicated that poaching was highly organized and interlinked with transnational organized criminal networks that traded ivory, rhino horn, drugs, stolen cars and engaged in people trafficking (Bonner, 1993; Ellis, 1994; Reeve and Ellis, 1995).

Following these high-profile campaigns, the issue of poaching has not gone away, although its profile is slightly different. In general, there have been two different types of response from authorities engaged in conservation including national governments and conservation NGOs. The first is related to the community conservation debates, and revolves around giving local communities a stake in conservation efforts. For example, programmes referred to as turning 'poachers into game guards' are focused on giving paid employment to former poachers as rangers for protected areas. These kinds of initiatives are discussed more fully in Chapter 5. The second kind of response is coercion. Peluso argues that a state's capacity to control and extract resources is a function of relations between state and society, but that the state's ability to enforce policy varies widely (Peluso, 1993). Extraction of resources has included allocation of land for tourism and rights of access to wildlife and this has led to the state and local people holding competing claims over national parks and wildlife. As a result, the state has used conservation as a means of coercing local people (Neumann, 1997, 1998). Successive governments have excluded local people from national parks and outlawed the use of wildlife in order to preserve a national asset for tourism, sport hunting and game viewing, which are mostly the realm of the wealthy.

Poachers cannot all be considered in the same way because there are different motivating reasons for poaching. But in a number of NGO campaigns in the 1980s all poachers were treated as equally culpable. The reasons for poaching were not generally explored since the fact that animals were being poached formed the basis of the campaigns (Peluso, 1993, pp205–209). In NGO campaigns poachers are often vilified as criminals or characterized as poverty stricken individuals driven to make money through illegal activity.

Coercive anti-poaching efforts are often reliant on an alliance between the state, donors and international green NGOs. For example, Bonner (1993) documents the use of a helicopter donated by Prince Phillip to the World Wildlife Fund for nature (WWF) for national government anti-poaching operations in Zimbabwe. After it was found that the helicopter had been authorized to engage in shoot-to-kill campaigns in the Zambezi Valley, WWF International withdrew the helicopter amidst claims by Amnesty International that the 'wildlife wars' in sub-Saharan Africa were responsible for massive human rights abuses (Bonner, 1993; Duffy, 2000). The use of various coercive methods, including violence and shoot-to-kill, raises questions about who gives authorization for the use of coercion and violence. These questions are all the more pertinent with the development of privately owned reserves and the use of private companies employed to carry out anti-poaching strategies.

Ferguson (2006) suggests that the commitment to privatized violence is visible in the realm of environmental politics because of the apparent 'need' to secure protected areas for internationally valuable ecotourism. States and international environmental NGOs have carved out spatial enclaves to protect biodiverse hotspots. In the zeal for protecting species, NGOs and states have presided over an expansion of use of mercenary forces to carry out anti-poaching patrols. Ferguson highlights the scheme by African Rainforest and River Conservation (cf. Shanahan, 2005) operating in Central African Republic where the sale of diamonds dug up in the area they control are used to fund the reserve; management of the reserve includes hiring ex-South African and Rhodesian mercenaries to organize anti-poaching patrols that attack groups of poachers operating from Sudan. As Ferguson suggests, these might seem like extreme measures but unfortunately they are not uncommon in conservation practice (Ferguson, 2006, pp42–47).

These schemes may begin with genuine goals of conserving species, but the commitment to the 'global good' of conservation can result not just in misfortune for certain groups and individuals, but can in fact end up legitimizing and justifying serious human rights abuses. This in turn reinforces the negative view (especially in Africa) that wildlife simply matters more than people. The development of private armies to protect reserves and species also raise complex ethical questions (Neumann, 2004): On whose authority do such private entities engage in violence against suspected poachers? Who legitimizes their use of shoot-to-kill policies? It is important not to forget that these private conservation armies generally deal with people who are only suspected of, and not convicted of, illegal hunting.

Poverty, conservation and local support

The poverty and conservation debate is hotly contested between those who feel that conservation policy should address poverty issues, and those who do not. Among the latter a common theme is that conservation is not about reducing poverty but about saving habitat, wildness and biodiversity. Advocates of this position argue that conservation is not responsible for the high levels of inequality and poverty visible globally, and the conservation movement should not try to become responsible for addressing these ills. Many of the places that conservationists are interested in for biodiversity reasons just happen also to be poor, and conservationists should not seek to become responsible for tackling the thorny issues that cause this poverty. Rather they should recognize that development and poverty reduction is a hard and complex task, and they should accept the limitations to their expertise and restrict themselves to saving species and habitat (Sanderson and Redford, 2003).

This position was strengthened by the widely recognized problems with so-called 'Integrated Conservation with Development' Projects, which had tried to combine conservation with development goals. This idea had won widespread support among donor circles. Many projects had been attempted at the cost of millions of dollars, but few could show any tangible gains for conservation objectives; in many cases they may have disrupted them (Wels et al, 1999). Consequently many observers felt that it was better to 'decouple' the objectives of development and conservation, pursuing both separately (Barrett and Arcese, 1995).

In response critics of that proposed separation of duties observed that there were many cases where conservation, as we have seen above, was responsible for the impoverishment of rural people. It was quite wrong, they argued, to ignore the poverty for which conservation policies were responsible. Moreover it was self-defeating as poverty drove the environmentally damaging behaviour with which conservationists were struggling. Ignoring development, and 'decoupling' conservation from it denied the possibility of 'win–win' scenarios where conservation and development gains could both be realized. The failure of IDCPs was real, but these were large donor-driven initiatives that were unsustainable without aid. More locally driven community conservation initiatives, while complex and difficult, have already demonstrated that conservation and development goals can be realized together.

The poverty–conservation debate is fraught and often confused. It gets particularly heated because the centres of biodiversity conservationists value most are often also located in the poorest parts of the world where development needs are greatest. Bill Adams, with minor assistance from his colleagues, made a valuable contribution in *Science*, which distinguished two normative stances and two empirical arguments in the debate (Adams et al, 2004).

The normative stances were:

1 **Conservation and poverty reduction are separate policy realms**
   Conservation policy should not consider development goals directly. Any incidental benefits such as improved ecosystem services, or the development of local tourism industries could be welcomed but should not made explicit goals. Rather conservation policy should be evaluated according to its impact on species or landscape conservation.

2 **Conservation should not compromise poverty reduction**
   The success of conservation policy is measured by its impact on species and landscapes, but in the process it ought not to impoverish people. Where it causes local hardship this needs to be compensated, even if it is not strictly necessary to achieve conservation's goals.

The empirical claims were:

1   **Poverty impedes conservation**
    Poaching and environmental degradation is often pursued by the poor in short-sighted ways. When people become richer they are more amenable to accepting conservation policies. Addressing poverty is therefore a means of directly and indirectly promoting conservation.
2   **Poverty reduction depends on sustainable resource use**
    Where livelihoods depend on living resources their sustainable use will promote both the resource and the livelihood associated with it.

It is worth noting another position in this debate, specifically adopted with respect to protected areas, which is sometimes adopted in verbal debates, but which we have rarely seen in print. This holds that parks are just good things and generate wealth. This is implied in works that only examine the benefits of protected areas and not their cost. It is also implied in the performance indicators of the Millennium Development Goals. One of the indicators used to evaluate performance of goal 7 (ensure environmental sustainability) is the proportion of land held in protected areas (target 9). The implication is that more protected areas will result in less poverty.

As noted above, this has been a central premise of international development since the 1950s and the idea of growth poles, which are large-scale generators of wealth that are assumed to have amplifier effects to the local economy. From this perspective, then, parks are seen as a kind of growth pole. But the empirical basis for this claim is weak.

Conversely other observers have argued that poverty increases with protected area growth. Geisler and de Sousa (2001) have argued that in Africa the poorest countries had the largest protected area estate. Geisler (2003) also observed that between 1985 and 1997 poorer African countries gazetted many more protected areas than richer African countries. But this position too does not withstand close scrutiny. Upton and colleagues examined the relationship between diverse indices of poverty and compared them to more recent editions of the WDPA. They found no relationship between them at the national scale, concluding that the local impacts of protected areas are just that – local (Upton et al, 2008).

If we parse practical conservation problems according to the scheme Adams and colleagues outline we suspect much more constructive disagreements become possible. Few people will dispute that, if conservation objectives are about preventing extinction and reducing the threat of extinction, then its success and priorities are best measured in terms of relative abundance of rare species. In this respect its distinctness from poverty reduction policies are important. Equally few conservationists believe that it is acceptable for biodiversity reduction to cause or enhance poverty, particularly where the people affected are already disadvantaged. In terms of empirical positions, where it can be shown that conservation objectives are being threatened by poverty, or where they can be enhanced by diverse strategies of pursuing local prosperity, then few conservationists would object to strategies that reduce the one and promote the other.

This parsing does not necessarily make the decision making easy. For example, how can we determine how much poverty is caused by conservation? How closely do schemes to promote prosperity have to be tied to conservation outcomes for them to be valuable to conservation's remit? For example consider one of the first experiments in community-based conservation and ecotourism development in southern Belize: the Cockscomb Basin Jaguar Preserve. The preserve was initially designated as a forest reserve in 1984, and was later expanded and converted into the world's first jaguar sanctuary, supported by WWF International and Jaguar cars. In 2000 the EU agreed to a €1.28 million grant to support co-management of the Cockscomb Basin Jaguar Preserve and other protected areas by the Belize Audubon Society, in conjunction with local communities.[4]

Like many other protected areas the creation of the Jaguar Preserve required relocation of local communities to a new site: the Maya Centre Village. The initial rationale was that Cockscomb would be a community-managed conservation area, and that the people of Maya Centre Village would directly benefit from the ecotourism revenues generated by the scheme. These revenues would then be used to compensate them for loss of access to areas they had historically used for subsistence agriculture and hunting. This was intended to ensure that the local communities did not have to live with all the costs of creating and enforcing protected areas without any of the benefits.

The creation of Cockscomb meant that agriculture and hunting became illegal in the preserve, even though they were vital subsistence activities for local people. As a result, the establishment of the jaguar sanctuary led directly to a significant reduction in access to resources contained within the reserve, including locally important spiritual and religious sites. The preserve was managed by the Belize Audubon Society, while the community was supposed to develop the institutional capacity to take over running the preserve. This led to criticisms that the jaguar sanctuary merely replicated the traditional relationship between communities and state-run conservation agencies. Despite the promises that Cockscomb would constitute a significant departure in conservation policy local communities have failed to gain substantial economic benefits or genuine participation in the management of the preserve (Duffy, 2002, pp105–107).

Such complex situations as these demonstrate how difficult it can be to see clearly with respect to the problems of conservation and poverty. Has the scheme made people poorer, or just failed to make them richer? Has it caused them any material harm, or has it marginalized them more, or has it merely failed to address, or worse intensified, existing inequalities of power? It might bring more economic benefit at some point in the future; else its market-guided alterations might not be associated with any meaningful changes.

A second area of confusion has arisen from the strongly held beliefs among advocates of community conservation that parks cannot survive without local support. This belief, called 'the principle of local support' (Brockington, 2004) is reiterated constantly in the conservation literature. It is one of the main reasons why strong approaches to conservation that impose protection laws (often called 'fortress conservation') have been criticized in recent years. David Western, once head of the Kenyan Wildlife Service, wrote that 'a fallacy of protectionism is that we can ignore costs locally' (Western, 2001, p202). The President of IUCN, opening the fourth World Parks Congress in Caracas, stated the importance in bald terms, claiming that 'quite simply, if local people do not support protected areas, then protected areas cannot last' (Ramphal, 1993, p57). Ed Barrow and Christo Fabricius, prominent conservationists in East and South Africa, stated that '[u]ltimately, conservation and protected areas in contemporary Africa must either contribute to national and local livelihoods, or fail in their biodiversity goals' (Barrow and Fabricius, 2002). Adrian Phillips, a leading figure in the IUCN, when asked to name one key lesson to be gleaned out of interactions between protected areas and their neighbours, found the answer 'very simple'; it was 'the iron rule that no protected area can succeed for long in the teeth of local opposition' (Borrini-Feyerabend et al, 2002).

Conservation undoubtedly becomes easier with the support of a sympathetic local population. There are many occasions when wildlife, vegetation and landscape have suffered because their conservation is unpopular locally. David Western recorded several instances when Maasai pastoralists expressed their antipathy to conservation policy by killing animals in and around the Amboseli National Park (Western, 1994). Saberwal and colleagues note that the heavy handed and exclusionist enforcing of conservation policy in India has created many local enemies of protected areas (Saberwal et al, 2001). The problems that conservation causes people have meant that, ironically, there are even a number of cases where parks have, unwittingly, initiated or enhanced nature's destruction. Fearing interference from governments and restrictions on resource use, villagers have killed chimpanzees in Tanzania, diverse wildlife in Uganda and felled trees and forests in Nicaragua, Nepal, Norway and China (Walsh, 1997; Brandon, 1998; Harkness, 1998; Nygren, 2000; Murray, 1992, cited in Hulme and Infield, 2001).[5] Analysts of sustainable forestry have observed forest reserve creation can be made possible by increasing the intensity of production on other forest lands, with adverse results for biodiversity conservation (McAlpine et al, 2007).

But it is not true that parks will always fail in the face of local opposition. The principle of local support can, oddly, ignore the politics of protected areas. It fails to recognize that protected areas distribute fortune as well as misfortune, that they make allies as well as enemies. Often the local communities who oppose the existence and policies of their neighbouring protected areas tend to be politically weak rural groups. They can be opposed to powerful alliances of central and local government and other rural groups, the police, park guards and paramilitary units, and national and international NGOs raising money and awareness for the cause of the protected areas. These are contests that the rural groups may be ill-equipped to win, especially when (as is often the case) the most powerful and educated members of a particular community are positioned to take advantage of economic opportunities presented by conservation and/or are being recruited as 'community representatives' by the powerful groups that other local people are resisting. Asserting the necessity of local cooperation, therefore, ignores the realities of power.

The principle of local support fails to recognize the power of the international biodiversity conservation movement and the important local power relations that sustain it. It can be, paradoxically, inimical to effective promotion of conservation policies that are fairer locally because it fails to recognize where the real power lies. If we are to understand the local impacts of conservation policy we require a much better grasp of its politics. If we want conservation practice that is more just then we have to understand what sustains injustice. Each local situation will have a different set of factors sustaining particular conservation policies.

To put it another way: there are countless examples throughout history of inequalities and injustices being perpetrated and perpetuated despite resistance to them, and despite the opposition and hatred they generated. The Roman Empire was not brought down by its slaves, enclosure in England and highland clearances in Scotland were not prevented by the people who lost their rights to the commons, nor were the iniquities of England's factory system overturned by a workers' revolt.[6] Indigenous peoples in Latin America, North America and Australia have been removed from their lands and violently treated for hundreds of years. Why should the injustices perpetrated by conservation be any different?

Conclusion

Protected areas have expanded rapidly in recent decades. They continue to proliferate. Many more are needed and will be needed in diverse regions and habitats that are not well protected. And as they spread they will have all sorts of consequences, both expected and surprising. As the reach of conservation areas expands, and the influence of parks grows we can expect these changes to become more common. The issues we have examined above will become more pervasive.

But to understand their importance properly we must recognize, first, that protected areas are also just one type of conservation strategy. The reach of conservation policy is extending far beyond protected areas boundaries. It has to if its objectives are to be achieved. We must therefore examine more carefully what happens when rural groups become involved in implementing conservation policy. Second, we must realize that protected areas are being incorporated into new networks of international governance, and new development strategies and programmes, such as the growth of ecotourism. To these issues we now turn.

Notes

1   This work is dated because over 120 protected areas of some 600 protected areas in India were established since that work was carried out. More are proposed (see Bhomia and Brockington, forthcoming).

2   This work too is dated as the extent of category 1 and 2 protected areas on the continent has increased by more than 10 per cent since its publication.

3   Since that original analysis has also been lost (Sebastian, pers. comm. 2005), it will be impossible to improve on that statistic.

4   *Belize Audubon Society Newsletter*, January–April 2000, vol 32, p1.

5   Although in the Norwegian case, when a landowner felled his forest on receipt of a letter announcing it was to become protected, it later emerged that the letter was in fact a practical joke sent by a neighbour (Svarstad, pers. comm. 13 October 2004).

6   Polanyi states 'The labouring people themselves were hardly a factor in this great movement [of social reform] the effect of which was, figuratively speaking, to allow them to survive the great Middle Passage. They had almost as little to say in the determination of their own fate as the black cargo of Hawkin's ships' (Polanyi, 2001 (1944)). Their demands were relatively easily ignored. In the UK when millions of Chartists demanded the vote in the 1840s, they were refused by a parliament representing only a few hundred thousand.

5

Local Management of Natural Resources

It [does not appear] feasible to achieve 50% coverage of exclusive protected areas, at least not without imposing considerable state-led coercion, and disenfranchising rural people from traditional practices and losing their co-operation, as so often happens (with) such areas... Given these circumstances, it ... appears more pragmatic to recognize that most conservation will have to be achieved through cooperation in human social space... The clear objective is a much more biodiversity-friendly mosaic of land uses driven by the livelihoods that are derived from the sustainable use of wild living resources instead of landscapes with small islands of biodiversity in a sea of agriculture ... In the tropics, for example, could 80–90% of tropical terrestrial biodiversity be conserved on 5–15% of the land, compared with 10–30% on 1–2% as at present?

Hutton and Leader-Williams (2003, pp219–220)

A great deal of hope and expectation can be placed in the ability of rural communities to conserve wild nature. Conservation by local communities is often claimed to be a more equitable and/or effective alternative to many types of protected areas, particularly to the misfortunes of fortress conservation. It is also widely perceived to be a means of expanding the conservation estate, ensuring land is managed for conservation purposes beyond the boundaries of protected areas. Advocates insist that it will result in more support for conservation values and more prosperous and/or empowered people.

While these ideas are appealing on many levels, it is important to understand the complexities of the relationships involved. For example, what happens when the idea of local people as natural environmental stewards meets the reality of the impoverished condition in which these people live? Consequently, advocacy of local natural resource management has been decried as trying to 'dress environmental problems up in Indian blankets' (Igoe, 2008) or using a false ideal of an 'ecologically noble savage' (Redford, 1990) to further their cause. Else consider the simultaneous emphasis on equity and market-driven approaches to conservation, which will encourage local people to 'value their surroundings'. As this chapter will show, there are many contexts in which small groups of people at the community level are positioned to take advantage of conservation-oriented market opportunities, while many others bear the cost of conservation while not realizing significant benefits.

In this chapter we consider four sets of ideas and related policies and actions that are essential to local management of natural resources:

1   The concept of 'community'.
2   Devolution of rights and responsibilities over natural resource management.
3   Common pool resources and common property resource management.
4   Co-management of protected areas.

We also examine how these ideas and policies relate to the realities that they are meant to describe and improve, and also how they relate to each other. The concept of community is obviously important, since all community-based interventions must have a target that is called a community. As we shall show below, however, such a target is difficult to define and depends a great deal on the specific intervention that is being proposed. The concept of devolution is closely related to the concept of community, since if communities are going actually to manage natural resources then they will need to have the rights and responsibilities necessary to do so. And if power is devolved how might management actually work? Debates about commons are vital in the realm of community conservation for these examine how groups (communities) can collectively take effective action sustainably to manage natural resources. Finally co-management of protected areas deserves special attention both as an increasingly popular trend in conservation, and as a form of local natural resource management that combines all the issues in this chapter.

Throughout this chapter and the next our argument is simple: just as fortress conservation arrangements distribute fortune and misfortune unequally to different groups within society, so also does conservation by communities and indigenous people. Community conservation merely introduces a different set of inequities to protected areas. It also introduces a different set of interactions with capitalism and market forces. The analyst's task is first to examine who these winners and losers are; and second, to consider how the distributions are shaped by globalization, the economy and demarcations of identity.

Community

Community conservation interventions often revolve around collective agreement and decision making as necessary steps in doing conservation. Its imperatives are reflected in often unstated assumptions that rural communities are harmonious and homogenous. They draw on the romantic tradition of the Noble Savage, which views rural communities as the ideal stewards of 'their nature'. This perspective has long been abandoned by field workers studying rural communities. To quote anthropologist Keith Hart:

> Social life organised through kinship ... is fundamentally disunited,
> and it is in response to this disunity that participants stress the
> opposite in their ideological pronouncements, emphasizing the idea
> of community and pretending that kinship ties express only
> solidarity. We, who retain in our language and sentiments the
> ideology without the substance of a society organized through
> kinship, project our own romantic nostalgia onto the faction-ridden
> and anxiety-prone family life of African villages.
>
> (Hart, 1982, p40)

In fact, the many and diverse things that members of rural communities share in common are often most obviously visible through conflicts between them. Their common geography can be seen in disputes between neighbours over land and access to resources. Their common ethnic identity can be seen in disputes over who is actually an 'authentic' member of a particular group and who behaves (or not) according to the prescribed standards of that group. Common livelihoods entail disputes over how resources should be used, what kinds of outside enterprises should be welcome to a community, and how the benefits from those enterprises should be distributed. Common kinship can be seen in family disputes. Of course these fights can also reveal the heterogeneity of particular communities, as they frequently – though by no means always – occur along lines of ethnicity, kinship, length of residence, livelihood practices, educational status, age, gender, social class, affinities to political parties and NGOs, and in perennial disputes between 'cultural traditionalists' and 'modernizing elites'. Accordingly, it is often much more interesting to find issues on which communities appear to unite and to ask what motivated people to set aside their differences in this particular case? From this perspective communities are produced, brought together, and divided by particular sets of historical circumstances.

This perspective on communities has been most popularly expressed in Agrawal and Gibson's seminal article, 'enchantment and disenchantment' (1999) (cited over 150 times). The article heralded an explosion of literature, which Fay (2007) describes as a 'now familiar litany of critiques' concerning the normative and prescriptive ideas of communities prevalent in conservation projects and practices. Agrawal and Gibson's paper made the usual points that communities are diverse and heterogeneous, and are as likely to be fraught with conflict as they are to be harmonious. They took this argument further, however, pointing out that communities are not clearly bounded entities. Rather, they are shot through with networks that are often transnational in scope:

> The local and the external, they are linked together in ways
> that it might be difficult to identify the precise line where local

conservation begins and the external – that helps construct the local –
ends.

(Agrawal and Gibson, 1999, p640)

This is particularly true with the case of community conservation, as it is
increasingly taken up and promoted by global networks of NGOs, donors and
International financial institution (IFIs). Rural groups engaged in community
conservation are increasingly incorporated into new networks of actors, including
NGOs, IFIs, international organizations, bilateral donors and private companies.

Can these types of transnational institutions develop genuine partnerships with
local communities involved in conservation schemes? Agrawal and Gibson
confidently wrote that proponents of community conservation viewed markets
and states as central obstacles to conservation success. Today the suspicion of
states remains, but the question of markets has become much more ambiguous.
With the neoliberalization of conservation, private enterprise and profit motives
have become widely accepted features of conservation, whether such conservation
strategies engage communities or exclude them. Increasingly, rural people are
targeted as potential partners in conservation-oriented business ventures.
Conservation NGOs, for their part, now openly broker these types of ventures,
such that conservation-business partnerships are becoming as common as
conservation-community partnerships.

All of these issues and developments have profound implications for the role of
rural communities as units of environmental governance. To begin with, taking
Agrawal and Gibson's arguments to their logical conclusion, what constitutes a
community depends on specific historical encounters of local people with states,
NGOs and private enterprise, and the types of interventions that these external
actors and institutions have sponsored over the years. For instance, powerful local
elites who have benefited historically from extractive industries are unlikely to
cooperate with conservation interventions that threaten these industries, though
they may be interested in profits from things like ecotourism. In cases where
economic opportunities are scarce, government agencies, conservation NGOs
and private enterprise are often in a position to handpick groups of local people
to represent the communities with whom they 'partner'. Finally, local people may
organize themselves to do conservation, but lack access to the external networks
that control the resources they need to make their efforts viable. This is especially
the case with neoliberal conservation, since rural communities frequently do not
control the types of resources that make them attractive to private investors.

What constitutes 'community', in any particular situation, therefore, is often
based on these interventions, how different local people have been positioned to
respond to them, and how these interactions have continued into the present.
While the boundaries that define communities may be difficult to draw, the
realities of bureaucratic interventions, and for-profit investments, demand they
be drawn somewhere. Even the most flexible and enlightened intervention must

have a visible target of intervention. Defining these targets will depend on who is seeking to define a community and for what purposes.

The processes by which these lines get drawn (or erased as the case may be) around communities, necessarily entails exclusion. Mosse (2004, p654) highlights the fundamental contradiction between the need for messy participatory processes and the simultaneous need for vertical control over programme outcomes in order to ensure quantifiable success indicators. (With the increased involvement of private enterprise, he could also add profit as a special type of quantifiable success indicator.) He argues that the types of communities that really count in this context are what he calls interpretive communities. These are networks of people spanning the village level to the transnational level. Their function, he argues, is to work together to make specific interventions appear as successes according to prevailing policy paradigms. At the grassroots level, members of these interpretive communities are usually chosen for their 'capacity to aspire' (Appadurai, 2004) and their ability to mobilize a critical mass of local people in support of a particular intervention.

One of the inherent dangers of this arrangement is the possibility of corporatist agreements: private negotiations between state agencies and selected private interests (Young, 1990; Bianco and Alder, 2001; Lane, 2003; Fortwangler, 2007), which have significant potential to undermine public deliberation. In developing countries, where weak states have been further weakened by structural adjustment, networks of governance are in some cases replacing more traditional types of states in the management and control of people and natural resources (see also Fortmann, 1997). In such contexts, networks of powerful actors spanning states, NGOs, private enterprise and local communities frequently operate according to hidden transcripts and extra-legal arrangements that are not readily visible to outsiders (Mbembe, 2001; Ferguson, 2006). They often operate at the expense of local people and even circumvent their legal rights. They may also be predatory towards communities in cases where they need to claim 'partnerships'.

For example, donors and environmental NGOs have been involved in directly running state-owned national parks in Madagascar, which is again an unusual level of involvement in the state sector by external actors. In particular, Association Nationale pour la Gestion des Aires Protégées (ANGAP), the national agency responsible for managing protected areas in Madagascar, is run and funded by a group of international NGOs and donors in conjunction with Malagasy state agencies. This has resulted in a complex public–private network that effectively manages ANGAP and has received funding from Conservation International (CI), the World Bank, World Wide Fund for Nature (WWF), United States Agency for International Development (USAID), the German development agency (GTZ), and the French and British governments. The Board of Directors is drawn from government ministries, such as the Ministry of Tourism and the Ministry of the Environment, but donors including the World Bank and WWF also have seats on the board. Ordinarily, Parks Departments have been the preserve of the state sector, but the semi-private status of ANGAP reflects the growing global pressure for privatizing public utilities. (The powers and challenges associated with public–private networks are more fully discussed in Chapters 8 and 9 (and see Duffy, 2006a, c)).

Communities, then, need to be understood in terms of networks. It is not enough, however, simply to argue that networks infiltrate communities and sometimes provide opportunities for local people. We need to move beyond asking how to maintain the smooth functioning of networks that solve a specific set of predefined problems; instead we need to understand the complex politics and inherent inequities of transnational networks of people that play a prominent role in defining both communities and the success of interventions designed to benefit those communities, especially as members of these networks are most likely to benefit from the interventions they define. These dynamics have significant implications for our second set of issues: the devolution of rights and responsibilities.

Devolution

Devolution is 'the transfer of power to elected local authorities' (Ribot, 2004, p8). It is sometimes called 'democratic decentralization'. It should not be confused with 'deconcentration', or 'administrative decentralization', which transfers powers to local government agencies who are not downwardly accountable to local electorates, but who remain upwardly accountable, to government officials in higher office.

Effective devolved management of natural resources by rural communities is in many ways the Holy Grail of effective community-based conservation. In theory devolution has much to offer, and is potentially a useful alternative to the inefficiencies and inequities of central state control. Indeed devolution might not just enhance natural resource management, it may be a vehicle for promoting stronger democracies (Wily, 2002). However, it is also important to note that devolution of decision making is often conflated with the types of deregulation associated with the promotion of free market development models. While both ostensibly involve the reduction of centralized state control, devolution also ideally entails the decentralization of decision-making responsibility to local people. If actually given these responsibilities local people may make decisions that are not in line with the spread of free market development models, or mainstream conservation interventions for that matter.

If done well, however, the potential benefits of decentralization for local communities, and healthy democracies, and the environment, are great. Ribot (2004, 2006) states:

It can promote equitable distributions of benefits from resource use, because allocation of benefits is determined by local democratic decision making.

It is likely to be more efficient. It can bring more local knowledge to bear on management decisions, it can mean decision-makers more aware of the needs of local people, it can reduce the transaction costs of administering the resource, improve co-ordination and facilitate growing environmental consciousness in the local electorate whose decisions now help govern the resources.

Ribot's major review of the experience of devolution in forests internationally concluded that there were numerous incidences of local authorities and people increasing revenue from forests, sustaining strong management, protecting them from commercial depredation and improving their management capacity (2004, 2006).

There are, accordingly, advocates of strong devolution policies because they are perceived to bring diverse benefits to local communities' economies and because of the potential benefits to be gained from effective management of local resources. Liz Wily, who has been a strong advocate of local control of forest resources in many parts of Africa, enthuses that:

> ...once customary/informal rights are made state law interests, not only individual customary rights but also those held in common by communities gain new legal respect. Communal forests and woodlands move virtually overnight from policy perception as un-owned open access resources into recognition as the private property of communities ...The incentive to communities to really start managing these resources is enormous.
>
> (Wily, 2002, pp5–6)

Empowering local groups, however, may not help local authorities achieve national, or international biodiversity priorities, which, by definition, cannot be seen in parochial terms (Borgerhoff Mulder and Coppolillo, 2005). Global conservation priorities are premised on their over-riding local values. Devolution can only serve conservation objectives to the extent that it empowers people who hold those values dear.

On the other hand such values are not cultural givens. They are learnt, encouraged and induced. They can change. Many rural people's antipathy to wildlife and conservation policy derives from their experience over many decades of being marginalized, impoverished or disempowered by conservation policies. For many African villagers wildlife was (and is) a forbidden resource. Hunting licences were prohibitively expensive, or the revenue from their sale disappeared into state coffers. Wildlife was therefore just a cost to rural residents, eating their crops, livestock, occasionally their friends and family. Forests and other wildlife habitat merely gave the miscreants a good home and denied people good agricultural land. The challenge of devolution is to provide not just power and responsibilities to local people over wildlife and its habitat, but also to provide effective revenues from them that are locally enjoyed in order that wildlife and its habitat can be seen as a benefit not a cost. As Child put it:

> if wildlife is permitted to contribute meaningfully to their welfare, people will not be able to afford to lose it in their battle for survival. If wildlife does not contribute significantly to their well-being, people will not be able to afford to preserve it except as a tourist curiosity on a few protected areas.
>
> (Child, 1995, p235. Quoted in Murphree, 1996, p177)

Unfortunately, however, despite all the talk about devolution, there are few cases where it has really been tried. We lack sufficient material about what happens to global priorities when they are put in local hands. One of the main findings of Ribot's work was that devolution has often been incomplete and has rarely actually been tried properly. Often the key obstacle is the state itself, or agencies within it, which are reluctant to relinquish the power, and revenues that they command. Local powers are captured by local elites, or by national elites working in particular localities, none of whom are properly accountable to electorates (Oyono, 2004a, b, c). Else power can be devolved to unaccountable local institutions such as customary authorities or NGOs (cf. Igoe and Kelsall, 2005). The outcomes of these failures are often highly unsatisfactory. They can be detrimental to local livelihoods, facilitate commercial exploitation by large-scale corporations that receive permission to enter from the new gatekeepers and increase exclusion, and disempowerment generally.

One of the most extensive experiments in empowering local control of natural resource management has been Joint Forest Management in India. This scheme arose out of initiatives by forest officers in West Bengal in the 1970s and was promulgated nationally with the National Forest Policy of 1988, and formally adopted in 1990 (Sundar, 2000).[1] It allows for the Forest Department to enter into agreements with specially formed forest management groups (often called Forest Protection Committees) from particular village communities. The protection committees help manage the forest to prevent village illegal use, while the villagers in return are allowed access to non-timber forest products and receive a proportion of the profits of timber sales. Sundar describes three types of local forest management arrangements – there are those initiated by the communities, those promoted by the forest department and those begun by the NGOs. She notes that power is rarely shared, with much influence remaining with the forestry department.

Estimates vary of the number of committees in existence, from 10,000 to over 60,000.[2] They manage about 150,000km^2 land (this compares to a protected area estate of about 170,000km^2 land). The results of the programme vary enormously. In many cases it is a substantial improvement on the poor relations between villagers and forestry department officials that pervade rural India (Gadgil and Guha, 1993). Saberwal and colleagues describe it as broadly a success (Saberwal et al, 2001); Agrawal and Ostrom find it difficult to generalize (2001). They note that forest cover has improved in many cases, but it is difficult to attribute this to Joint Forest Management. Positive impacts on rural livelihoods are clearer, although Kumar cautions that the rural non-poor gain most (Kumar, 2002).

There are close parallels between the work of Joint Forest Management and new village forest reserves in Tanzania. These originated at the village of Duru-Haitemba, where villagers there faced the imminent gazettement of their local forest by the District Council to form a forest reserve but resented that prospect. District control of woodland was associated with exclusion and corrupt management. Instead, with the help of enlightened District Forestry Officers they demarcated their village boundaries within the forest and established a forest management committee that sanctioned some uses and excluded others. These were enforced by village bye-laws passed by the district councils. The consultant who facilitated this process, Liz Wily, has been effusive at the consequences, insisting that local democracy has been revived by the empowering experience of controlling local resources, that local livelihoods have benefited and that forest condition has improved (Sjoholm and Wily, 1995; Wily and Haule, 1995; Wily, 2001; Wily and Dewees, 2001).

It was not clear, however, from Wily's work how these changes were really possible. She attributes it to the empowering of people for whom the resource mattered. But the same sorts of people throughout rural Tanzania regularly participate in electing village and district governments and chairmen generally renowned for their poor performance and corruption (Fjeldstad and Semboja, 2000, 2001; Fjeldstad, 2001; Brockington, 2006). It is not clear why village forest reserve should be any different (Brockington, 2007).

On the other hand it is clear that the similar experiment to revive the *Ngitili* (private and village grazing reserves, a traditional institution of the Sukuma people) in central Tanzania, which hinges on strong institutions protecting poor villages against the depredations of powerful livestock owners, is having an effect on the ground, with improvements in diverse forms of biodiversity (Monela et al, 2004). Something is clearly changing in institutions of village government, and quite possibly in local expectations of how they are meant to perform. There are some encouraging signs in some places, and in some types of environments, but we cannot yet report any rigorous comparison (Petersen and Sandhovel, 2001; Lund and Nielsen, 2006; Topp-Jorgensen et al, 2005; Blomely and Ramadhani, 2006).

One of the earliest examples of devolved natural resource management was the Communal Areas Management Plan for Indigenous Resources (CAMPFIRE) in Zimbabwe, and arguably it provided a model for conservation and development practice that was used as a template in sub-Saharan Africa and beyond (Hutton et al, 2005, p345). Consequently it attracted international attention as a programme that was at the forefront of what seemed to be an innovative and workable approach to negotiating the potential conflicts between people and wildlife and between sustainability and development. For donors, NGOs and national governments alike, community-based natural resource management presented a more socially and politically acceptable rationale for conservation in the context of the creation of new 'democracies' in Africa in the post-Cold War 1990s (Hutton et al, 2005, p344). Traditionally, wildlife conservation and rural development have been considered as conflicting goals (Brockington, 2002; Wolmer, 2007). This is because there was an assumption that conservation required existing areas of land for wildlife to be maintained, if not expanded, whereas development meant industrialization or the expansion of land available for crops and livestock. This conflict between conservation and rural development was most sharply demonstrated by the national parks systems of sub-Saharan Africa. Therefore community-based natural resource management, and CAMPFIRE in particular, appeared to offer a workable solution to this conflict. Furthermore, it had the added advantage in that it seemed to 'pay its way' through careful development of sustainable use of wildlife (through production of meat, skins and ivory, or the sale of wildlife as sport hunting trophies and for photographic/cultural tourism). As a result it was attractive precisely because, in financial terms, it was not 'donor dependent' unlike some other forms of wildlife conservation in sub-Saharan Africa. It resonated with the new-found faith in local communities and individuals as 'rational' resource managers, which neatly fitted with the fashion for decentralization and participatory development.

During the 1990s CAMPFIRE became internationally renowned for its efforts to reconcile the needs of conservation and development. Begun in 1986, it aimed to ensure that the rural communities living in Zimbabwe's semi-arid and marginal Communal Areas were able to capture the benefits from wildlife utilization, in all its forms. This was to be achieved by devolving responsibility for wildlife management to the smallest possible unit through investing new powers in the Rural District Council; the local CAMPFIRE representatives would then decide how to use wildlife in their area to generate revenue For example, the CAMPFIRE Committees would work with the Parks Department to determine the 'sustainable offtake' level for local elephant populations and then sell the rights to hunt the animals to safari/trophy hunting companies, which oversees hunters. Given that safari hunters will pay between $10,000 and $20,000 (in 2000, see Hurt and Ravan, 2000) to hunt elephants, as well as thousands of dollars to shoot lions and leopards, not to mention a string of other animals as part of a three-week package, the returns can be lucrative.

It is often suggested that CAMPFIRE began as an idea hatched by a group of white liberals in the Zimbabwean Parks Department, which Murphree referred to as the 'khaki shorts brigade' of wildlife enthusiasts; in developing CAMPFIRE, this group rapidly found themselves at the forefront of debates about rural development (Murphree, 1995). Despite this perception and its association with the Parks Department, it was quickly embraced by a number of rural districts. The legislative changes in the post-independence period provided the context for the development of community-based natural resource management in Zimbabwe. Once Zimbabwe gained independence in 1980, the 1975 Parks and Wildlife Act looked discriminatory and colonial, therefore the 1982 Parks and Wildlife Act allowed district councils in the communal areas to be designated as an appropriate authority to manage wildlife. This legislative change allowed the concept of CAMPFIRE to be further developed during the 1980s, but the first CAMPFIRE areas were only established in 1989 in Guruve and Nyaminyami. CAMPFIRE was intended to strike a workable and ethical balance between wildlife conservation and meeting the basic needs of rural people. Furthermore, during the 1990s CAMPFIRE provided the key argument for the Parks Department in Zimbabwe for its controversial approach to wildlife based on sustainable utilization (particularly the commitment to sport hunting); and it was especially important on the international stage as the major justification for Zimbabwe's stance on reopening a limited ivory trade in order to capture the full economic value of elephants through sales of ivory produced by natural death, culls and Problem Elephant Control (PEC) programmes (see Duffy, 2000).

The problem was the distribution of the resulting revenue. Spread out over a whole district the benefits were hard to see, because they were shared among too many people, including those who did not have to live with wildlife on their lands. However, if returns were spent locally, at the ward level, and if village populations were small, then the value of wildlife could be remarkable and make a significant difference to people's lives. In two villages in particular, Mahenye and Masoka, Murphree has documented substantial improvements (Murphree 2001, 2005).

But there are many discontented voices. In some places these derive from the failure of district councils to pass on revenues to the wards where the wildlife lives. But sometimes it is because rural Zimbabweans simply do not want to live with the animals. They see the rural backwaters in which buffalo and elephant thrive as out of the way places, with few services and not enjoying the development provisions that they fought so hard to win (Alexander and McGregor, 2000). In other cases benefits are being distributed, but there are local politics of exclusion and dispossession at work and traditional uses of wildlife are being displaced (Dzingirai, 2003). Else it can simply be awkward and unpleasant dealing with safari hunting operators who are steeped in racist values that define some white cultures in southern Africa. These are not people many African villagers want to choose to do business with (Murombedzi, 2001, 2003).

The ways that the CAMPFIRE model has been taken up and expanded to numerous contexts by multiple organizations means that in some ways it has been the victim of its own success. Over the last 20 years the concepts and practices of community-based natural resource management have been picked up and expanded so that they have become the depoliticized 'catch-all' justification for conservation schemes. In this way community-based natural resource management has shifted from being an *approach* to conservation to being a *component* of conservation schemes. Community-based natural resource management can be used to legitimize conservation initiatives in ways that mask potential problems, dynamics and challenges. Therefore, while many projects are criticized for engaging in 'green-washing' to satisfy environmental concerns, it could be argued that many projects run the danger of 'participation-washing' to answer concerns for local communities (Swatuk, 2005).

The model of transferring powers and revenues to the village and ward level is proliferating in southern and eastern Africa (Swatuk, 2005). The debate about it is often cast in terms of whether it 'works', or whether it is a 'success' or 'failure'. As before, we do not see it in those terms, but rather want to consider how they distribute cost and benefits to different groups, and affect relationships between them, and how they alter relationships and interactions with nature. Child and Jones' enthusiastic advocacy of using safari hunting revenues to fuel community-based conservation initiatives in Zambia and Namibia hinges on the valuable revenues they generate to rural villagers (Child, 2000a, b; Child and Dalal-Clayton, 2001; Jones and Murphree, 2001). Child also notes that the revenues facilitated the introduction of more transparent village government and better accountability over the use of village revenues (Child and Dalal-Clayton, 2001). The revenues of elite photographic safari hunting in Tanzania have similarly fuelled local development in the village of Ololosokwan, close to the Serengeti, and strengthened village institutions, including an independent quarterly audit of village accounts (Nelson and Makko, 2003; Nelson, 2004).

More money is often a good thing for many people in these places but note the consequences here. In Zambia selling the right to hunt wildlife means prohibiting local hunters from doing so, many of whom's prestige and identity arose from their position in village society as hunters. Ken MacDonald has observed a similar process in Pakistan where tourist hunting of ibex removes control over their meat and value from one group of villagers and gives a different sort of reward (money) to another. This project took place in the absence of any decent data documenting trends in ibex populations (MacDonald, 2004, 2005). Sullivan has shown in Namibia that conservancy operations value hunting and wildlife over other natural resources and can reinforce and perpetuate discrimination against women's resources and participation in resource management (Sullivan, 2000). She also notes that these schemes are based on commodifying and selling, or distributing, previously hunted meat. All the joy and complexity, the experience of the hunt with its smells, sights and memories are lost to local experience as a result (Sullivan, 2006). There is a curious echoing of deep ecology here – reducing our interactions with nature to dismal dollars is a poor way to cultivate lasting conservationist sentiment.

Community-based conservation will not be effective if it does not account for actually existing resource management systems and how these have changed over time. Devolving management for natural resources to local people becomes a hollow exercise if this devolution is already oriented to specific types of outcomes and assumes that existing resource management practices are irrelevant, or perhaps even inimical to conservation goals. However, unless local resource management practices are understood, then their relationship to conservation goals remains an unresolved question. This can be seen in the existing debates surrounding common pool resources.

The commons

Local attempts to manage resources and promote conservation outside private land and state-protected areas will require the cooperation of groups of resource users. To understand the likely success of these initiatives we must know more about the circumstances in which groups are able to cooperate successfully and those which make successful cooperation less likely. There is a substantial and systematic body of research that has examined precisely this question.

We must clear up two confusions at the start. Cooperative management practices that govern resource use of resources not owned by the state or individuals are generally called common property regimes, abbreviated to 'CPRs'. Resources that are not easily privatized, like fish in an ocean, or small pockets of rangelands in trackless wastes, and whose use is subtractable (i.e. what I use, you cannot), are called common pool resources, also abbreviated to CPRs.

There is an obvious overlap between the two, in that common pool resources are good candidates for common property management regimes, but this is not a *necessary* relationship. Some common pool resources will be not be managed at all – these are called 'open access regimes'. Others will be managed, at least nominally, by the state. Nor are common property regimes restricted to common pool resources. Individuals can agree to share the management of resources that they could cope with on their own; communes (or married couples) can share ownership of a house. The literature uses 'CPR' freely for both terms, despite their obvious differences. Sometimes authors fail to specify which they are referring to. For clarity we eschew abbreviations below.

The second source of confusion is the late Garett Hardin. Most people's understanding of common pool resources and common property management regimes begins with his infamous essay 'The tragedy of the commons' (Hardin, 1968). Published in *Science* this essay (which is superbly written) is about the perils of overpopulation and the need to control reproduction. It is founded on a well known analogy. 'Picture a pasture', Hardin begins 'open to all'. On this 'commons' are a number of livestock owners. Now imagine what will happen as the livestock owners using that pasture try to get wealthier. Each will want to increase their herds, and so each will add more stock to the pasture. They enjoy the benefits of each extra animal completely, they do not have to share its revenue, meat or milk. The costs of declining condition of the rangeland are shared by all the other herders. And therefore the pasture will inevitably degrade, because it is in each herder's interests to become more prosperous and none has to pay the full costs of their decision. Thus the rangeland will fill up with animals even as it degrades into nothing.

> Ruin is the destination toward which all men rush, each pursuing his own best interest in a society that believes in the freedom of the commons. Freedom in the commons brings ruin to all.
>
> (Hardin, 1968, p1244)

It is a dilemma that has long fascinated many observers (Hardin himself noted that he was making popular an old idea first written up in 1833). For it suggests that people, acting rationally and reasonably but individually, can collectively cause disaster. Our own individual intellects and desire for preservation and prosperity that have kept us alive, and helped us evolve into such a competitive species, could become our undoing.

The essay has been enormously influential (it has been cited over 3300 times, and ever more so each year recently, although later use is also an indication of disapproval). And although its topic was really the dangers of overpopulation its analogy about resource management has been particularly well disseminated. But although this analogy is a good place to begin in order to understand the literature on common property, it is a bad place to begin if you want to understand common property regimes themselves.

Hardin was not actually writing about common property regimes at all. His 'commons' was nothing of the kind because it was open to all. There were no rules governing who could use it or when, which is one of the defining attributes of a commons. He was describing the inevitable degradation of open access resources.

Hardin was also not using an empirical example; it was a thought experiment, a model. And as a model it had some unusual features. For example the herders did not appear to talk to each other much. They did not appear to have the capacity to observe the condition of the rangeland and act on it to prevent its degradation. They were slaves to their own desires for more wealth. These are simplifications that do not apply to all societies.

Fortunately Hardin's model produced clear predictions that we can use to test his ideas. If 'freedom in the commons' brings ruin then it will be impossible for open access resources to become well managed. Either they must be controlled by the state, which would have the oversight to govern and restrict use according to the ecological limits of the pasture, or the land would have to be privatized, so that any overstocking would damage each herder's property individually.

And on this point Hardin has been refuted. There have been cases where common pool resources have become managed by common property regimes, where the resource users have agreed to restrain their own use for the good of the resource. The author who has done most to challenge Hardin's model is Elinor

Ostrom (Ostrom, 1990; Ostrom et al, 1999, 2002; Ostrom and Nagendra, 2006). She began her work in California examining the evolution of groundwater management. Complicated rules had rendered groundwater extraction virtually unmanageable but fears that the resource was diminishing, and being invaded by seawater near the coast, facilitated the introduction of a common property management regime. Ostrom described how agencies fighting over an open access resource came, in this instance, to cooperate and regulate their use of a managed resource (Ostrom, 1990).

Now the research task is to establish what conditions make for effective common property management regimes, and under what circumstances they are likely to perform poorly or fail. Since then there has been a prominent collaborative research effort to document diverse cases of common pool resource management governing irrigation, fisheries, grazing and forestry (Wade, 1988; Berkes, 1989; Bromely and Cernea, 1989; Feeny et al, 1990; Ostrom, 1990; Baland and Platteau, 1996). The Digital Library of the Commons has a bibliography of over 50,000 references and a digital library with over 1000 papers from conferences and published literatures.[3] This work has found that robust common property management regimes are typically characterized by clear rules of who is allowed to use the resource and often when they are allowed to use it. They will exclude some uses and some users. In practice this means clear social and spatial boundaries with respect to use. Use is monitored to ensure that there are no infringements and that infringements are punished, generally with a gradation of punishments.

The research has identified a number of traits with respect to the communities involved, the nature of the resource, the political context, the type of use and other factors that have been synthesized by Arun Agrawal (Agrawal 2001, 2003). He examined work by Wade (1988), Ostrom (1990) and Baland and Platteau (1996) to draw up a list of factors that facilitated effective and durable common property regimes, and supplemented it with his own suggestions (Table 5.1). He notes that the abundance of factors makes it difficult quantitatively to analyse the fortunes of common property management regimes because it is hard to undertake studies that control some variables and observe variation on others. However, he also observed that many of these variables are causally related. Group interdependence for example, was likely to be a function of group size, and mobility, market pressure and resource size. He argued for analysis of the large collections of case studies to understand how causality works and to reduce the number of variables in the analysis. It is precisely this undertaking that the International Forestry Resources and Institutions Program is undertaking, some of whose work we reported in the previous chapter (Hayes, 2006).[4]

There is, however, an important complication in that conceptual framework. The assumption of this research programme is that the strength of the common property management regime is the dependent variable, and that other aspects – community

Table 5.1 *Conditions facilitating common property management regimes*

1   The characteristic of the resource
- small size
- well-defined boundaries
- low levels of mobility
- possibility of storing benefits from the resource
- predictability

2   The nature of the user group
- small size
- clearly defined boundaries
- shared norms
- past successful experiences
- appropriate leadership
- the group is internally interdependent
- heterogeneity of endowment; homogeneity of identities and interests
- low levels of poverty

3   Relationship between characteristics of the resource and the group
- overlap between the group's residence and the location of the resource
- high levels of dependence by the group on the resource
- equitable allocation of benefits from common resources
- low levels of user demand
- gradual change in levels of demand

4   Institutional arrangements
- rules are simple and easy to understand
- access and management rules are locally devised
- rules are easily enforced
- graduated sanctions
- adjudication cheap
- monitors and other officials accountable to users

5   Relationship between resources system and institutional arrangements
- match restrictions on harvests to resource regeneration

6   The wider social and political environment
- exclusion technology is low cost
- adaptation time of technology suited to resource's dynamics
- low levels of articulation with external markets
- gradual change in articulation with external markets
- the State:
  - central government does not undermine local authority
  - external sanctions supportive
  - aid supports conservation activities
  - nested appropriation, provision, enforcement and governance

Source: Agrawal, 2001, p1659 (Table 2)

homogeneity, government support, the nature of the resource and so on – are the independent variables. In other words, that the nature of the management regime is explained by these other factors. That is not always the case. It is quite possible for the birth and development of common property management regimes to affect the nature of other variables, sometimes quite fundamentally.

For example Johnson's work on fisheries in Thailand has shown that quite diverse and heterogenous communities have united and overlooked their differences in order to exclude outsiders. This involved setting up common property management regimes of fisheries that advantaged the wealthier members of the community. In other words, community homogeneity was a product of the success of the establishment of the regime, not a condition of success (Johnson, 2001). There are other cases. In Tanzania, village forest reserves, and wildlife management areas, have been set up in anticipation of the central government legislation allowing their creation, and long before many central government actors have been sympathetic to their existence (Nelson and Makko, 2003; Brockington, 2008).

We must also avoid a common error with respect to the benefits of common property management regimes. It is often assumed that, because common pool resources are difficult to privatize, they are vital for the livelihoods of the poorest rural groups. These are resources that it is difficult for the wealthiest to dominate or exclude others from. This can be true of the resource but we must also note that common property management regimes depend upon establishing clear rules of inclusion and exclusion and monitoring and enforcement of infringement of the rules. Thus common property management regimes that exclude the poor and which enforce those rules will not be 'pro-poor' – quite the opposite. Equally, common property regimes that exclude the poor in theory (according to their rules) but not in practice (because the rules are not enforced), could be quite beneficial to the rural poor because they do not prevent resource use by those whose need drives them to break local laws.

For example Klooster has studied the community forestry regimes in Mexico (Klooster, 2000). He found that there were high levels of resistance to timber control in community-managed forests. Tree poachers would fell valuable trees in the forest, cut them into planks on the spot with a chainsaw and sell them privately. This was curious because these problems had characterized precious state management of the forests. Why did community control not result in a more popular forest management regime and more rural obedience? Klooster's analysis of the politics of community control of the collectives that managed the community forests showed that the benefits were being enjoyed and distributed by a few village elites, who had also been able to control the distribution of revenues during the previous management regime. Significant groups within the communities managing the forests were still excluded. To put it another way, community control had been 'captured' by elites. Community control had slightly altered the distribution of fortune and misfortune that characterized previous regimes, but not in ways that appeased disgruntled factions.

It is also important to realize how fraught common property resource management can be. The water management whose emergence Ostrom recorded in Los Angeles was born out of conflict and litigation. Successful regimes are characterized by high levels of surveillance and monitoring, of people checking up on others and disciplining themselves; they are characterized by the punishment of infringements, formally and informally. These are not necessarily pleasant places to live and work. They can deliver effective resource management, but they do so by managing and mitigating conflict, not by removing it. Campbell and colleagues have claimed that reading the literature left an impression of optimism and that 'CPR (*sic*) management is a relatively easy task' (Campbell et al, 2001, p590). Compared to Hardin's doom it is optimistic; most things would be. Some authors may also be guilty of a romantic approach (as Wily's work demonstrates). But we cannot recognize this characterization of common property management regimes as 'easy'.

Finally we must also note that just as the impact of common property management regimes on poverty varies, so will the impact on conservation objectives. Few common property management regimes are set up with wildlife conservation objectives in mind, although some common property management regimes manage wildlife resources. The outcomes of common property management regimes can nonetheless be most valuable to conservation objectives. The second largest population of the endangered Ethiopian wolf (*Canis simensis*) lives outside a formal protected area on communal grasslands in Guassa, where they appear to cope with the presence of people and livestock (Ashenafi et al, 2005). Similarly the critically endangered Bengal florican bustard (*Houbaropsis bengalensisi*) are thriving on grasslands in Cambodia that are subject to periodic and patchy burning by local groups (Gray et al, 2007).[5] Lekking males seek out relatively open areas and the low levels of disturbance people cause may actually be conducive to their needs.

However, such beneficial consequences for wildlife conservation are not a necessary property of the management regime's success. They are serendipitous. In an extensive review of the role of customary resource management in marine conservation Cinner and Aswani (2007) concluded that the two were compatible, and that customary resource management could further conservation objectives, but that attempts to hybridize the two had explicitly to recognize the differences between them, if they were to be successful in marrying their contrasting goals.

Co-management of protected areas

The label 'co-management' is problematic. It implies equality between the participants. It also conceals a considerable diversity of practice, and a variety of specific historical and political circumstances that have given rise to the arrangements. Many cases of *de facto* co-management are often not recognized as such either because the resident people have historically been seen as a special kind of endangered species (as is the case in Brazil), a perennial problem (as is the case in Tanzania); or no legal category for co-management exists and so such arrangements must be made on a case-by-case basis and so will not officially be called co-management (as is the case in the continental United States).

The Xingu National Park in Brazil was in fact created in part to protect the Kayapo people living there as another type of endangered species (Villa Boas and Villa Boas, 1968). In a move that could only be construed as collaborative from the most ironic perspective, they even kidnapped the director of Xingu National Park, demanding that the Brazilian government continue to protect the boundaries of the park, and therefore their traditional homeland, as sacrosanct.

More typically co-management arrangements occur in wealthier developed countries like Australia, New Zealand, South Africa and the US, where the state is trying to redress historical grievances. In the US a variety of arrangements exist between the National Parks Service and indigenous communities (for a full discussion see Burnham, 2000). The Badlands National Park, for instance, overlaps with the Pine Ridge Reservation of the Oglala Sioux in South Dakota. Through a memorandum of agreement between the Oglala and the Park Service this part of the park is jointly managed with benefits (gate receipts) going directly to the tribal government (Igoe, 2004b).

In South Africa, as part of the post-apartheid land restitution process, portions of the country's protected area estate are now 'under claim' from evicted communities. This includes a large portion of the Kruger National Park and 80 per cent of the protected areas of Mpumulanga Province in the north-centre of the country. Some conservationists in the country are alarmed at the extent and implications of these claims. However, the history of claims thus far shows that the loss of conservation estate that was feared has not been realized (Fabricius and de Wet, 2002). In almost all cases thus far, people moved from protected areas, who have won back their land, have chosen *not* to return to the protected areas. Reasons for this are diverse. In part it is because these are now urban-orientated people. Often many years have passed since they were moved, and the current more numerous generation call their new place home. The remote unserviced rural locations that they win back are not their preferred place to live. Else they have become part of broader societies, often composed of people displaced from diverse areas, in which identity and place are not well connected.

The other reason for the persistence of protected area estate are the innovative and beneficial co-management arrangements that the South African government has initiated in order to maintain the integrity of its protected areas (Reid et al, 2004; Reid, 2006). The most famous incident is the 20,000ha Makuleke claim at Pafuri in the northern end of the Kruger National Park. This community was moved off their land in 1969 and to claim it back formed a Common Property Association of about 15,000 people. They negotiated the return of their land, but agreed instantly to lease it back to the government for 50 years (cancellable after 25). A joint management board of three community representatives and three

South African National Parks representatives manages the land. This portion of the Kruger National Park has been reclassified as a 'contractual park'.

It is important to note that the Makuleke community receive no rent from their lease. The agreement instead gives them control over tourist income, including hunting. They have built a lodge aimed at the luxury market. Most are in a much better position now than they once were with respect to their land. But, as always, what matters is the distribution of cost and benefit. Many of the older generation did not want to sign away their rights to the land, but return to it (Reid, 2001). The current arrangement still results in their exclusion, and in the strange commodification of their knowledge and interaction with the landscape into something tourists will pay to watch. The lodge has the potential to generate significant revenues for other families.

It is all very well setting up a joint management board, but what matters is how well it functions. These can be mixes of unequal capacity, with experienced national parks officials, for whom management boards are their natural habitat, and long-marginalized rural communities who lack the capacity and experience to flourish in these institutional environments. According to Reid the South African experience of these sorts of imbalances is mixed. In Makuleke, the community representatives have grown rapidly to fit their roles, and they are increasingly dominant in joint management board meetings; in the Richtersveld the experience is much less satisfactory (Reid and Turner, 2004). Other arrangements have resulted in sustained conflict. The handback of the Dwesa-Cwebe forest reserve in the former Transkei has also resulted in the land continuing as a protected area leased back from its new owners by the South African government. But there is a continued conflict within the affected communities that has left many aggrieved (C. Fabricius, pers. comm. 2005).

Co-management will be hard. It makes possible all sorts of local and small-scale conflict, which simple exclusion obviated. But it could also increase the local legitimacy of conservation activities, a more just distribution of resources (Reid and Turner, 2004). It also makes possible one great potential dividend. Throughout the African continent national parks and game reserves have been set up on lands in which people used to live. Tourists will walk through and drive past former homesteads or ancient burial grounds in complete ignorance of the social history of the landscape, and of the violence necessary to render it empty for them to enjoy. But awareness of the role of eviction in creating protected areas is growing. Discerning tourists tend not to enjoy holidays that depend on these processes. South Africa is unique in the continent in addressing the violence in the history of conservation. Tourists can not only go there with a clean conscience, they can be more certain that their fees are being put to good local use.

Australia too has sought to address the troubled relationship between the state and Aboriginal peoples through more inclusive conservation policies. Few, if any, protected areas in Australia were established by removing indigenous inhabitants (Poirier and Ostergren, 2002). This was because in many regions the damage had already been done, with entire groups killed off and others split up and forcefully assimilated into white society. Rather the impetus for co-management here has come from the enormous social dislocation which Aboriginal communities face following decades of marginalization and discrimination. Following an enquiry into the high rates of Aboriginal death in custody, the central government, and federal states, recognized that more efforts must be made to strengthen Aboriginal communities and their associations with country (the land) that colonization had so brutally severed. Co-management of state protected areas is one means by which this can be achieved, for it could restore contact and connection with the nourishing terrains so central to identity and belonging (Rose, 1996).

As a federal country the fortunes and practice of co-management vary according to the state in which it occurs. The Northern Territory was the first to act establishing co-management arrangements over the Gurig National Park in 1981 (Smyth, 2001). The Commonwealth government (central state) co-manages three protected areas – Uluru-Kata Tjuta (often known as Ayers Rock), and Kakadu and Booderee National Parks. In all cases the land was managed for conservation by the Australian government before co-management began. Title to the land was then granted inalienably to land trusts that hold it on behalf of traditional owners, and, as in South Africa, at the moment title was granted the Commonwealth simultaneously began to lease the lands back from the Aboriginal owners. Each lease lasts for 99 years, and each involves substantial annual payments: A\$235,000 plus park management contracts (Booderee); A\$150,000 and 25 per cent of tourism income (Uluru); and lease money plus 39 per cent tourism revenues, worth A\$1.3 million in 2000 (Kakadu).

Aboriginal representatives constitute the majority on the boards. But the key question here is not numbers, but, as in South Africa, the capacity to make the boards work for the community. The establishment and development of co-management arrangements are scenes of perpetual conflict. This is inherent to such arrangements. In Kakadu they are further complicated by the presence of a large uranium mine, and the diversity of traditional groups who reside in different parts of the park (Lawrence, 2000). In all parks various forms of traditional use of natural resources by Aboriginal groups continue, specifically hunting and fishing. But, as Smyth observes, these arrangements hinge on their ability to promote the development and community aspirations of the groups whose opportunities can be argued to have been curtailed by conservation restrictions (Smyth, 2001). The story is mixed here. In Kakadu tourism enterprises employ considerable numbers of residents, but jointly owned tourism companies are still in their infancy. For many traditional owners tourism remains an alien activity, and catering to the needs of tourists is not a straightforward operation (Lawrence, pers. comm. 2006). At Uluru despite the majority the traditional owners enjoy on the board they have not been able to restrict the practice of climbing on the rock (which they dislike because every year people die and are injured on it) and are only able to advise tourists against it. The economy of the local area is highly dependent on the income the park and its lease provides, but as yet the income has done little to address the chronic pathologies of alcohol and drug abuse and community dislocation that plague the local Aboriginal settlement. Nevertheless Reid and colleagues felt that, in general, compared to South Africa, the Australian parks service were investing much more in promoting local employment and training (Reid et al, 2004).

Australian co-management is characterized by greater openness to local cultural uses of natural resources and interpretations of the landscape. South African national parks are subject to a much more stringent interpretation of the legislation even in co-managed areas. However, in Australia this can generate a further set of interesting ecological questions. Aboriginal groups interpret value in biodiversity differently from western scientists (Reid et al, 2004). Some feral introduced species (buffalo, rabbits) are 'good tucker' (food), so why try to exterminate them?

Fortunes in the different states of Australia vary. In New South Wales legislation allows a schedule of state parks to be returned to Aboriginal ownership. The benefits of this process are numerous. The state pays a substantial lease (often over one hundred thousand Australian dollars) to the owners, who comprise a majority on the management board. The cultural heritage in the landscape is managed by those whose heritage it is and people are reconnected to country in new powerful ways. For example the handback of Biamanga and Gulaga National Park followed years of wrangling and disputes in which local Aboriginal groups had fought the logging and desecration of sacred sites on Mumballa Mountain and Mt Dromedary respectively (Egloff, 1979, 2004). Staff managing the parks and local traditional leaders enjoy a productive and close relationship.

But note these problems with co-management. In order to be considered as an owner claimants have to subject themselves to a rigorous invasive inspection of their past and social links in order to establish their significant cultural associations with the place. This can be disturbing and generates conflict, as people who feel they have strong associations are omitted. Waters' study of co-management and well-being noted that:

> it could also be argued that the processes of co-management have been detrimental to wellbeing as a result of the social conflict produced by the processes determining the issues of the identification of who can 'speak for country'.
>
> (Waters, 2006, p10)

Furthermore, the NSW legislation stipulates that the lease be compulsorily renewed and that funds must be spent on the upkeep of the park. The committees are still exploring the latitude allowed in determining what can be included in park expenditure.

Still, the situation is better than Queensland, where there is a more recent and active history of exclusion and dispossession. The worst case was that of the former residents of the Archer River Pastoral Station who raised the funds necessary to buy the pastoral lease from its owners and thus win back land taken by European settlers. The government of Queensland, however, which normally rubber stamps all such sales, decreed that they were not allowed to own it because it was not their government's policy to allow Aboriginal ownership of ranches. The Aborigines successfully contested the government's decision, saying that it was racist discrimination. When they lost the case the government promptly compulsorily purchased the land and turned it into the Ben Archer National Park (now Mungkan National Park). But then the story gets worse. Upon the introduction of legislation allowing joint management of national parks the same mob applied to have that park leased back to them and then jointly manage it with the government. They went through the same invasive and exhausting process of establishing significant historical and cultural ties to the land – and, having been identified as the rightful owners, were told by the Queensland government that their terms for leasing the park were that it would be given back to the government for free, and in perpetuity. The traditional owners have declined to pursue the issue.

In the face of this sort of hostility from the state there are still concrete ways, however, that conservation can become more meaningful to Aborginal groups, and can value their connections to the land. This depends on the informal associations and friendships between park staff and local groups on which also hinge the success of the formal co-management arrangements (Smyth, pers. comm. 2006). Renaming of sites within the park using local vernacular terms and the informal granting of collecting activities can be more valuable given the general desire of the state to deny and restrict such associations (Smyth, pers. comm. 2006). Similarly, in New South Wales even if the legal process can be obstructive and impeding, it cannot block people's claims on and belonging to country. One of the more moving interviews Brockington conducted in Australia was near Biamanga and Gulaga National Parks, with an Aboriginal councillor. The councillor's husband was present, a man whose personal history demonstrated some of the violent extremes of Aboriginal life in Australia, and he frequently joined in the discussion. He described how he had been taken from his family as a child on the night his mother died and was raised in a boys' home. He spent 30 years of his life as an alcoholic, with no self-respect. He did not know who he was until he took a course in Aboriginal studies. Now he does, he knows where he belongs, and although not a recognized traditional owner or an elder, and although he was not intending to seek formal recognition, he said repeatedly of Biamanga, gesturing towards the mountain with satisfaction and certainty, that 'I own that place'; nourishing terrains indeed.

Co-management therefore is a complicated tool. It can be a means by which states empower marginalized and disadvantaged groups. But it is also a means by which state control is extended and confirmed. It can restore relations to country and to lands indigenous people value, but rarely on terms they determine. In New Zealand Coombes and Hill have shown that moves to 'co-manage' the Te Urewera National Park in the northwest of the country are being met with hostility because residents fear that it will weaken the unresolved land claims that the Maori residents of the area have already made against the Crown (Coombes and Hill, 2005). Similarly Tofa (2007) has brilliantly examined co-management arrangements at Taranaki National Park in the northeast of New Zealand. This region experienced some of the worst injustices of suppression and land alienation prior to the park's establishment (Waitangi Tribunal, 1996). The settlements that have followed the Crown's recognition of its mistake involve giving Maori iwi control over some conservation land and eventually some say in the management of Taranaki National Park itself.[6] Tofa argues that these arrangements are themselves further impositions as they have required the construction of governance entities that have reshaped iwi into forms that the government can negotiate with, and in the act of giving control over sites to particular iwi the settlements are at the same time closing off other areas. Nevertheless she observed that Maori were willing to cooperate with these arrangements because they offered a stepping stone to more satisfactory relations. Purists (and some Department of Conservation staff in New Zealand) insist, however, that co-management should only be applied to the country's national parks if the land is being handed back to Maori ownership.

Many co-management arrangements are pursued specifically with indigenous peoples in particular countries. It is important to note these groups typically enter these arrangements from positions of weakness. Handback is often made conditional on protected area status continuing, with leases being renewable in perpetuity. Moreover, entering into these types of arrangements often has divisive effects on the groups of concerned communities, accentuating existing divisions and creating new ones. In the case of Badlands, the memorandum of agreement was signed during the period of civil unrest described above. It was signed by a pro-Goon (a pro-government faction) tribal president and still strongly resisted by traditionalist factions who have occupied the reservation side of the park since 2002 (Igoe, 2004b). To understand these dynamics properly requires a more detailed examination of the politics of indigeneity. This we explore in the following chapter.

Conclusion

All of this discussion suggests the need for much more complex and empirical approaches for doing conservation with local communities. Approaches to working with communities often begin with certain types of assumptions about communities and certain desired outcomes that are essentially non-negotiable. Such a way of looking at communities presents two problems. The first is that it results in a sort of reverse engineering when it comes to working with communities. This approach begins with assumed outcomes and asks how can we get communities to perform in ways that will bring about these outcomes. In many cases this results either in disappointment when communities do not perform in ways that the desired outcomes require, or in the need for handpicked interpretive communities that will be predictable enough to bring about desired outcomes or at least be able to create and talk about interventions in ways that present the appearance of realizing the desired outcomes. The second problem is the assumptions themselves. They can involve odd ideas about what constitutes a community. They often include notions of synergies between decentralized resource management and free market economies. Closely related is the assumption that people will only conserve natural resources if they value them, and they will only value them if they have a cash value.

Perhaps the biggest problem with this approach to community-based conservation is that it systematically filters out those problems and challenges that do not meet its criteria. A more open ended, empirical approach is much more likely to help us find approaches that are effective, equitable and more in line with local needs and values. This type of approach can also allow us to ask much more productive questions, about which types of approaches seem to work best in which contexts, and how are costs and benefits distributed in the process? What kinds of patterns emerge in terms of how community-based conservation actually interacts with the environment and local livelihoods? And how can understanding these patterns help us to improve the ways in which conservation gets done? This may not be so effective at mobilizing resources for large-scale interventions. However it will allow a far more nuanced and flexible approach to community conservation. It also sets the stage for the types of learning that are essential to improved design and practice over time.

Notes

1   Sundar also notes that it is not entirely new and lists several precedents before the 1970s.
2   Sundar (2000) gives 10–15,000, citing a source published in 1996; www.rupfor.org/jfm.asp gives 63,000 (accessed 19 December 2007).
3   www.sristi.org/cpr/display.php3 (accessed 15 December 2007).
4   www.indiana.edu/~ifri/ (accessed 15 December 2007).
5   It is not clear whether these grasslands are subject to a common property management regime. The authors describe them as 'open access' and 'community-managed'. They describe practices of management and burning but do not describe the decision-making processes that result in this management being carried out.
6   An iwi is approximately equivalent to a tribe in English. It is a named, distinct sub-group of the Maori people.

6

Conservation and Indigenous Peoples

We Eskimos would like to join the Sierra Club Inuit Activist
William Wiloya, 1969 in Catton, 1997, p4

In 1970 a group of Inuit activists joined forces with conservationists to protect the Alaskan Wilderness from oil exploration and the construction of oil pipelines that were threatening both the environment and the Inuit way of life. This alliance ultimately led to the creation of Gates of the Arctic National Park in 1980. Gates of the Arctic was the first park within the US National Parks system that allowed for human habitation (Catton, 1997, p2). Throughout the 1970s and 1980s, alliances based on the common interests of indigenous peoples and conservationists grew but remained limited in geographic scope. By the 1990s, however, the protection of biodiversity was becoming discursively and institutionally linked to cultural diversity and indigenous rights (WWF, 1997; Stepp et al, 2004). Conservation interventions targeting indigenous peoples proliferated (Chapin, 2004). Indigenous peoples and indigenous issues became increasingly common at international conservation events. In 2000, IUCN established a theme on indigenous and local communities, equity, and protected areas (see Igoe, 2008 for a detailed discussion).[1]

These discursive and institutional transformations coincided with the emergence and growing success of the global Indigenous Peoples' Movement following the Soviet collapse in the late 1980s. During this period the global spread of NGOs and funding for initiatives that were clearly beyond the purview of states, created new opportunities for transnational activism by indigenous peoples. It also created new opportunities for 'space making' inside transnational institutions like the UN and the World Bank (Li, 2000; Muehlebach, 2001; Hodgson, 2002a; Niezen, 2003; Igoe, 2005, 2006a; Dove, 2006). These developments were accompanied by the rise of what Niezen (2003, pp4–5) calls the rise of 'global indigenism': a nascent global ideology that the experiences of the world's 'first peoples – those who are strongly attached to the world's "last wild places" and who share a claim to have survived on their land through the upheavals of colonialism and corporate exploitation'. The association of 'the world's first peoples' with the 'world's last wild places' suggested opportunities for 'space making' within the institutional structures of transnational conservation, such as the IUCN and large conservation NGOs.

These events and processes appeared to portend a convergence of global indigenism and global environmentalism. Indeed, at the turn of the millennium encounters between conservationists and indigenous peoples were intensifying in unprecedented ways, thereby creating unprecedented opportunities for more effective alliances and collaborations (Tsing, 2004). Even the World Bank began to support indigenous environmental knowledge, declaring itself 'the knowledge bank' (Dove, 2006, p195).

Unfortunately, these encounters also revealed that conservation interventions targeting indigenous peoples were often failing (Chapin, 2004). They also revealed that indigenous ways of valuing and using natural resources were frequently out of step with those of conservationists (Niezen, 2003), a revelation that contributed to a backlash known as the 'back to the barriers movement' (Roe et al, 2003; Hutton et al, 2005); for examples, see Leakey (2003) and Sanderson (2004). At the same time, indigenous peoples in many parts of the world have become suspicious and disdainful of anything called conservation (Dowie, forthcoming).

This chapter will lay out some of the institutional and historical context of these encounters and the types of effects they have had in different times and places. Indigenous peoples play a significant and active role in conversations about indigenous people and conservation, which we will examine. However, for the most part these are not conversations among equals. Inuit people who worked to create Gates of the Arctic National Park have found themselves increasingly excluded from that park (Catton, 1997); Aboriginal groups in Australia found themselves being used as pawns between mining companies and conservationists (Allen, 1981). Transnational conservation NGOs aggressively pursued alliances with indigenous peoples in Latin America, but then wound up with the lion's share of the funding (Chapin, 2004). From 'the local' to 'the global' the putative link between biodiversity has put tremendous pressure on indigenous leaders to cultivate certain images that are exceedingly difficult to live up to in practice.

From a historical perspective protected areas have two starkly different, and at times paradoxical, consequences for indigenous peoples. On the one hand, they have been instrumental in dispossessing people of land and resources. Viewed from below there is little difference between protected area establishment and other large-scale development projects (Brockington, 2002; Dowie, 2005). Both are planning exercises carried out by states that require significant changes in the way that rural peoples live their lives. On the other hand protected areas can be the instruments by which indigenous people win control over land and resources and defend themselves against the transformations of modernity. Indigenous leaders must negotiate this precarious paradox as best they can.

In this chapter we explore the paradoxical relationships of indigenous people and protected areas in the context of conservation encounters. We look at protected areas as a literal 'common ground' for these encounters. We examine the consequences for people and nature of the alliances that have developed. We then turn a more critical eye upon the concept of indigeneity itself, especially the ways in which ideas of indigenous and ideas of nature can become mutually constituting in the context of transnational biodiversity conservation. We consider the problems of the category 'indigenous', the types of pitfalls it can create both for conservation and indigenous activism and the exclusions it can entail and the politics of its application.

Initial encounters

As we noted in Chapter 2, mainstream conservation traces its roots to the creation of national parks in the 19th century in the United States, especially Yosemite and Yellowstone. We further noted that while this particular 'creation tale' is problematic, it is nevertheless powerful. Moreover, it focuses on a historical moment when the 'collaborative legacy' of mainstream conservation was being established in the context of westward expansion in the US. This was a process of contact and displacement, and parks were integral to this process.

This history does not begin in the US, but in western Europe, where changes in rural capitalism and land tenure laws led to the emergence of elite landscape ideals in which human beings or any evidence of their activities did not belong, and were therefore actively excluded. These ideals were imprinted on landscapes throughout Great Britain and other parts of western Europe through the creation of a stark divide between landscapes of production – set aside for the production of wealth – and landscapes of consumption – set aside for the viewing pleasure of rural elites. Landscapes of consumption were most commonly created as part of country estates, which revolved around the idea of a 'pleasing prospect' (Williams, 1973; Olwig and Olwig, 1979; Cosgrove, 1984). Through these transformations, enjoyment of nature and outdoor leisure activities became part of aristocratic distinction. Contemplation of nature and scenery in the West, and therefore mainstream western conservation values, is intimately related to the changing rules and circumstances by which land was controlled and its proceeds distributed (Daniels and Cosgrove, 1988; Pringle, 1988; Daniels, 1993; Neumann, 1998; Igoe, 2004b).

The creation of parks in the US was instigated by urban elites from the eastern part of the country, who were strongly influenced by European ideals of the 'pleasing prospect'. As we have seen, the original call for parks is commonly attributed to George Catlin who, during his trips along the Missouri River in the 1830s, was taken by the beauty of the American prairie and its native American inhabitants. He correctly feared that these landscapes and people would become decimated by westward expansion and therefore proposed national parks for the landscape and its residents (see page 19, Chapter 2). Catlin's vision of a landscape for people and nature never came to fruition. By 1865 a new champion of the conservation in the West emerged – Samuel Bowles. Bowles celebrated the magnificent beauty of what he called the Switzerland of America, a land of:

wide elevated Parks, lying among her double and treble folds of the
continental range … surrounded by mountains that rise from …
plains green with grass, dark with groves, bright with flowers.
(Spence, 1999, p23)

Unlike Catlin, however, Bowles wanted this to be a land from which Native
Americans were restricted and contained. He met many on his travels but
supported the new and treacherous system of reservations that the government
was proposing as they looked to the west and to the Indian lands therein for
expansion. He wrote:

We know that they are not our equals … we know that our right to
the soil, as a race capable of its superior improvement, is above theirs
… Let us say [to them] you are our ward, our child, the victim of
our destiny, ours to displace, ours to protect. We want your hunting
grounds to dig gold from, to raise grain on, and you must move on.
(Spence, 1999, p25)

Reservations would be awarded, but if:

the march … of empire demands this reservation of yours, we will
assign you another; but so long as we choose, this is your home, your
prison, your playground. (Spence, 1999, p27)

This language was accompanied by a new sense of nationhood and purpose
summed up in the belief in America's manifest destiny. After the conquest of
northern Mexico, and the ceding of territory from the British in Oregon,
America came to celebrate in the 1840s 'its manifest destiny to overspread and
possess the whole of the continent for our yearly multiplying millions'. At the
same time as it was seeing a great future for itself, Americans were also seeking
out suitable symbols for their increasingly auspicious nation – and it was this that
in part inspired Bowles. He saw in the magnificence of the mountains, in the
scenery of Yosemite and in the ancient big trees suitable symbols with which to
celebrate America as the exclusive domain of the white man.

The result was that national parks in the US became instruments of dispossession
at the same time as they were conserving landscapes from developments by settlers
and as they were also promoting nascent tourism industries. Yellowstone was
created on lands that had been allotted as hunting grounds to neighbouring Indian
groups four years earlier. Rights to hunt there were revoked, and the first task the
government faced was to clear the hunters out. The first park headquarters was a
heavily fortified blockhouse, located on an isolated hill that offered a good defensive
position. Hundreds of people died in efforts by the US Cavalry to establish the park
and clear Indians from the area.

The Glacier National Park was established in 1910, when there was less active conflict with native American groups and more nostalgia for their vanishing world. The park featured opportunities to see traditional dances and to have Indian-dressed golf caddies. But at the same time there was fierce opposition to Indian interference and hunting in the eastern edge of the park where it adjoined their reservation because it was perceived to be unnatural. Ironically this was also a time when park staff were witnessing an explosion of elk and other wild grazers in the park resulting in problems of overgrazing because the park staff were killing off unwanted predators like wolf, coyote and mountain lion.

In fact there are no major protected areas in the American West that have not had significant conflicts with native American communities. This aspect of the early history of national parks was marginalizing at best, and violent and traumatic at worst. But it is one that is simply erased from the popular history of Yellowstone. A recent volume on the topic was sub-titled *The Hidden History of American Conservation* (Jacoby, 2001). It is not a story that is widely known and is absent from Nash and Runte's popular histories. Moreover, as Spence (1999) argues, wilderness preservation based on the Yellowstone model spread throughout the world in the 20th century, thereby becoming 'a model for native dispossessing the world over' (p85).

Neumann (2005, pp134–135) takes this argument further, asserting that protected areas are linked to the expansion of state control. Parks are certainly often associated with the control and containment of indigenous communities. However, they are also frequently spaces uniquely beyond state control. Parks in Africa and Latin America have become staging grounds for guerrilla movements (Dunn, 2003; Tapia, 2005), as well as for drug trafficking (Stepp, 2005; Tapia, 2005). Protected areas in the US shelter marijuana plantations and methamphetamine labs, as well as people seeking to enter the country illegally. They have also sometimes enabled indigenous people to elude state control and other forms of incursion. The Ute Mountain Tribal Park in Colorado was created by the Ute Mountain tribe in part to protect their land from being taken over by the Mesa Verde National Park (Igoe, 2004b). The Xingu National Park in Brazil was essential to Kayapo resistance to commercial mining and hydroelectric dams on the Xingu River (Turner, 1993). The Kuna Park in Panama was instrumental for the Kuna in protecting their homeland from colonization by formerly urban settlers and cattle ranchers (Chapin, 2000).

As contested spaces, sometimes beyond the reach of states and global capitalism, parks have brought together indigenous peoples and western conservationists in landscapes around the world since at least the 19th century. In an effort to protect these landscapes, sometimes from each other, both groups have sought support and resources from distant but powerful institutions. Over time, their externally oriented strategies have engendered transnational institutional structures like the IUCN and the UN Forum on Indigenous Issues.

Relationships that began in the context of protected area encounters have been reproduced in these structures, with the added complexity of distance, institutional survival and funding cycles.

The rise of global indigenism: Problems of definition, identity and articulation

The global Indigenous Peoples' Movement emerged at a time of transformation in the global environmental movement. Conservation NGOs have become more numerous, with funds concentrated onto a powerful few (Chapin, 2004; Khare and Bray, 2004; Dorsey, 2005). Their growth was achieved through a diversification of funding strategies to include funding from corporate, bilateral and multilateral sources. This has also been the period, as we examine in the final three chapters, when conservation has turned increasingly to neoliberal rhetoric to justify its policies. These developments have increased possibilities for encounters between conservationists and indigenous peoples, while simultaneously defining the contexts in which these encounters will take place. Especially since, as Chernlea (2005) argues, there is an increasing trend in some parts of the world of environmental NGOs moving away from 'facilitation to domination' and from 'local partnering' to 'local production' (cf. Chapin, 2004; Dove, 2006; Igoe and Croucher, 2007).

Transnational indigenous activism has been going on for as long as transnational environmental activism. As with environmental activism, the transnational structures of indigenous activism have their roots in colonialism and European expansion (for a detailed discussion see Niezen (2003) and Igoe (2008)). In 1974, indigenous leaders from North America, Latin America and Australia established the World Council of Indigenous Peoples, the first of 11 indigenous NGOs with official UN consultative status (Sanders, 1980). However, it was not until participation in 'international consultations and standard setting was extended to self-identifying indigenous peoples from Africa and Asia in the 1990s, that the indigenous peoples' movement became more fully global' (Niezen, 2003, p26). The reasons for the initial exclusion of people from Africa and Asia, as well as their later inclusion, in the global Indigenous People's Movement are complex and controversial (Li, 2000; Sylvaine, 2002; Kuper, 2003; Niezen, 2003; Igoe, 2005). However, they are closely tied to the global spread of NGOs during this same period, which presented activists in Africa and Asia with unprecedented opportunities for gaining access to international forums (Niezen, 2003; Igoe, 2008).

These developments have clearly increased the political clout of indigenous activists. Not only this, they have contributed to the creation of a new international legal category, which indigenous activists can use to bolster their claims to cultural autonomy, political sovereignty and natural resources. Most recently this has resulted in the ratification of the UN Declaration of the Rights of Indigenous Peoples in September of 2007.[2] They are also the basis of increased and intensified encounters between indigenous activists and conservationists. This convergence has in turn resulted in both conflicts and collaborations between conservationists and indigenous activists, a matter that will be addressed in detail below.

Before turning to the issue of conflict and collaboration and correspondence, it is important to note an inherent paradox in the global Indigenous People's Movement, which Niezen (2003, p3) succinctly describes as follows:

> The clearest expression of human diversity can now be found in a category now widely referred to as 'indigenous peoples'; yet the very creation of this category involves common origin, is predicated on a global sameness of experience, and is expressed through mechanisms of law and bureaucracy, the culprits most commonly associated with gains in cultural uniformity.

This paradox has presented a fundamental challenge to indigenous activists, while sparking intense debates between anthropologists and other social scientists. As Dove (2006) explains, most anthropologists agree that the concept of indigeneity is fraught with problems and contradictions, but disagree on the implications of those problems and contradictions. In his article 'Return of the native', Adam Kuper (2003) argued that the term 'indigenous' is little more than a euphemism for the term 'primitive', and that it fosters 'essentialist ideas of culture and identity that may have dangerous political consequences'. He further asks, 'should we ignore history for fear of undermining myths of autochthony' (p400)? By contrast, David Maybury-Lewis, founder of the organization *Cultural Survival*, has admonished that anthropologists should 'know better' than to write critically about the appropriateness of indigenous status for people in Africa and Asia.[3] Governments might use their works to justify policies that adversely affect disadvantaged ethnic minorities in their countries (cf. Colchester, 2002). Much of the anthropological writing on this topic, especially critiques of Kuper, revolves around 'the politics of Science' (Dove, 2006, p193). These critiques question the ethics of interfering in the efforts of indigenous activists to strategically invoke specific categories, identities and histories in their struggles against the forces of globalization. These writings highlight 'place-making' by indigenous activists in transnational institutional structures like the UN, the World Bank, and the IUCN (Muehlebach, 2001; Colchester, 2002; Hodgson, 2002b; Niezen, 2003; Igoe, 2004a).

As Dove (2006) also points out, indigenous activists engaged in 'place making' usually do not have the luxury or the inclination of this type of analysis. Rather, they must develop the necessary skills and language to negotiate the paradoxes and contradictions of indigeneity in a global context. They must be simultaneously 'modern' and 'traditional'. In her excellent book *Methodology of the Oppressed*, Chela Sandoval (2000) argues that effective activism by all previously colonized peoples requires what she calls 'differential consciousness'; this is a kind of mental mobility, the ability to move between different contexts and audiences, and even contradictory ideas, in ways that achieve specific purposes. She argues that many colonized peoples have already achieved differential consciousness as a matter of survival in response to the contradictions forced upon them over generations by European colonialism. She argues that westerners also need to develop differential consciousness in order to learn how to operate effectively in our convoluted and contradictory globalized world. She warns, however, that differential consciousness must be accompanied by a democratic ethic, in which differential consciousness is used to bring about egalitarian social justice. Differential consciousness without a democratic ethic leads to what philosopher Roland Barthes (2000 (1957)) called 'cynical consciousness', which begins with 'a concept wedded to power (value) and then seeks a form to represent it' (Sandoval, 2000, p94). This is the approach that marketing professionals use to sell a product or idea.

From this perspective the job of anthropologists is not exactly to critique definitions of indigenous per se, but to understand how they are created in different contexts and how different groups of people and individuals struggle to articulate with them in order to advocate on behalf of their communities or to further other sorts of causes. Tania Li (2000, p169) conceptualizes an 'indigenous slot' with which some groups are able to articulate. Certain preconditions are necessary for this articulation, three of which are apropos of international 'space making': outsiders interested in finding and helping indigenous groups, a capacity to make local cultural identity intelligible to outsiders, and individuals mandated to speak on behalf of the group.

Understanding how different groups of people manage to articulate with this 'indigenous slot', will give us a much more solid understanding of the different types of encounters that are likely to occur between indigenous activists and conservationists, and which shape the outcomes of those encounters are likely to look like, as well as how they get reported. Anthropologists, policy makers and indigenous activists have struggled to create definition of indigenous that is broad enough to include people from a broad diversity of contexts, while being narrow enough to still be meaningful. Colchester (2003, p18) claims to have resolved the paradoxes of this exercise in category making by defining indigenous peoples as a 'self-ascribed polythetic class' that is global in scope (see also Burger, 1987; Khan and Talal, 1987; UN High Commissioner for Human Rights, 1989).[4] According to this type of analysis, this class has emerged through the interaction of indigenous activists at transnational forums promoting indigenous sovereignty. They attend these forums with 'little doubt about their own status of indigenous, and few open doubts about the claims of others' (Niezen, 2003, pp18–23).

This way of looking at indigenous identity apparently alleviates the need for pedantic scholarly discussions about which groups are indigenous and which groups are not. Unfortunately, it can only achieve this by conflating indigenous place making at the transnational level with the dynamics of actual indigenous communities, such that 'indigenous cultural politics are always also the politics of land ... and all struggles for and about land are also struggles about identity and culture' (Muehlebach, 2001, p425). International indigenous activism is irrefutably tied to local land struggles, though not always and not always in the ways that these pundits imagine. The main problem with these types of narrative, however, is that they ignore the exclusivity of the international forums in which 'space making' by indigenous activists takes place. The idea of indigenous peoples as a global self-ascribed polythetic class is only unproblematic as long as it also ignores the inherent exclusivity of these forums.

When this exclusivity is ignored, whether or not a group of people becomes indigenous appears as a matter of choice. Colchester's (2002, p2) discussion of this issue smacks surprisingly of Sartrean free will:

> Not all marginalized ethnic groups choose to consider themselves
> indigenous. Some apparently see greater advantage in assimilating
> into the national mainstream. Others, like many Kurds, apparently
> feel that the indigenous struggle is too parochial and claim rights to
> full nationality by other means.

As Li (2000, p151) demonstrates, however, not every marginal ethnic group can 'choose' to be indigenous:

> A group's self-identification as indigenous is not natural or
> inevitable, but neither is it simply invented, adopted, or imposed. It
> is a positioning, which draws upon historically sedimented practices,
> landscapes, and repertoires of meaning, and emerges through
> particular patterns of engagement and struggle.

Before these preconditions can come into play, however, more fundamental preconditions must be met: knowledge of the Forum for Indigenous Issues, money for travel expenses and the courage to travel to unknown places, not to mention passports, visas, the possibility of foregoing opportunity costs and a group of outsiders with the will and resources to support a specific indigenous cause. Ironically, this means that some people are too marginal to claim indigenous status (Beteille, 1998; Jackson, 1999; Fisher et al, 2005; Dove, 2006; Igoe, 2006a).

It is also important not to underestimate the extent to which indigeneity represents an important form of symbolic capital, which indigenous leaders use to make alliances with, and leverage resources from, international actors – not the least of whom are representatives of international conservation organizations. Arguments about 'indigenous self-identity' notwithstanding, effective use of this symbolic capital often depends upon meeting externally defined criteria of indigenous legitimacy, which may be quite different from local ideas of what this might mean (Conklin and Graham, 1995; Hodgson, 2002a; Niezen, 2003; Igoe, 2005, 2006a).

These dynamics are complicated by the fact that indigenous struggles are not always about land (cf. Sylvaine, 2002, p1076). Most notably, they are also about monetary resources associated with interventions targeting indigenous peoples. These external resources are crucially important to communities that have been impoverished by the historical alienation of their natural resource base. Tribal governments and indigenous NGOs are not only vehicles for indigenous advocacy, but also one of the few (if not only) opportunities for gainful employment in many indigenous communities.

Struggles over issues of identity and representation, which are frequently tied to access to outside resources, are source of frequent allegations that indigenous leaders are not operating according to the type of democratic ethic that Sandoval advocates. An organization called 'the Accountability Coalition' has documented corruption and rights abuses by tribal government throughout Canada (Niezen, 2003). At the Pine Ridge Reservation in South Dakota, US, conficts over representation resulted in a period of bloody civil unrest, in which when a pro-government faction known as the Goons fought violently with Oglala traditionalists who had joined the American Indian Movement. These conflicts became visible again when Oglala traditionalists occupied the tribal offices in 2000, as well as by their current occupation of the Badlands National Park (Burnham, 2000; Igoe, 2004b; Igoe and Kelsall, 2005). In southeast Alaska, a coalition of landless communities struggled against native leaders who had cut them out of their 'village corporations'. Members of this coalition rejected the indigenous label, identifying instead with the Pentocostal Church (Dombrowski, 2002). In Brazil, some Kayapo leaders stand accused of selling out their communities to benefit their factions, to the extent that they are no longer welcome in their own villages (Turner, 1993; Nugent, 1994; Conklin and Graham, 1995). Struggles over identity and external resources also resulted in the near breakdown of Tanzania's indigenous NGOs movement in the late 1990s (Igoe, 2003a, 2004b).

There are two systematic inequities inherent in current arrangements: 1) inequities between indigenous groups; and 2) inequities between indigenous groups and other marginal groups, who for one reason or another cannot choose to define themselves as indigenous. The first type of inequity is best summed up as 'some indigenous people are more indigenous than others'. San groups in Namibia, for instance, have become a permanent underclass of agricultural workers. Members of this group are unable to articulate the same claims to indigeneity as San groups in neighbouring Botswana (Sylvaine, 2002). In Tanzania, Barabaig NGOs leaders complain that Maasai NGOs dominate the Tanzanian indigenous peoples' movement. The Maasai enjoy global recognition, while the Barabaig are barely known outside of Tanzania. As a result, Barabaig leaders claim, Maasai leaders command more than their fair share of NGO resources (Igoe, 2000, 2004c; Hodgson, 2002b). San leaders in Botswana have made similar allegations against Maasai NGOs (Suzman, 2002/3, p8). Maasai opposition to the evictions from the Mkomazi Game Reserve excluded and alienated local groups that had been in the area longer than the Maasai (Kiwasila, 1997). In Colorado, over 600,000 tourists a year flock to the Mesa Verde to visit ruins of ancient Anasazi peoples, who were the ancestors of contemporary Hopi groups. What most of these tourists don't know, and which they will never find out at the Mesa Verde visitor centre, is that the park was excised from the reservation of the Ute Mountain Ute, who are in no way related to the ancient Anasazi and benefit very little from the areas booming tourist economy (Burnham, 2000; Igoe 2004b).

Next, indigenous people are not always the most marginal people displaced and impoverished by protected areas. While the impoverishment of Native Americans by national parks is a little known story, the impoverishment of Appalachian communities is an even lesser known one (Horning, 2004). Members of these poor white communities, derisively referred to as hillbillies by many Americans, have been forcefully displaced by the establishment of the Shenandoah National Park (Jacoby, 2001) and the Blue Ridge Parkway (Wilson, 1992).

The situation is more complicated in contexts where poverty takes a more 'equal opportunity approach' and where the line between indigenous and non-indigenous is more directly influenced by the perceptions of western conservationists, human rights activists and eco-cultural tourists. Nugent's account of conservation in Amazonia poignantly captures this dilemma:

> In its attempts to make the world over in its own image, Europe's portrayals of society at the fringes have frequently betrayed a kind of stereo tunnel vision: in one eye is presented that which typifies the legacy of civilization, the other observes primitivism. Out of focus, if not out of view, is the nether world, that vast region of social and historical marginality where images are less pristine and for which more explanation is required than can be summed up in a flattering archetype. Ragged urban infants selling ices are neither gratefully European nor charmingly primordial. The canoe paddling fisherman wearing a t-shirt emblazoned with 'Miss Nudity Concourse U.S.A' is on the wrong set. (These) out of focus Amazonians ... appear when needed as guides, they are present when laundry needs to be done; they drive cabs and serve up beer, but they are almost incidental, populating the transitional zone between the airport and the Amazonian Indian theme park.
>
> (Nugent, 1994, pp17–18)

Because it is so unpleasant and so complicated, residents of Nugent's 'nether world' are frequently overlooked by conservationists and conservation interventions. They are also overlooked by social scientists as people who have 'chosen to assimilate'. The problem with this perspective is that being assimilated into poverty only means that you are poor with nothing to distinguish yourself in the eyes of outsiders who may bring resources to your communities. Studies from Indonesia (Li, 2000), South Africa (Kuper, 2003), and Tanzania (Igoe, 2003a) illustrate that people descended from displaced groups frequently make up significant minorities of the rural populations in developing countries. These groups are also frequently the most marginal and least ethnically distinct. In fact, Gupta goes so far as to suggest that these 'out of focus people' represent the majority of the world's poor.

We wish to emphasize here that this discussion is not meant to let anyone off the hook when it comes to working with indigenous peoples. Redford (1990) is certainly correct that advocates of indigenous rights frequently construct indigenous peoples as 'ecologically noble savages'. It does not follow, however, that indigenous peoples should not have rights to land and natural resources and that their well-being should not be the concern of conservation. Rather, we are arguing here that the global project of nature conservation is inextricably intertwined with the global project of cultural conservation to which Gupta refers above. Just as effective nature conservation must engage with the full complexity of living ecosytems, which include the people who live within them, cultural conservation must engage with the full complexity of the experiences of formerly colonized peoples, whether or not these people are able to lay claim to indigenous status. Conservation interventions, by definition, have and will continue to encounter people living in landscapes. The discussion that follows, therefore, is designed to present a more complex understanding of the dynamics of these encounters, and whether they are likely to result in collaboration or conflict.

Conservationists and indigenous activists in the 'shifting middle ground'

Understandings of encounters between indigenous activists and western conservationists must begin with the ways in which both groups market their activities through appeals to external supporters (for a detailed discussion see Niezen, 2003, pp187–190). This situation is made doubly difficult by the fact that, in many parts of the world, indigenous activists depend on conservation organizations for funding. This means in effect that conservation organizations are marketing themselves to their funders and the general public often in oversimplified ways that conceal many of the complex problems that we are addressing in this book, and indigenous activists must in turn market what they are doing with reference to the marketing discourses of conservation organizations.

These concerns reflect more fundamental problems with convergence between the global indigenous peoples' movement and international conservation, which is perhaps best described as an 'encounter of strangers predicated upon assumptions of vaguely similar values: environmental preservation, appreciation of "different" cultures, and rejection of poverty, misery, and illegitimate death' (Niezen, 2003, p191). The problem with the 'vagueness' of this overlap, is that it frequently obscures pressing local concerns (Hodgson, 2002b; Sylvaine, 2002; Kuper, 2003; Igoe, 2004a). By treating indigenous communities as just another 'stakeholder group' community conservation discounts their primary goal of self-determination and gaining control of the natural resources on which their livelihoods depends (Conklin and Graham, 1995).

Landscape preservation is also frequently at odds with indigenous pursuits of prosperity and economic development (Redford, 1990; Niezen, 2003). Conservation has taken peoples' land, imposed changes to culture and custom, and marginalizes them politically (Colchester, 1997; Gray et al, 1998; Colchester and Erni, 1999; Chatty and Colchester, 2002; Nelson and Hossack, 2003). It is one of the means by which states exert control over them. In Botswana, Ethiopia and Thailand ongoing evictions or attempts at eviction are continuing to disrupt the lives of indigenous people (Buergin and Kessler, 2000; Ikeya, 2001; Sato, 2002; Buergin, 2003; Pearce, 2005a, b). Mac Chapin and Mark Dowie have controversially alleged that major conservation organizations are substantially implicated in the marginalizations affecting indigenous peoples (Chapin, 2004; Dowie 2005, 2006).

Conklin and Graham (1995, p695) describe the context in which indigenous activists and western conservationists encounter one another as a 'shifting middle ground' through which indigenous peoples and western conservationists construct a 'mutually comprehensible world' characterized by new systems of meaning and exchange. 'Middle grounds are forged on the basis of assumptions about the Other and what (they) can contribute to specific goals' (p696; also cf. Rangan, 1992). This middle ground represents a paradox of the convergence of conservation and the indigenous peoples. Indigenous activists around the world invoke the idea that their relationships to the environment are consistent with conservation principles in their efforts to enter into alliances with western conservationists (Alcorn, 1993; Redford and Stearman, 1993a, b; Turner, 1993; Catton, 1997; Li, 2000). Such strategies are often essential in their bids to maintain control of their natural homelands. However, they also carry an implicit premise that indigenous communities are only worthy of remaining on a landscape as long as they remain 'ecologically noble' (Li, 2000, p170 and Niezen, 2003, p197). In this context, Dove (2006, p194) argues that indigenous identity is 'a narrow target that is too easily overshot or undershot'. People always run the risk of being too modern or too primitive.

In her ethnography *Friction* (2004), Anna Tsing documents the ways in which networks between activists in Indonesia's Merapus Mountains were able to use transnational standards to critique national policies in ways that allowed them to enter into alliances with international conservationists to protect their homeland from deforestation. In the process they were able to define a community by social relationships inscribed in the forests where they live. She hastens to add, however, that this fortuitous outcome is not the result of a particular formula that was successfully applied to doing conservation with indigenous communities.

In fact, she describes in detail how attempts to export successful collaborations can spell disaster in other contexts. Specifically she describes the ways in which experiences of collaborations between Brazilian rubber tappers and North American human rights groups to stop deforestation in the Amazon basin were exported to Malaysia with disastrous results. Where environmentalists and local people were successful in making deforestation an Indonesian cause, collaborations in Malaysia were treated as interference by outsiders, ultimately ending with the disappearance of a Swiss adventurer named Bruno Manser who championed the cause of the Penan people whose rainforest was threatened. Tsing's conclusion is that effective collaborations between indigenous communities and conservationists will only occur in specific configurations of circumstances in which both groups are able to use globally circulating universal ideas – like biodiversity, democracy and human rights – to work towards goals that they are able to identify in common. It is also important to note that these configurations of conditions will not remain static, but inevitably change over time.

From this perspective, there appear to be three main contexts in which effective collaborations do occur. First, there are collaborations in which indigenous communities cooperate with conservationists to co-manage protected areas on their traditional homelands, which we discussed in the previous chapter. Second, are cases when conservationists and indigenous people have a common cause and a common enemy, as with the case that Tsing has documented for Indonesia. This is what prompted Inuit activist William Willoya's assertion that the Eskimo wanted to join the Sierra Club to protect the Alaska wilderness from oil exploration. This type of alliance is especially prevalent in Latin America. The most famous of these is the case of the Kayapo and their struggles to stop hydro-electric dams on Brazil's Xingu River (Turner, 1993). In this context Sting and Kayapo activist Raoni appeared on national television in both the UK and US, and Sting released his rainforest CD (Nugent, 1994).

Beyond these types of arrangements, there are also cases in which indigenous communities establish protected areas of their own accord and on their own land. Such an arrangement is now recognized by the IUCN under the category of 'Indigenous Protected Area' (IPA). Like co-management, however, this category obscures the particular political, economic and historical circumstances under which indigenous people establish protected areas. In Australia, indigenous protected areas account for 19 per cent of the country's protected area estate (Langton et al, 2005). Australia's IPA programme is widely celebrated, but early assessments indicate that Aboriginal communities have started IPAs in the hopes of capturing external resources. In the process many have become dependent on non-aboriginal management experts, as an IPA must meet specific criteria in order to be officially recognized by the Australian government.[5] The Ute

Mountain Tribal Park in Colorado, by contrast, was established explicitly to keep Ute land from being taken over by the Mesa Verde National Park and to keep outside conservation experts off of the reservation (Igoe, 2004b). As we outlined in Chapter 2, indigenous peoples have been creating protected areas for centuries in the form of sacred groves, vision quest sites, drought reserve and the like. The extent of these types of protected areas must be substantial on a global scale. Unfortunately they are poorly documented and not usually recognized as IPAs according to IUCN criteria. But as we have seen they can be particularly effective: lands in the Amazon basin are as effective as national parks in preventing fire and deforestation, and do so in regions that are at the forefront of the advancing wave of landcover change (Nepstad et al, 2006).

Finally, there are collaborations that occur through benefit sharing of the type that we examined in the previous chapter. These arrangements most typically involve people setting aside land for wildlife conservation in exchange for a cash benefit and/or a private business venture. A notable example of the latter is Kenya's award winning Il Ngwesi Group Ranch, where have set up their own high-end tourist lodge, which they staff themselves. They benefit from bordering the Lewa Conservancy, another high-end tourist destination, and have imported a white rhinoceros, which grazes freely (one of very few to do so in the region), and are curbing their warriors' tendency to hunt lions.

Whether or not these arrangements can be called collaborations, and the extent to which they actually benefit local people, is often in the eye of the beholder. They can easily be portrayed as simple success stories because conservation organizations and their funders use images of happy communities and conservation-minded indigenous people as part of marketing what they do as both good for the environment and good for local people. But, as we concluded in the previous chapter, it is more likely that they will distribute fortune and misfortune – even Il Ngwesi distributes its benefits unevenly (Castillo, 2004). The community that runs it is, of course, a divided and troubled one. The willingness to believe and portray good news stories means that two essential questions are rarely asked: 1) do the benefits from these types of enterprises offset the livelihood costs of protected areas and other conservation interventions, especially in contexts where people have been displaced; and 2) whether the people who realize the benefits of these arrangements are the same people who have borne the livelihood costs (Igoe, 2006b). Beyond this it is important also to know about levels of transparency and participation. Only with this kind of information can we begin to say whether such an arrangement is a collaboration, what kind of collaboration it is, who is benefiting from it and in what ways.

Conclusion

The analysis presented in this chapter is doubtlessly discouraging to practitioners who are looking to develop and implement specific types of models for doing conservation with indigenous peoples and other rural communities. However, a more nuanced and contextual approach is more likely to present possibilities for doing conservation with indigenous communities that is both effective and equitable. Once we recognize that indigenous cultures are dynamic and that resource management practices can come into existence, and decline, for all manner of reasons, it is possible to have a much more sophisticated view of how indigenous people interact with conservation interests, and place indigenous cultures within a much wider framework. Consider Dombrowski's extraordinary study of the politics of indigenous identity and timber in Alaska (2002). He examined the village and regional corporations set up in Alaska to meet Native Alaskans' financial needs while avoiding large welfare payments. Some corporations, whose lands held oil, were highly profitable, but most were not. To improve their profitability Congress allowed the corporations to exploit a special tax loophole previously available only to timber companies. The tax rules allow companies owning tracts of timber to claim a paper loss on tracts of timber that are deemed to have decayed and lost value between when they were taken over and when they were felled. These losses can be offset against tax. The native corporations had large timber stands, and although they paid little tax, were allowed to sell these paper losses to other companies who needed them (by virtue of another tax loophole). Thus millions of dollars could be raised on the free market, but there was a catch. The losses could only be realized once the timber stands had been felled. The consequence of the legislation was to initiate large-scale clear cutting of forests on native Alaskans' land. Dumbrowski goes onto analyse the complicated politics of identity these changes brought, for the native corporations excluded many native Alaskans, and many of those worse affected by the forest-felling were among the excluded.

This kind of situation is unfortunately far more common than self-promoting reports are likely to reveal. Understanding the types of variables that come into play in these complex situations will allow us to begin finding ways of understanding the types and nature of outcomes that are likely to occur in different contexts. It will help us understand, for instance, why Kayapo leaders entered into alliances with transnational conservation organizations, while a Maasai leader from Tanzania described his people as 'enemies of conservation' during a session at the 2004 World Conservation Congress. It can help us understand why the World Wildlife Fund worked to block hydroelectric dams in Brazil but became part of a consortium of multilateral institutions promoting hydroelectric dams in Laos (Goldman, 2001a, b). It explains why conservation BINGOs (big international NGOs) support the idea of people living in parks in Latin America, but not in Africa. It explains why the Ute Mountain Tribe was successful in establishing a tribal park but not the Oglala Sioux or the Maasai. The type of analysis presented in this chapter can be applied to all of these questions and many others that have direct relevance for how conservation with indigenous peoples gets done.

From this perspective, it is impossible to predict specific outcomes. And yet these outcomes are not random either. They have patterns that are recognizable, and can be attributed to certain variables that are present in some circumstances and absent in others. For instance, alliances between conservationists and indigenous communities appear to be more likely in contexts where indigenous peoples have legal authority over specific resources; where they have been historically allowed to live inside protected areas; where indigenous leaders have good accountability to their constituency; and where indigenous peoples initiated the relationship with conservationists rather than vice-versa. In situations where conditions are opposite to those described here antagonisms are more likely to prevail. Though it may seem obvious, it unfortunately also needs to be said that in situations where relationships between conservationists and indigenous communities have been historically antagonistic the reasons for these antagonisms will need to be addressed before fruitful collaborations can be expected to occur (Igoe, 2004b).

While understanding these types of historically and geographically contingent variables will allow conservationists to determine whether or not specific indigenous communities are likely to be inclined to work with them, and on what terms. By the same token it would allow them to ask whether a specific indigenous community is likely to have historical grievances against conservation that will need to be addressed before effective alliances can occur.

It is also important to be cognizant of the ways in which competing, and sometimes collaborating, forces and interests might bump encounters between conservationists and indigenous peoples along certain trajectories. The vast financial resources of corporations, for instance, have tempted both indigenous leaders and conservationists, and sometimes both at once. Moreover, as this chapter has shown, both indigenous and environmental activism has become increasingly oriented to transnational bureaucracies. In the context of transnational bureaucracies it is possible to believe that 'sound science' supported by well-funded BINGOs represents the salvation of our planet's environmental future. It is also possible, and indeed tempting, to ignore, and indeed conceal, processes of social and political marginalization that are not easily explained by 'flattering archetypes' of 'ecologically noble savages'. It bears repeating here, however, that the fact that such archetypes are inaccurate does not let conservationists off the hook for working with local people. It merely means that working with local people will be more difficult and complex than originally presumed.

From a distance, these arrangements make it possible to believe that 'the rainforest' or 'the Kayapo' can be saved by the push of virtual button, after typing one's credit card information into the funding website of a conservation BINGO. As we will discuss in detail in our concluding chapter, the belief that only distant and exotic landscapes and people are worth saving externalizes both the problems and the solutions. Most fundamentally, it spares people in the global north the discomforts of the social and environmental impacts of their most mundane activities. It also conceals on a day-to-day basis the types of social and environmental problems that are closest at hand.

This chapter has made it clear that direct and localized engagements with environmental and social problems will almost certainly be complex and fraught with difficulty. However, if we continue to ignore these types of complexities and problems we do so at our peril. Chela Sandoval is certainly correct that in order to engage with this kind of complexity will require new types of mobile consciousness combined with a democratic ethic. These two things are more broadly connected to an ethic that recognizes one's own connection to social and environmental problems. In this respect we stand to learn a great deal from the recent convergence of global environmentalism and global indigenism – most immediately the ways in which our vertically integrated and electronically mediated world distorts the most basic relationships of humans to each other and to the natural world.

Notes

1   www.iucn.org/themes/ceesp/Wkg_grp/TILCEPA/TILCEPA.htm (accessed 30 December 2007).
2   For details please visit the website of the International Working Group for Indigenous Affairs, www.iwgia.org/sw248.asp (accessed 8 January 2008).
3   In a keynote speech at the meetings of the American Ethnological Society on Friday 4 May 2001 in Montreal Quebec, entitled 'The Cultural Survival of Indigenous Peoples: Theoretical and Practical Dilemmas'.
4   A polythetic class is defined in terms that are neither necessary nor sufficient for membership. In other words, there may be a number of criteria by which people identify themselves as indigenous. A group may meet all these criteria and still not qualify as indigenous, while another group may meet only some and still qualify as indigenous. As Igoe (2006a) argues, these criteria are frequently reduced to particular types of 'cultural distinctiveness', which resonate with the ways in which western audiences imagine 'the primitive'.
5   www.environment.gov.au/indigenous/ipa/index.html (accessed 11 November, 2006).

7

The Spread of Tourist Habitat

Adventure has been an essential part of the A&K experience ever
since Geoffrey Kent started offering his Kenyan safari's back in 1962.
But adventure 'Abercrombie & Kent style' doesn't mean you have to
live without your creature comforts – like the finest cuisine,
indulgently comfortable beds and that essential chilled glass of
champagne to accompany the sunset.

(Abercrombie and Kent, advertising for adventure safaris in 2007)

This chapter focuses on tourism as one of the most important ways in which conservation is justified and legitimated. In the last two decades tourism has become the key rationale used to underpin the maintenance of protected areas through claims that conservation will 'pay its way' via the development of tourism. It is assumed that nature-based tourism and ecotourism are dependent on the environment as the 'core attraction'; they revolve around particular charismatic species (elephants, tigers, gorillas, whales) and landscapes/seascapes (Himalayas, Victoria Falls, limestone pinnacles of the South China Sea). Therefore, promoters of tourism are able to muster a powerful argument: that since 'nature' is the attraction it makes long-term financial sense to protect it. In 2006 the United Nations World Tourism Organization (UNWTO) reported that world tourism had seen record growth for the fourth year in a row. The first half of 2007 had a higher than expected rate of growth. From January through April, international tourist arrivals worldwide rose by over 6 per cent to 252 million, representing an additional 15 million arrivals as against the same period in 2006; Asia and the Pacific (+9 per cent) achieved the strongest growth, followed by Africa (+8 per cent), the Middle East (+8 per cent), Europe (+6 per cent and the Americas (+4 per cent).[1] International tourism receipts totalled US$2 billion per day in 2006; and while there were 845 million visitor arrivals in 2006, the UNWTO estimates there will be 1.6 billion visitor arrivals in 2020.[2] Therefore, tourism is a significant growth industry and one which is particularly attractive to the South.

The expansion of ecotourism into one of the fastest growing sectors of the global tourism industry has provided an additional and strong rationale for committing resources to conservation on the grounds that such investment will pay significant dividends. Tourism, and particularly ecotourism, has been a central driver in the shift in debates about the direction of conservation, so that it is commonly couched in terms of turning nature into a lucrative resource instead of being justified in terms of debates about the intrinsic or ecological values of wilderness, ecosystems, biodiversity and so on. The ways that conservation is defined in terms of tourism means that it intersects with neoliberal and market-oriented understandings of environmental management and economic development. Tourism resonates with and is a driver of global neoliberalism, but the extensive claims attached to it as a force for 'global good' means that its supporters include (amongst others) grassroots community groups, conservation scientists, national governments, private companies, the World Bank and international donors. Its neoliberal appeal means that tourism and especially ecotourism has emerged as a key policy agenda for international financial institutions (IFIs), national governments and the private sector. As a result, ecotourism has been identified as a strategy by which many states (especially in the South) can diversify their economies and produce environmentally sustainable development (Harrison, 1992; King and Stewart, 1996; Bramwell and Lane, 2005). This chapter will examine the relationship between conservation and tourism and how they intersect with the global context of neoliberalism. We will then provide an analysis of the complexities involved in using tourism to legitimate specific forms of conservation and protected areas. We examine first the tourism and development debate; second we explore the relationships between tourism and sustainability; and finally we explore the complexities associated with specific forms of tourism, especially ecotourism, ethnotourism and voluntourism.

Tourism and 'development'

In order to understand the ways that conservation debates have been reconfigured and redefined through appeals to tourism, it is useful to examine how tourism intersects with neoliberalism. The development of tourism has (in part) been shaped by wider global changes, notably the end of the Cold War and the onset of globalization.

The expansion of the tourism industry occurred at the time the world was experiencing a major geopolitical shift as the Cold War ended. This period was also characterized by the growth in the faith in markets and an increase in the demands of multilateral institutions on the South (such as economic liberalization under Structural Adjustment Programmes). From the mid-1980s the renewed emphasis on outward-oriented growth, the rise of neoliberalism and expansion of the global tourism industry has meant that tourism has been identified as a key growth sector; and the UNWTO figures cited above certainly support this position. Neoliberal understandings of development emphasize economic diversification, particularly a commitment to non-traditional exports, such as tourism (Brohman, 1996; see also Reid, 2003). This approach has also been favoured by the IFIs including the World Bank and the International Monetary Fund (IMF), and by bilateral donors, which have supported the development of market-based economies (Harrison, 2004).

The rise of neoliberalism was also accompanied by the expansion of the influence and activities of international organizations and the growing importance of the language of sustainable development (Walley, 2004, p32; West and Carrier, 2004). At the same time global tourism flows rapidly increased in response to greater prosperity and social and economic shifts in the industrialized world, which allowed larger numbers of people to engage in overseas travel; and this has further developed into markets for ethical/responsible/green travel, which reflects and draws on the changing holidaying tastes of societies in the North (for further discussion see Butcher, 2003).

Supporters of tourism as a development strategy point out that it neatly fits in with neoliberal strategies of basing economies on comparative advantage. Advocates of this position argue that each state should concentrate on exporting goods that it is 'naturally' best at producing (Amsden, 1990; Porter, 1990). For example, during the 1980s many governments in the Caribbean were encouraged by IFIs and donors to diversify their economies away from single cash crops such as bananas and sugar by developing a tourism industry based on the three S's: sun, sea and sand (Pattullo, 1996; Reid, 2003). Countries in the South are portrayed as having 'comparative advantage' in tourism since they attract tourists from the industrialized North; they are presented as offering a chance to experience a pristine nature, and at worst they are promoted as 'primitive Edens'; as such they are highly attractive to tourists from the industrialized world who seek sunshine, beaches and other natural and cultural attractions.

Promoting tourism that appeals to international tour operators and visitors can cut out a whole series of choices about the development of tourism infrastructure to meet the needs of internal or regional tourists. Azcarate (2007) argues that the development of the 'pink package' to view flamingos in Celestun (Mexico) was designed to appeal to foreign visitors, who have progressively displaced Mexicans who used the area for their vacations. In Celestun, local authorities and tour operators oversaw the development of infrastructure including roads, hotels and boat moorings to facilitate the speedy transfers of visitors from Cancun and the Mayan Riviera to visit the flamingos and petrified forest. As a result, the riverside and beach areas of Celestun have been effectively colonized by international tourists, leading to the exclusion of internal tourists who can no longer use the areas. Tourism is clearly a highly political policy choice. Choosing tourism as a means of producing development and paying for conservation also means that overt and covert development objectives are pursued at the expense of other objectives. As Hall (1994) suggests, the selection and implementation of certain political and economic values will depend on the winners and losers in the development of tourism.

Since the interest in embracing tourism as a development strategy can be regarded as part of the global context of neoliberalism, it raises questions about the conceptual underpinning, purpose and potential impacts of tourism. Tourism is credited with being a major provider of employment, often in areas where there is little other opportunity for waged labour. Tourism provides employment in direct and indirect ways. Direct employment is provided within the services and industries that comprise the tourism industry, including hotels, tour operators and casinos. Indirect employment is provided in sectors that are affected by tourism, such as local transport, craft production, restaurants and bars used by locals and visitors alike.

A great deal of direct and indirect employment that is created by tourism is in the informal sector. In the informal sector, local people provide services to tourists on a casual basis, such as selling local crafts as souvenirs (Abbott-Cone, 1995; Pattullo, 1996; Hitchcock and Teague, 2000). The extent of employment creation in the informal sector is unquantifiable; even so, such opportunities can make a significant contribution to finances from the individual and household level to the national budget (Pattullo, 1996).

Bianchi's critiques of tourism centre on the close relationships between tourism development and the expansion of capitalism (Bianchi, 2004). Similarly, Reid (2003, p6) notes that because of the sheer size of tourism as a global industry, any critique of it must also involve a critique of the system in which it operates. Reid suggests that tourism is at present a major force in the organization of Barber's *McWorld*, which is marked by corporate globalization; tourism is a worldwide phenomenon dominated by transnational corporations, which export western culture to the developing world and which drains the developing world of its resources. For Reid, tourism is a product of the hegemony of the West and it starkly highlights the 'development' gap between the world's richest and poorest nations (Reid, 2003, pp2–3). This critique of tourism is in many ways applicable when we consider the ways that tourism is promoted as a green or sustainable form of development.

Tourism and the sustainability debate

In debates about the prospects for sustainable development, tourism is often identified as a potential solution to the problem of how to achieve national economic development whilst conserving the environment. As will be made clear below, the expansion of tourism has driven a process whereby market-based mechanisms of valuation and management have been extended and deepened. If we argue that tourism is not necessarily the solution for development, then we also need to explore whether it can achieve conservation objectives as well.

As we have already stated, one of the challenges facing the nature-based tourism industry is how to develop and expand without destroying the environment as the core attraction. Despite the temptation to lump them together, there are important differences between nature-based tourism and ecotourism. Nature-based tourism is tourism that uses nature as the main attraction, while ecotourism encompasses a much wider set of concerns about the environmental impact of accommodation and the levels of local ownership, amongst other things. In terms of labelling trips, hotels and activities, the label of 'eco' is often misapplied to nature-based tourism, which is essentially a form of conventional tourism.

The precise definition of ecotourism is still subject of much debate; however, it is clear that it relies on the idea that places and cultures are pristine, unspoiled and untouched by westernization, industrialization and even mass tourism (Fennell, 1999; Ceballos-Lascuráin, 2003; Cater, 2006; Sharpley, 2006). There is no single definition of ecotourism, but in general, ecotourism should satisfy conservation and development objectives (Lindberg et al, 1996). It is often defined as travel to natural areas that conserves the environment and improves the welfare of local people. Defining ecotourism is particularly difficult, and in many ways it has become a loose, catch-all term for tourism that is concerned with visiting and experiencing some aspect of the environment, be it wildlife, rainforests, coral reefs or even beaches. One definition of ecotourism is provided by Boo (1990) who broadly defines it as nature tourism that consists of travelling to a relatively *undisturbed* or *uncontaminated* natural area with the specific object of studying, admiring and enjoying the scenery and its wild plants and animals as well as existing cultural manifestations in the areas (our emphasis) (Bottrill, 1995). Along similar lines the Ecotourism Society defines it as responsible travel to natural areas that conserves the environment and sustains the well-being of local people.[3]

Furthermore, ecotourists themselves are also a relatively difficult type of global traveller to categorize. However, in general ecotourists can be described as vacationers with an interest in outdoor pursuits, they tend to be financially comfortable, well educated, older people with free time to travel (Ballantine and Eagles, 1994). Ecotourists are more likely to desire vacations that provide an opportunity to learn about the host culture, society or environment and they emphasize visiting wilderness areas and seeing as much as possible in the time available (Ballantine and Eagles, 1994, pp210–212). The ideas of remote, untouched, unspoilt and even primitive are used as markers of ecotourist desirability, and the Other is presented as the antithesis of industrial society, where local cultures in the ecotourist destination are often portrayed as extensions of the natural world (Dann, 1996, pp67–71; Edwards, 1996, pp200–204; Mowforth and Munt, 1998, pp44–83). Ecotourism also relies on the individual exercising power through choices about consumption rather than acting as a citizen engaged in collective and organized protest (Duffy, 2002a). Since ecotourism emphasizes the ways that green forms of consumption can 'save the environment' and contribute to economic development, it does not present any kind of challenge to the existing neoliberal framework. It clearly operates within neoliberal understandings of conservation and development.

The UNWTO claims that ecotourism can contribute to conservation of natural and cultural heritage in natural and rural areas, as well as improving living standards in those areas.[4] 2002 was declared the International Year of Ecotourism by the United Nations, which focused attention on it as a growing niche market.

Global environmental NGOs, the World Bank, national governments and the private sector have all made claims about the beneficial effects of ecotourism for conservation, national development and community development. However, while it is clear that there are benefits for conservation and for some stakeholders, the focus on and promotion of these positive outcomes can mask the complexity of power relations produced by a commitment to ecotourism.

Although ecotourism is often presented as significantly 'different' from mass tourism it is far from unproblematic. This is because it exists in a context of global neoliberalism that is part of it and entirely compatible with it. Ecotourism suffers especially from being promoted as a kind of magic bullet that can simultaneously hit multiple targets. As a result it has been promoted by a range of organizations, including the United Nations, The World Bank, national governments and environmental NGOs, as a means of achieving sustainable development for North and South alike. In terms of debates about the development, tourism is regularly presented as the answer. At the 2003 World Parks Congress in Durban, South Africa, IUCN passed a key recommendation that tourism (and especially ecotourism) was the key to conservation of biodiversity and maintenance of protected areas (IUCN, 2003). Therefore, the notion that tourism is a means to produce sustainable development and secure conservation of biodiversity constitutes the dominant orthodoxy; while there are clear advantages for conservation in developing tourism initiatives in terms of provision of funding, the social and political dynamics of following these policy choices is often overlooked or obscured.

There are numerous case studies that demonstrate the utility of ecotourism, especially with regard to wildlife conservation (see for example Barnes et al, 2002; Novelli et al, 2006). In many ways the arguments around conservation are taken as a given: that ecotourism, which relies on 'nature' as the core attraction, will automatically be 'good' for the environment. However, Bramwell and Lane argue, there is often an implicit assumption that tourism leads to sustainable development, which is then not subjected to systematic research and criticism (Bramwell and Lane, 2001, 2005, p54). There are a few examples that trace the links between ecotourism and environmental damage; for example, Bulbeck (2005) carried out a detailed study of the negative ecological impact of tourism at Monkey Mia Dolphin Resort in Sharks Bay, Western Australia. Monkey Mia states that it is 'known to be one of the most reliable meeting places for dolphins in the world. Dolphins have visited everyday in the last five years excluding only four times. It is the only place in Australia where dolphins visit daily, not seasonally'.[5] It is the case that the dolphins are not captive, they are 'wild' in the sense that they are not fenced in. However, the practice of feeding the dolphins has created a set of behaviours that means that the dolphins do appear to choose to visit the resort and interact with tourists every day. However, this raises questions about what 'wild' means and whether such forms of tourism can in fact be ecologically damaging. According to Bulbeck the practice of dolphin feeding led to dependence on humans for food, and because of the narrow diet provided by visitors at Monkey Mia, the local dolphins have a shorter life expectancy and lower birth rates.

Bulbeck argues that ecotourism increasingly relies on close contact with specific charismatic species; ecotourists want tactile and emotional forms of engagement with animals, which can be seen in the proliferation of 'swim with dolphins' experiences at a number of luxury resorts in the Caribbean. One such resort is Xcaret, on the rapidly developing Mayan Rivera in Mexico; it defines itself an Eco-Archaeological theme park and offers cultural tours, archaeological tours and swim with the dolphins experiences.[6] The resort claims:

> During the Delphinus Interax dolphin swim program at Xcaret, a group of majestic dolphins will swim freely with you long enough to allow time for play and time for touching them and to feel that special connection they have with man... Then, into the water, join them in their interactive and 'mime' games. Find out how dolphins breathe, eat and sleep. The grand finale is the thrilling experience of the dolphins leaping over your head![7]

Despite the company's claim to offer an 'eco' experience, it has not escaped without criticism. When the company attempted to open a sister resort in Belize, named Cangrejo Caye, their claims that they supported conservation of dolphins and engaged in education through swimming with dolphins were rejected by the existing tour operators, hotel owners and environmental organizations in Belize; opponents claimed that the dolphins held in 'semi captive' conditions at Xcaret had a lower life expectancy and suffered from disease, because they lived in extended pens, so they were not able to cover the large distances needed to feed themselves properly (see Duffy, 2002, pp84–85). Nevertheless, the Xcaret model has been expanded on the Mayan Riviera coast to satisfy tourist imaginings that their holiday engages with 'nature' and contributes to its conservation. For example, Xpu-Ha Palace resort is a curious combination of being an 'ecological all inclusive resort'; it offers 'animal rescue and treatment programmes' and ecological 'jungle tours' as part of their sports and entertainment programmes. Xpu-Ha, along with a growing number of large-scale luxury resorts, offers tours with a qualified ecologist to provide explanations of the surrounding environments.[8]

Critics of attractions like Monkey Mia, Xcaret and Xpu-Ha cast doubt on whether they constitute genuine 'ecotourism'. Herein lies one of the problems with ecotourism: the definition of ecotourism has been expanded so far that it encompasses a wide range of projects, activities, hotels and tours. However, the argument that any tourist practice with negative impacts does not constitute genuine ecotourism is in a sense irrelevant. It is clear that any project/initiative, whether it claims to be hard-core or strict ecotourism or conventional forms of nature-based tourism, is filled with complexities, contradictions, costs, benefits, problems and challenges. The argument that anything that is 'good' is genuine ecotourism and anything that is 'bad' is conventional tourism is an easy get out clause for promoters of ecotourism. Such arguments largely miss the point that all forms of tourism have costs and benefits: there is no fabled 'win–win' situation.

Ecotourism and community empowerment

Apart from the claims made about ecotourism as a force for conservation, one of the other key claims associated with 'genuine' ecotourism is that it brings empowerment, poverty alleviation and economic opportunity for local communities. The International Ecotourism Society defines ecotourism as responsible travel to natural areas that conserves the environment and improves the *well being of local people*; for the International Ecotourism Society, ecotourism should *provide financial benefits and empower local communities* (our emphasis).[9]

However, the extensive claims centring on the benefits of ecotourism to local communities obscure the complexities and problems associated with it. For example, ecotourism projects do not appear in a vacuum; rather they intersect with existing community dynamics. This inevitably means some members of the community will benefit more than others. However, communities are often treated as homogenous and static units to be 'developed' and 'intervened in'; this fundamentally misunderstands the dynamic and complex nature of communities (Honey, 1999; Scheyvens, 1999; Barrow and Murphree, 2002, p4). For example, Southgate's study of Kimana community in southern Kenya clearly indicates the disgruntlement caused by the decision of Kimana Group Ranch officials to enter into an agreement to lease land to the African Safari Club for the creation of a private reserve and luxury eco-lodge. The decision brought significant benefits to some members of the community, but most felt excluded. According to Southgate, when the African Safari Club put up signs to designate the area as 'private property', they were defaced within days. It is clear that many in the community resisted the reserve and its eco-lodge through acts of poaching and vandalism, which were the only means through which they could express their opposition to the scheme. As Southgate argues, at one level ecotourism can offer opportunities for economic diversification, but it can also exacerbate existing resource management conflicts that are rooted in the historical context of local power relations (see also Mowforth and Munt, 1998; Southgate, 2006).[10]

The notion that communities can manage natural resources and develop ecotourism fits well with neoliberal ways of thinking about regulating, organizing and implementing methods of conservation that include extension of the market as the most efficient manager of natural resources. In particular, it intersects with the argument that decentralized networks of 'stakeholders' can govern resources rather than leaving them in state hands (Western and Wright, 1994). This in turn fits with the agendas of IFIs and NGOs that claim to engage in participatory methods of development and conservation with local communities. As such, the notion that ecotourism provides a community-oriented and participatory approach to producing economic development in a sustainable way results in a very powerful argument in favour of it, and one that presents a significant challenge to critics of it. Ultimately, the extensive claims attached to ecotourism means that, especially for local communities, it is often very hard to resist schemes to develop it in poorer and more marginalized areas. This is especially the case when there appears to be no alternative means of generating income, because their remoteness or seeming 'lack of economic development' means it is difficult to attract in other forms of investment or establish new schemes to alleviate poverty.

Tourism Concern, a UK-based NGO, has been working since 1989 to raise awareness of the negative economic, cultural, environment and social impacts of tourism. It points out that communities often find they have tourism imposed on them by governments and foreign developers and tourism businesses. There is little linkage between tourism, especially at a mass scale, and local industry, such as agriculture. Land and natural resources are frequently co-opted, often illegally, and cultural traditions are appropriated and commercialized.[11] This raises the question of whether communities have the ability to develop ecotourism 'on their own terms'. This is especially acute when the national governments, the donor community, IFIs, the private sector and international environmental NGOs constitute the core drivers in developing and marketing new 'eco destinations'. Therefore, it is important to interrogate what the term 'partnership' means in practice when such partnerships encompass marginalized local communities as well as powerful IFIs and transnational advocacy networks engaged in promoting and implementing wildlife conservation initiatives.

Luxury ecotourism

The debates about the importance of engaging local communities in participatory management of wildlife and other natural resources through ecotourism has been enthusiastically taken up by the private sector. This is visible in the proliferation of new luxury ecotourism resorts that define themselves as private sector, profit-driven companies, but which also market themselves as playing a key role in local community development. These new luxury resorts are intended to tap into a new and growing market for ethical travel that offers a high-end luxury experience but which promises community participation and economic development. In general community-based ecotourism has been associated with basic accommodation and facilities, and it has been marketed at independent and low-budget travellers who do not expect (or want) high-end tourism facilities. However, the development of new luxury eco-lodges that blend community-based conservation initiatives is a significant new departure.

One interesting example of a privately owned but community-oriented ecotourism initiative is the resort of Anjajavy, located in north-east Madagascar. Its combination of luxury ecotourism with community development has attracted the attentions of the global media, including the BBC. While Anjajavy is owned by South African business people, all staff that are employed in the resort are from the neighbouring community, and the income from the resort has been used to build a clinic and a school in the area.[12] The Anjajavy resort offers guests the opportunity to take a tour of the village of Ambodro Ampasy to see the dispensary and primary school established by the Ecole du Monde NGO, as well as the craft shop set up by the Association des Amis d'Anjajavy. Their promotional information reassures visitors: 'You can take part in the village's development and help the local populace by purchasing Malagasy handicrafts made on site by the villagers.'[13] The Anjajavy project is indicative of new directions in Community Based Natural Resource Management (CBNRM) and ecotourism (Duffy, 2008b). It is a privately owned and run luxury lodge that goes one step further in terms of community engagement: rather than simply offering employment, the lodge is involved in community development projects and poverty alleviation on a wider scale in the local area. In terms of marketing, the owners draw attention to the ways that, by choosing the Anjajavy eco-lodge, ecotourists will be directly contributing to poverty alleviation, community development and conservation in the surrounding area. This effectively blends the approach of luxury nature-based tourism with elements of the rationale for community-based ecotourism that are centred on poverty alleviation and environmental conservation. This is beneficial for some but raises questions about the meanings and purposes of partnership in this context. It may well mean that the development of private luxury eco-lodges that have a community rationale merely offers communities 'more of the same' rather than developing and offering pathways for them to develop initiatives that operate on their own terms. There is the danger of replicating the problems associated with mass tourism and conventional forms of tourism, where operators (often foreign owned) make the greatest level of profit while local communities benefit in a very minimal way through employment in menial tasks rather than taking a central role as managers, owners and tour operators (for further discussion see Pattullo, 1996; Honey, 1999).

In conservation terms, the commitment to luxury eco-lodges has also led in some cases to very specific forms of wildlife and landscape management to meet the expectation of tourists from the industrialized North. Botswana has also developed a National Eco-tourism Strategy (NES) that aims to produce sustainable use of resources, revenue for reinvestment in conservation, and engagement of local communities in tourism ventures; this is heavily linked to community-based tourism (CBT), sport/trophy hunting, photographic tourism and culture tourism. Currently, tourism is the second largest income earner after diamond exports and government statistics assume there will be a 10 per cent per annum increase in tourism arrivals between 2000 and 2020.[14] Botswana has been keen to develop a sector based on luxury/high-end nature-based tourism and ecotourism; however, it is clear that the luxury eco-lodges actively work to manage landscapes and wildlife populations in order to satisfy tourist imaginings of *the wild*. Wildlife or nature-based ecotourism redefines, presents and can even *create* areas of 'wilderness', which are, more often than not, based on notions of people-free landscapes (West and Carrier, 2004). For example, luxury eco-lodges in Botswana are beginning to engage with ecotourism opportunities that allow for close encounters with wildlife, particularly elephant-backed safari rides. For example, Abu Camp Elephant Safaris in the Okavango Delta offer four-day safaris on elephant back through the delta;[15] Abu Camp offers ecotourists a 'luxury eco-experience' in a private concession that has links to the national park; such public–private partnerships are an increasing trend in conservation and in tourism. In the case of elephant-back safaris in Botswana, operators have been keen to exploit a specific niche market in emotional and tactile encounters with animals (see Bulbeck, 2005, for further discussion). These initiatives are indicative of the ways that ecotourism is increasingly tied to the wider tourist industry and the capitalist system it inhabits. Ecotourism has gone 'upscale' and luxury, which in turn raises questions about how far it can empower and benefit some of the world's poorest communities. This problem is all the more acute in current forms of ethnotourism as discussed below.

Ethnotourism

Numerous studies on the impacts of conservation point to poor integration of local communities who live with wildlife and their associated costs (such as crop damage and bans on hunting for subsistence purposes). These have demonstrated that external policy frameworks and interventions from states, IFIs and global NGOs have the potential to negatively impact on community–environment interactions and damage prospects for conservation in the longer term (see for example Hulme and Murphree, 1999, 2001; Brockington, 2002; Hutton et al, 2005). For example, where local communities have been allowed to remain within protected areas or been allowed to continue to use their resources, their everyday practices (e.g. hunting, grazing livestock, collecting wood) have tended to be constrained to fit within a particular framework set by the government in conjunction with tour operators and conservation NGOs. Communities are often encouraged, or even required, to perform particular roles and dress in particular ways to act as part of the tourist attraction. Communities can then be repackaged as part of the landscape, as wild, primitive and pre-modern. Wolmer (2007, pp151–153) suggests that early colonial framings and understandings persist in some current forms of ethnotourism in Africa; this is prevalent in discussions about how communities should behave and dress if they are to be allowed to continue to live within protected areas in Africa.

Ethnotourism in sub-Saharan Africa perhaps provides the best example of the ways that cultures are commodified and marketed to appeal to international tourists, to such an extent that people are often portrayed as just another attraction alongside wildlife and landscapes. For example, the 'Tribes and Wildlife on the Rift' overland tour from Addis Ababa to Nairobi, offered by Dragoman, is promoted using just such language:

> This is a thoroughly tribal adventure travel trip. In Southern Ethiopia, we travel overland into the depths of the Rift Valley, visiting the amazing lakes, witnessing the wildlife and meeting the local tribal people... We will travel into one of the most unchanged tribal regions in Africa and meet peoples who lifestyles have changed very little in the last two hundred years. At Konzo we will explore the Konzo tribal culture and villages before heading deep into tribal southern Ethiopia towards the Omo Valley.[16]

Destinations and their cultural attractions tend to be homogenized and packaged in ways that appeal to external tastes. For example, the Caribbean is often 'sold' on the international tourism market in ways that evoke very specific images of colonial plantations, reggae music, laid back cultures and sunshine (Pattullo, 1996). One of the world's biggest tour operators, Thomson, markets Jamaica in the following way:

> When you think of holidays in Jamaica what do you picture? Sugary soft, white beaches. Grand plantation houses. And gallons of golden rum. Well, granted, you can while the days away stretched out on the sun-bleached sand. Take a river raft ride past the sugar plantations that are home to those colonial great houses... All to the mellow background heart-beat of Reggae – it's the lifeblood of all holidays in Jamaica.[17]

One of the most extreme and highly criticized versions of ethnotourism is so-called 'first contact' tourism. This is when tourists are promised a genuine interaction with communities that the guide claims are 'uncontacted peoples': that is peoples that have decided not to communicate or interact in any way with the outside world. According to Survival International, an NGO that campaigns for the rights of indigenous people, estimates that the majority of such 'uncontacted societies' are located in West Papua. Stephen Corry, Director of Survival International, has condemned the development of 'first contact' tourism, and the organization is concerned that uncontacted peoples might be negatively affected by such practices.[18] However, we should not automatically assume that communities are inert, static and 'impacted upon' by this form of visitation. A BBC documentary, *First Contact*, shown in February 2007, followed a first contact tour to West Papua, and argued that the tour was in fact a hoax that was elaborately staged by communities and the operator to extract revenue from tourists.[19] We should not assume that communities simply passively conform to what tourists want to see.

Voluntourism

'Volunteer tourism' or voluntourism is a rapidly growing niche, and one that is important in the expansion of new forms of nature-based tourism and ecotourism. Voluntourism is part of the increased interest in ethical travel, and it has been fed by the rise in organized 'gap year' experiences; furthermore, it resonates with wider debates about fair trade and corporate social responsibility. In effect, voluntourism is based on the idea that an individual's holiday choices can be used to 'deliver' anything from wildlife conservation to economic development. Cater (1994) suggests that conservation volunteers constitute the 'hard edge of ecotourism'. A number of conservation organizations are defined as part of the growing ecotourism market. Munt suggests that this indicates a desire for holidays that are in keeping with post-modern culture (Mowforth and Munt, 1998). For example, tourism may no longer be about travel per se, but include other activities such as trekking or mountain biking. Tourism has become interwoven with education and learning new skills, encapsulated by the development of special-interest activity tours, such as art courses, wine tasting, architectural tours, mountain biking and so on (Urry, 1990, p154). As Mowforth and Munt suggest, the mass tourists' interest in the three S's of sea, sun and sand has been replaced by the independent tourists' enthusiasm for the three T's: trekking, trucking and travelling (Mowforth and Munt, 1998, pp125–155).

Voluntourism can be regarded as part of this wider shift in holidaying practices. From the relatively well established volunteer organizations such as Earthwatch Foundation and Raleigh International to the more recently formed Operation Wallacea, Voluntourism, Greenforce, Frontiers and Coral Cay Conservation, these organizations are located at the interface between commercial tourism (specifically ecotourism) and charities or NGOs. However, they are not without their critics, and their presence is often fraught with local conflicts that intersect with broader struggles over environment, development, resource exploitation and the global expansion of tourism. Voluntourism can often replicate the problems associated with conventional forms of tourism. Indeed, in 2007 the UK-based Voluntary Service Overseas (VSO) has argued that the expansion of 'gap year' projects have little real benefit and that 'gappers' might just be better off backpacking rather than paying to join voluntary projects.[20] For example, Coral Cay Conservation operates a marine conservation project in a number of countries. Its President is a well known environmentalist and broadcaster, Professor Ian Bellamy. It won the 1993 British Airways Tourism for Tomorrow Award and was 'long listed' for a Virgin Holidays Responsible Tourism Award in 2007. It places volunteers to undertake reef surveys in Papua New Guinea, Honduras and the Philippines, amongst other locations.[21] However, the organization has been hit by controversy. In 1998 the Belize government did not renew its licence to continue working in Belize. This was as a result of a deteriorating relationship with the University College of Belize. The organization was accused of recreating colonial patterns of behaviour and exploitation between host and tourist, of failing to make significant investment in local economies, of social exclusion of local people and of environmental damage. While the organization denied this, the problems at the marine research station on Calabash Caye eventually hit the national newspapers in Belize, and the organization was no longer allowed to operate (Duffy, 2002, pp64–70).

The case of Coral Cay Conservation is indicative of the potential for conflict at the local level which can be associated with 'charities' operating in the South. In fact, Tourism Concern[22] criticized the expansion of voluntourism and questioned the claims that these projects were beneficial. Tricia Barnett, Director of Tourism Concern, has suggested that ill prepared and poorly directed volunteers can do more harm than good and stated that Tourism Concern had been contacted by numerous volunteers complaining about the negative aspects of the projects they had joined. In many ways, then, the projects were criticized as 'overpriced guilt trips' that had little value to the communities and countries they claimed to 'help'. As a result, Tourism Concern has begun to develop a code of practice for the voluntourism sector.[23]

The ecotourism bubble

A final aspect of ecotourism that is important for understanding the interconnections between international conservation and the ascendancy of global neoliberalism is what Carrier and Macleod (2005) refer to as the 'ecotourism bubble'. They derive this idea from Marx's notion of commodity fetishism (Marx, 1976 (1867)) from which he argues that commodities within the capitalist economy circulate in ways that obscure their social and historical context. (Towards the end of his life Marx also extended this argument to include ecology.) The basic argument of fetishization is that commodities appear for our consumption in ways that appear as almost magic. We know nothing of the historical transformations that occurred so that they could become available (cf. Wolf, 1982; Mintz, 1985). We know nothing of the people whose labour produced the commodity, or the types of hardships they may have endured in the process. We know nothing of the loss of access to natural resources that people may have experienced so that we could consume this commodity. Finally, we know nothing of the ecological effects of producing and transporting the commodity we consume or where the waste from this commodity might go when we are finished with it.

Debord (1995 (1967)) took this argument one step further, arguing that through mass media it is not only possible to fetishize commodities in the ways described above, but it is also possible to fetishize their experiences. Through mass media, he argued, people experience their lives as a collection of spectacles, images and experiences that appear divorced from their social and historical context.

According to Debord, the logic of the Spectacle is a very simple one: 'whatever appears must be good and whatever is good must appear'. Debord believed that this basic assumption is implicit in the way many people in societies dominated by mass media and the consumption of commodities tend to see the world.

The 'ecotourist bubble', by extension, is the idea that ecotourist experiences are often packaged thus. From within this bubble, ecotourists see the environment in simplified (a-social, a-historical and a-ecological) terms, which obscure the socio-ecological implications of the global infrastructure and economic relationships that make ecotourism possible in the first place. Carrier and Macleod (2005) especially emphasize the fact that ecotourism relies very heavily on air travel, which is strongly implicated in global climate change. The ecological footprints of ecotourists who fly to different parts of the world on a regular basis, therefore, is usually several orders of magnitude more significant than the footprints of the local people who live in the places that ecotourists visit. Because of their proximity to putative pristine nature, however, these local people are often ironically seen as a threat to nature, and ecotourists as its saviours.

Other forms of travel also frequently have significant ecological impacts, to the point that environments in protected areas can actually become threatened by the very people who visit them. Traffic jams have been a notable problem at Yellowstone National Park since the 1960s, while animals at Tanzania's world famous Ngorongoro Crater and other East African honey pots are exposed to a daily parade of zebra-striped safari vans (Bonner, 1993). In the Azores, the zodiacs used for whale watching emit high-pitched underwater sounds, which disrupt the whales sonar, while tourists arriving at midday interrupt their sleeping patterns and the breast feeding of their young (Neves-Graca, 2004). The scenario is repeated in many places where ecotourism concentrates large numbers of people in close proximity to other species and in fragile ecosystems.

The ecotourist bubble also tends to obscure the broader ecologies of protected areas, by presenting them as frozen in time. So for instance, Tanzania's Tarangire National Park was created around the Tarangire River, because this is a place that wildlife congregates during the dry season. From the veranda of the Tarangire Lodge it is possible to see large concentrations of wildlife while having an evening cocktail and talking to friends about what animals people saw on that day's game drive. During the wet season, however, these animals migrate out of the parks to neighbouring landscapes. These migration patterns are now being disrupted by increased farming, which has resulted in part by the displacement of Maasai herders from the park when it was created. As such, ironically, the park has contributed to conditions that threaten the ecology of the animals that it was created to protected (Igoe, 2004b). None of this complexity is visible to the average ecotourist.

The ecotourism bubble also selects for certain types of interactions between tourist and local people. These interactions should be as friendly and positive as possible, as this reinforces the idea that tourists are doing something good by coming to a particular country and spending their money there. For these interactions to be possible, local people must do a great deal of 'emotional labour', which Bryman (2002, p59) defines as 'the act of expressing socially desired emotions during service transactions'. Emotional labour was perfected in the context of Walt Disney theme parks. As we will discuss in more detail in our concluding chapter, this is a fact that has significant implications for how conservation is conceptualized and carried out in the new millennium. Walt Disney always insisted that his employees, just as Malawi's former president for life Dr Kamuzu Banda always insisted that his citizens, should smile and wave at tourists without exception. Emotional labour is especially important to voluntourism, because voluntourists are especially concerned that local people should recognize that they are doing something virtuous and important. When voluntourism involves home stays this can be an around the clock performance.

In most major ecotourist destinations, people from the customs agent at the airport to the receptionists at the safari lodge, including the people on the side of the road where ecotourists pass, are engaged in emotional labour on a daily basis. One of us (Igoe) recently interviewed a group of Maasai women at a craft cooperative in Tanzania who were taught by their European donors that they should begin to sing, dance and smile as soon as they heard a vehicle coming up the road. Most of these women described the arrangement as good fun, but emotional labour often takes a negative psychological toll. An especially poignant presentation of this problem is Denis O' Rourke's ethnographic film *Cannibal Tours* (1988), which follows a group of western tourists up the Sepik River in New Guinea. The tourists describe what they are doing in glowing terms, while local people interviewed in the film express confusion and despair over the emotional labour they must perform to earn small amounts of money.

The ecotourist bubble, in short, shields tourists from the broader historical, social and ecological implications of their activities. Ecotourism is only made possible by global networks of relationships, many of which are highly exploitative. For the most part, however, tourists are only exposed to interactions that fulfil their fantasies of what these relationships should be. This is problematic for the types of social and ecological ethics it promotes. But it is equally problematic for the fact that the ecotourist bubble is an actual commodity with a great deal of value. Tourists spend billions of dollars every year for the privilege of consuming experiences that fit within this bubble (cf. West and Carrier, 2004). In the context of global neoliberalism, the types of experiences promoted and preserved in the ecotourist bubble can even come unmoored from particular people and places and circulate freely in a global economy of images, signs and virtual commodities. We return to this point in our final chapter.

Conclusion

It is clear that tourism plays a central role in justifying conservation, and especially the need to demarcate, enforce and maintain protected areas as important 'tourist playgrounds'. This in turn means that local communities can often end up being excluded from protected areas and economically important landscapes used by the tourism industry; paradoxically tourism also opens up new areas for tourists to visit while simultaneously excluding other communities. This ensures that landscapes and wildlife habitats conform to tourist imaginings of what the 'wild' looks like (West and Carrier, 2004). Tourists are often unaware of the social, political and economic processes that have conspired to 'produce' the attractions they want to visit. For example, they are not informed about the ways communities may have been persuaded (or even forced) to leave areas that are deemed valuable by the international tourist industry, often in conjunction with national governments and conservation NGOs. They are also unlikely to be cognizant of the ways that people and communities are drawn into the tourism industry, and are persuaded by arguments that the tourist trade provides employment and income for families that would not otherwise have access to wage labour. This obscures the ways that the tourism industry generally provides low-paid work, and does not recognize that other development options have often been scripted out of the decision-making process. These problems are all the more acute when we consider the ways that tourism often forms the centrepiece of policies aimed at producing 'sustainable development'.

This chapter has demonstrated that the interactions between tourism and conservation are highly complex. Even new forms of 'alternative tourism' such as ecotourism, ethnotourism and voluntourism need to be approached with caution. As we have shown, all these so called alternative forms of tourism also distribute different forms of fortune and misfortune. It is clear that they are interlinked with the wider tourism industry, which happily co-exists with and is dependent on the neoliberal global system. This means that even the most alternative forms of tourism can end up repeating the same problems as other forms of development. This is clear in the recent moves towards developing luxury eco-lodges that may not be able to deliver genuine empowerment and development to local communities. It is visible in the ways ethnotourism can engage in highly exploitative practices against the world's poorest and most vulnerable communities. Even that ecotourism might end up damaging the environment.

Notes

1   UN World Tourism Organisation (2007) 'Strong World Tourism Growth in 2007', *World Tourism Barometer*, available at http://unwto.org/facts/menu.html (accessed 28 September 2007).

2   www.unwto.org/index.php (accessed 28 September 2007).

3   See www.ecotourism.org/ (accessed 12 August 2003); also see www.ResponsibleTravel. com (accessed 20 August 2004) and Denman (2001).

4   UNWTO (2003) *UNWTO Assessment of the Results Achieved in Realising Aims and Objectives of the International Year of Ecotourism 2002* (UNWTO: Madrid), p2,

at www.world-tourism.org/sustainable/IYE/IYE-Rep-UN-GA-2003.pdf (accessed 5 July 2007).

5   www.monkeymia.com.au/site/awdep.asp?depnum=11526&menu=HOME (accessed 20 September 2007).

6   www.xcaret.com/ (accessed 19 September 2007).

7   www.xcaret.com/park-attractions/swim-with-dolphins.php (accessed 19 September 2007).

8   www.xpuha-palace.com/index.html?gclid=CKyb5vTh1I4CFQI_EAodA3fu-g (accessed 20 September 2007).

9   www.ecotourism.org/webmodules/webarticlesnet/templates/eco_template.aspx? articleid=95&zoneid=2 (accessed 14 August 2007).

10 Similar problems have been observed around the community-based lodge set up by the Il Ngwesi Maasai in Northern Kenya (see Castillo, 2004).

11 www.tourismconcern.org.uk/index.html (accessed 20 September 2007).

12 www.anjajavy.com (accessed 15 June 2007); also see pers. comm. Nivo Ravelojaona, Director, Za Tour, Antananarivo, 27 April 2004.

13 www.anjajavy.com (accessed 15 August 2007); also see pers. comm. Nivo Ravelojaona, Director, Za Tour, Antananarivo, 27 April 2004.

14 www.botswana-tourism.gov.bw/tourism_s/tourism_s.html (accessed 15 August 2007).

15 www.elephant-back-safaris.com (accessed 17 August 2007).

16 www.dragoman.com/destinations/tripdetails.php?cat=TWR (accessed 24 September 2007).

17 www.thomson.co.uk/destinations/caribbean/jamaica/jamaica/holidays-jamaica.html (accessed 24 September 2007).

18 www.survival-international.org/news/2191 (accessed 23 September 2007).

19 www.survival-international.org/news/2191 (accessed 23 September 2007); and see news.bbc.co.uk/2/hi/entertainment/5338876.stm (accessed 23 September 2007).

20 'You're better off backpacking', *The Guardian* (UK), 14 August 2007, www.education.guardian.co.uk/students/gapyear/story/0,,2148122,00.html

21 www.coralcay.org/ (accessed 20 September 2007).

22 www.tourismconcern.org.uk/index.html (accessed 20 September 2007).

23 'Vacationing like Branjelina' by Laura Fitzpatrick, *Time Magazine*, 26 July 2007.

8

International Conservation

Conservation of biodiversity is one of the most important global responsibilities mankind has to ensure its survival and this includes all species of plants, animals and other organisms; the range of genetic stock within each species, and the variety of ecosystems. Therefore, biodiversity conservation is a global issue and it must also be a global responsibility.

Himalayan Biodiversity Conservation Statement,
World Conservation Congress 2004

From the earliest stages of conservation's history the movement has been international in its scope and ambition. The name of one of the first major conservation organizations (the Society for the Preservation of the Wild Fauna of the Empire (SPWFE)) rather gives the game away. The well heeled and travelled aristocrats who populated that society were principally concerned about wildlife and habitat in far-off lands. They drew their models of nature conservation from American practices.

There are strong ecological, economic and political imperatives requiring an international approach. Many challenges facing conservation simply cannot be dealt with on parochial national bases. Controlling trade in wildlife, migratory species and meta-population management all require concerted international efforts.

Yet, as we have seen with respect to conservation and indigenous people, it is the work of international conservation apparatus that has also generated some of the most heated debates about what conservation does to people, and the ethics of conservation policy. Put simply, wildlife conservation is generally funded by the global north, by individuals, companies and foundations. International conservation organizations see themselves as vehicles for redistributing wealth to the poor areas where shortfalls in conservation funding are greatest (James et al, 2001; Balmford and Whitten, 2003; Balmford et al, 2003b). If conservation is progress, and its spread and influence a progressive force for good, then these institutions are doing good work. But from other perspectives international conservation institutions also expose themselves to accusations of imperialistic interference and neo-colonialism, of meddling in other people's affairs and countries. Their values and practices are often inspired by western and northern models of nature, and introduced where these values are alien and often unwelcome. In the worst cases this not only results in the imposition of ideas of nature and conservation, but also the physical displacement of generally poor rural people to make way for spaces that are then occupied by the transnational leisure industry, wealthy tourists, research scientists and conservation NGOs.

The stark inequities of these arrangements can result in a fierce debate. The situation on the ground, however, is inevitably more complex. Most international conservation groups decry such practices and insist that they work with people and spend a great deal of effort and time negotiating their alliances. Many are involved in a great many activities in addition to supporting protected areas.

In this chapter we first lay out the general terrain of international agreements and organizations that are important for conservation. We examine the ways that the international legal framework is defined by broader struggles over definitions of nature, appropriate management and who has the right to use nature and in what ways. We analyse how international conventions define conservation issues, attempt to regulate the environment and how they respond to the challenges of implementation. We then look at more specific international arrangements in detail, focusing on the Convention on International Trade in Endangered Species of Wild Fauna and Flora (CITES) and its role in elephant conservation, NGOs, Transfrontier Conservation Areas and transnational private–public partnerships.

Our argument throughout is that conservation strategies and policies involve significant reshaping of society as well as nature. These reshapings are not always bound up in ways that promote capitalism. In the case of CITES and elephants the explicit goal of many groups is not to allow a market to develop in ivory. But in the process these same people deploy arguments about the value of images of burning ivory, and the potential revenues that photographic tourism could bring. The regimes of environmental governance under which conservation, and particularly international conservation, has to work have been forged and negotiated in an era of neoliberal dominance.

The apparatus of international conservation

The transboundary nature of global environmental change has meant that it has become a key site for what has been called 'global environmental governance'. Oceans, forests, wildlife, the atmosphere and so on all cross human-constructed national boundaries. Good environmental management has largely been defined in terms of supranational conventions, policies and agreements. The environment has clearly become a key area for governance of local resources from the global level because numerous international regimes are deemed to operate for the 'global good'. However, an examination of these global environmental regimes reveals that they embody multiple and competing interest groups rather than representing a common global view that can be effectively implemented at the local level.

Global conventions have been established in response to transboundary activities and problems where domestic legislation has proved inadequate, and so they are especially significant in the area of environmental management. Young (1989) argues that international regimes have, in general, been formed by states seeking to control transboundary activities in order to guarantee benefits to dominant parties. In the case of international environmental agreements it is clear that certain norms, usually based in western political ideologies, also have a critical role to play. Nadelman (1990, p479) suggests that these norms strictly control the conditions under which states and other actors can participate in and authorize certain activities.

One form of global environmental governance can be found in international agreements that are intended to regulate a variety of local, national, regional and global processes. These include the Convention on Biodiversity (CBD), CITES, the International Whaling Commission and the Law of the Sea. The CBD, for example, arose out of the 'Rio Summit' in 1992. The Convention establishes three main goals: the conservation of biological diversity, the sustainable use of its components, and the fair and equitable sharing of the benefits from the use of genetic resources.[1] This final objective is also covered by the CBD Cartagena Protocol on Biosafety, which explicitly states its commitment to the precautionary principle.[2] This is a vitally important position, taken by a number of international conventions; at its most basic it means we must assume that any use (such as the trade) of species will be detrimental to its long-term sustainability, we must therefore take precautions and conserve remaining resources. Apart from this, there have been international level meetings including the Earth Summit in Rio de Janeiro, followed up with the World Summit on Sustainable Development (WSSD), in Johannesburg in 2002, as well as conventions to deal with issues such as climate change, notably the Kyoto Protocol and Inter-Governmental Panel on Climate Change (IPCC). We cannot cover all of these international agreements and conferences in any great detail. Here we have concentrated on CITES and on trying to understand its intersection with conservation at the global to the local scales.

Global environmental regimes raise questions about the contested nature and status of scientific knowledge. In particular, global regimes rely on ideas of positivist and uncontested science that can be used to draw up universally applicable forms of environmental management. The apparent 'neutrality' of scientific forms of management as promoted by international conventions provides the basis for international cooperation and agreement. These arguments about scientific neutrality can then be used to justify and legitimate highly political global interventions at the local level (Litfin, 1994; da Fonseca, 2003).

In the case of CITES the idea of neutral scientific management translates into the use of prohibition, or the threat of prohibition, as a norm – that is, a standard rule to regulate the behaviour of parties. The international trade in wildlife products operates under a global legislative framework that has been created as part of a broader landscape of conservation ideologies, which are presented as politically neutral environmental science. The formation of global regimes to govern the behaviour of state and non-state actors is often at odds with local norms that govern everyday activities and behaviours. One area where this is apparent is in the disputes over the global trade ban on ivory sales.

CITES and elephants

The function of CITES is to regulate the global trade in endangered species. The basic regulatory tools and principles of CITES are set out in a system of appendices, where an Appendix I listing constitutes a trade ban, Appendix II allows controlled and monitored trading, and an Appendix III listing means the species is subject to regulation and requires the cooperation of other CITES signatories to ensure that trade does not lead to overexploitation (Hutton and Dickson, 2000; Wijnstekers, 2001, pp393–421; Reeve, 2002). These appendices are the centrepiece of CITES' claims to be engaged in scientifically determined, politically neutral environmental management.

Appendix I listing is the mechanism that prohibits trade in elephant ivory. This has led to bitter debates because of southern Africa's burgeoning elephant population (Cumming and Jones, 2005). The problems associated with over-crowding by elephants have a number of implications for the wider environment and for biodiversity conservation. For example, large elephant populations that are contained within national parks can mean that they compete with other more endangered species (such as black rhino) for food and for space. Southern Africa's problem is that it has too many elephants rather than too few. Most signatories to CITES would accept that the debates held at the biennial Conference of the Parties (COP) meetings are highly politicized. But anti-ivory trade states and interest groups have maintained that CITES Appendix listings are scientifically determined (and therefore politically neutral).

This is a position that has changed over time according to context and circumstances. As investigative journalist Raymond Bonner documents in his book *At the Hand of Man* (1993), several prominent conservationists and conservation NGOs opposed a total ivory ban on scientific grounds – that it would lead to habitat destruction in southern African countries. However, the main organization supporting the ban, the African Wildlife Foundation, enjoyed a massively successful direct mail campaign raising money to save Africa's elephants. In fact, it was the most successful direct mail campaign in the history of American charities. Following the success of the campaign, conservationists and conservation organizations abruptly changed their position on the ban, such that when the CITES vote took place there were hardly any conservationists who were prepared to oppose the ban in public.

Before CITES the favoured method of dealing with overcrowding was culling. However, international outcry over culling as a cruel process has led a number of states (notably South Africa, Botswana and Namibia) to consider other options for fear that such negative publicity will have a detrimental impact on their tourism industries. Those in favour of culling point out that it solves the problem of overcrowding and also provides ivory, which is a potentially lucrative source of revenue that could be ploughed back into protected area management and wider forms of conservation.

Currently, and put briefly, the overall policy direction of western states, South Asian states, East African states, and many environmental NGOs has been informed by preservationist ideas that mean a total ban on the ivory trade is the only way to ensure the survival of elephants as a species. In contrast, local management practices of southern African elephant range states, Zimbabwe, Botswana, Namibia, Zambia and South Africa, have been determined by ideas of sustainable use, which allows for a limited ivory trade.[3] As might be expected, these vastly different philosophical positions lead to complex ethical debates about who has the right to use elephants, how they can be used, and for what purpose. The preservationist stance is informed by the precautionary principle, requiring parties to demonstrate that trade is non-detrimental to the survival of the species being traded. If there is any doubt, states are asked to cease all trade until non-detriment findings are proven (Environmental-Investigation-Agency, 1994, p5; Reeve, 2002, pp27–60). This has led to claims that long-term survival of elephant species can only be secured through a complete ban on the ivory trade. Preservationist interest groups have consistently argued that elephant range states can use elephants to generate funds for communities, private-sector operators and governments through tourism, especially photographic tourism and ecotourism. In essence, 'non-consumptive use' of elephants means elephants can be used but only in ways that mean the elephant is not killed. According to this conservation philosophy they cannot be sport hunted for trophies or used for meat, hides or ivory products. In general, this strategy requires a commitment to protected areas in the traditional sense: national parks and wildlife reserves that are separated from areas used by human populations for agriculture, livestock production and so on.

Critics of the preservationist approach argue that it effectively means that the poorest groups in the developing world (especially the rural poor) are expected to forgo the economic opportunities associated with the ivory trade but still live with all the costs of being in close proximity to elephants. For example, elephants in the communal lands of Zimbabwe have raided crops, which constitute the basic food supply of poor families. Those in favour of a utilizationist approach suggest it ensures that elephants will be conserved if they contribute to development and to meeting basic human needs through use of ivory trade, tourism and sport hunting revenues for community projects.

The pro-ivory trade states and interest groups have linked elephant management to the debt and aid question. In line with this, southern African states put forward a proposal for a debt-for-ivory buyout. Southern Africa's position has always been that the ivory stockpiles (produced through culling, natural death, problem animal control and seizures of illegal ivory) constitute an unacceptable waste of a natural and renewable resource. It was suggested that the World Bank Global Environmental Facility could provide funding to environmental organizations to buy ivory stockpiles from African governments (Duffy, 2008a). The newly purchased stockpiles could then be burnt to prevent them from entering a legal or illegal international trade. Those in favour of disposing of stockpiles in this way argued that the ivory would then have economic value to the producer states without allowing that ivory onto the international market where it might increase poaching and the illegal trade in ivory. In this way, burning stockpiles would neatly satisfy the demands of those advocating a utilization approach and a preservationist stance. However, very few offers of aid for ivory have been made, and those that have, have been very low. In 2002 the Humane Society of the United States offered to buy South Africa's stockpile of ivory and burn it. It offered US$250,000 for the 30-ton stockpile; the Humane Society argued that although the amount offered was low, South Africa would benefit from a significant increase in aid and donations to encourage 'non-consumptive use' options for elephants, such as photographic tourism and funding for protected areas. The South African National Parks Department described the offer as a joke, and pointed out that the ivory would be worth US$5 million on the open market.[4] In addition, CITES documents on ivory stockpiles have pointed to the failure of donors to fund elephant conservation plans and indicate that African elephant range states have also been unable to demonstrate they have adequate controls over the stocks.[5]

Challenges posed to CITES regulations by the arguments put forward by southern Africa were eventually successful, and at the 1997 meeting, Zimbabwe, Namibia and Botswana had their elephant populations down-listed to Appendix II (Milliken, 2002, p2). This decision came with the proviso that trading was only to be allowed in 1999 if adequate measures were introduced to ensure that trading was sustainable and free from illegally hunted ivory. The decision meant that in 1999 Namibia, Zimbabwe and Botswana reopened a restricted trade with Japan. The 1997 decisions paved the way for further relaxation of the ivory ban at the CITES conference in Chile in November 2002 that allowed Zimbabwe, Namibia, Botswana and South Africa to begin planning sales of ivory stockpiles for 2004.[6] However, a one-time ivory sale to Japan was only to be allowed in mid-2004 if range states could prove there were sufficient controls in place to ensure that no illegally hunted ivory entered the system. Although South Africa, Namibia and Botswana fulfilled these criteria, Zimbabwe did not. Nevertheless, the decision was immediately met with the concern that it provided a signal to poachers to restart the levels of commercial poaching witnessed in East Africa in the 1980s.[7] Given the current political situation in Zimbabwe, many were surprised, even greatly concerned, that the CITES 2007 COP authorized a one-off sale of ivory stockpiles by that country (as well as by neighbouring Botswana, South Africa and Namibia) (Duffy, 2008a).

International conservation NGOs

International environmental NGOs have been especially important in the arena of conservation. Organizations like the World Wildlife Fund and The Nature

Conservancy (TNC) grew rapidly in the 1970s. The 1980s witnessed a growth in the number and type of NGOs, some of which were especially powerful, not only in terms of their willingness to criticize governments, private companies and international institutions for environmental failures, but also because their unique position as expert 'knowledge brokers' or epistemic communities allowed them to frame and define the terms of the global environmental debate (Litfin, 1994; Princen and Finger, 1994; Keck and Sikkink, 1998).

The influence of environmental NGOs lies partly in their ability to disseminate environmental information through the media, and campaigning activity has been used against governments, private companies and international organizations (Keck and Sikkink, 1998; O'Brien et al, 2000, pp109–123). One good example of this was the Greenpeace campaign against Shell's activities in Ogoniland, Nigeria; this campaign revealed the 'soft underbelly' of global corporations and the ways they had to provide some sort of response to criticisms from global civil society (see Frynas, 2000, for further discussion). Following this, we might expect that NGOs such as World Wide Fund for Nature-International (WWF-International), the Wildlife Conservation Society (WCS) and Conservation International (CI) to operate in contestation with, for example, the World Bank. Surprisingly, and perhaps ironically, however, they often have a very close relationship, and can work to achieve common (often neoliberal) goals in the form of economic liberalization and environmental protection.

Of all international debates about conservation policy and practice, the controversies about conservation NGOs have probably aroused the most passion. Conservation NGOs are the means by which millions of people, mainly westerners, many of whose lives are characterized by day-to-day separation and alienation from nature, express their support and devotion to conservation causes. Conservation NGOs are the means by which people can make a difference in a world that does not seem to care nearly enough about wildlife and the damage we do to it. Yet conservation NGOs can also be harsh bureaucracies and callous in their imposition of alien policies. Their allegiances with corporations smacks of betrayal and dangerous compromise (Dowie, 1996). When Mac Chapin published his polemical critique of the big three NGOs in *World Watch* it resulted in the largest number of letters the publication had ever received on an article (2004; Seligmann et al, 2005). It was this debate that prompted Kent Redford (who works for the WCS) to marvel (as we reported in the Preface) at how conservation had now become equated with the destructive forces of the planet.

However, as Tsing (2004) clearly documents, the relationship between mainstream conservation NGOs and corporate interests is nothing new. Mainstream conservation emerged right in the middle of America's 'Guilded Age'. It was supported by the very same railroad companies that opened up the American West to exploitation and economic development. It was also supported by a broader diversity of Eastern elites with direct interests in the industrialization of the American economy. Land for conservation was acquired with support of the

Rockefeller family, who founded Standard Oil, and contributed significantly to the ecologies and economies of Latin America in the years following World War II through its purveying of petroleum-derived fertilizers and hybrid seeds (for a detailed discussion of these connections see Ross, 1998). In fact, only a myopic view of conservation could overlook these historical connections, which are mainstream conservation's collaborative legacy. A more fitting question from this perspective is not how conservation came to be equated with the most destructive forces on the planet, but why it took so long to get around to addressing the associations between them. A strong argument can be made to show that the roots of mainstream conservation are linked to destructive corporate interests. Dowie has documented how in the 1980s and 1990s the conservation mainstream in the US became increasingly wedded to, and unable to resist corporate capitalism (Dowie, 1996).

Conservation NGOs have been around since the beginning of the movement. John Muir and other preservationists founded the Sierra Club in 1892; the National Audobon Society began in 1896 (Dowie, 1996), the SPWFE in 1903 (Adams, 2004, p28). Organizations like TNC (1951) and the World Wide Fund for Nature (WWF) (1961) are youthful in comparison. However, the nature of the conservation NGOs has changed in two ways in the last 25 years. First, the number of NGOs working on conservation has proliferated. This was part of

Table 8.1 *The growth of conservation NGOs working in Africa*

Decade established	Number of organizations
1901–10	3
1911–20	0
1921–30	1
1931–40	0
1941–50	0
1951–60	5
1961–70	8
1971–80	14
1981–90	38
1991–2000	51
2001–present	19
Total	139

Source: Scholfield and Brockington, 2008

a global expansion of the third sector from the 1980s onwards. It is both the deliberate and unintentional result of neoliberal policies. Deliberate where finance institutions and donors have sought to strengthen and support civil society, and unintentional where NGOs have grown to fill the vacuum left by retreating states. The growth of over 130 conservation NGOs working in Africa demonstrated this pattern clearly (Table 8.1).

At the same time that NGOs have been proliferating, however, funds available for conservation have been declining. During the 1990s conservation funding decreased by 50 per cent, while funding to emerging big international NGOs (BINGOs) increased dramatically (Chapin, 2004) Moreover they have more recently been concentrated into the hands of increasingly few NGOs. Chapin names the main growth organizations as 'the Big Three', TNC, the WWF and CI (2004). Dowie, another critic of conservation practice adds to that list the WCS (Dowie, 2005, 2006). In different regions other organizations become prominent. In sub-Saharan Africa for example, TNC's presence is small and the African Wildlife Fund (AWF) spends nearly as much money as the WCS and CI. These are some of the world's biggest NGOs, collectively controlling billions of dollars and employing tens of thousands of people all over the world, and adopting increasingly corporate strategies, organization and cultures (Chapin, 2004; Khare and Bray, 2004; Dorsey, 2005). Their growth was achieved through a diversification of funding strategies to include funding from corporate, bilateral and multilateral sources.

There are two ways to assess the work of conservation NGOs – on their own terms, and according to a broader critique of their aims, methods and visions. To assess conservation NGOs on their own terms we have to see the extent to which they have been able to prioritize their spending to meet their declared priorities. This is a difficult task as the larger NGOs have only recently begun assessing their own spending this way. The conservation prioritizing models we examined in Chapter 2 are as much fund-raising tools as spending guides. They did not initially appear to have been used by their creators to evaluate conservation expenditure. Halpern and colleagues compared spending against identified conservation priorities at the global scale. They examined spending by the World Bank, the Global Environmental Facility, the WCS, TNC and the IUCN, with the priority sites identified by three other organizations – CI, Birdlife International (BI) and the WWF. They found that the presence of priority areas explained a small proportion of spending but concluded that 'global priority models are having little effect on how money is distributed among countries containing high-priority areas' (Halpern et al, 2006, p62). Remarkably they were unable to evaluate the geography of the three priority-setting institutions themselves because these organizations 'currently have no way of tracking spending at the regional or country level' (p58). The gaps and mismatches they identified point to substantial problems with existing priority setting exercises: we simply cannot tell how they are influencing current funding. Halpern and colleagues were quite critical in the conclusion of their study:

The credibility of extensive and expensive conservation planning efforts ... depends on our ability to find and quantify the link between priorities and effort. At the moment, we lack the data necessary to understand where on this continuum conservation actions fall... [C]onservation organisations should first ensure they have a system in place for evaluating how well spending matches stated goals and priorities before continuing to spend money prioritising. Conservation priority systems have the potential to be powerful and influential in this regard but it is time to balance enthusiasm for their potential with a thorough analysis of their actual impact on conservation action.

(2006, p63)

Similarly Castro and Locker's (2000) preliminary assessment of donor support to conservation projects in Latin America and the Caribbean found that some high priority regions were relatively neglected and recommended that the distribution of funding across regions be reviewed.

Only one review of spending by the conservation sector in a region has been carried out of which we are aware (Scholfield and Brockington, 2008). This found that overall spending by about 80 organizations in sub-Saharan Africa by country did follow the general distribution of biodiversity. However, spending was far from optimal once the costs of achieving conservation goals were taken into account. Comprehensive conservation is a long way from being put into practice.

The analysis of the conservation sector in sub-Saharan Africa also makes it possible to consider how much more money the sector might need in that region. Estimates of conservation need in the region, measured in terms of the shortfall of protected area funding alone, vary from about US$450 million to US$800 million. Actual spending was only about US$200 million. These funds supported only 20 per cent of protected areas on the continent (where support means any level of help however small), and they were spent on all manner of projects, not just in protected areas. Given the token levels of support some protected areas are receiving, given how many are not protected and given that so many other projects are also funded, it is possible to argue that, analysed on their own terms, African conservation NGOs need to scale up their activities by an order of magnitude.

But such a claim can only be legitimately made if existing funds are efficiently spent and deliver conservation objectives effectively. If there is waste then scaling up would scale up the waste as well. Unfortunately there are very few studies of which we are aware that examine the effectiveness of conservation NGO expenditure, or the consequences of recent increases in funding. The studies we know about are critical of existing use of funds (Austral-Foundation, 2007). Finally, if efficient and effective means of spending more money can be found it is also not clear whether a scaled up sector would mean more money to the same players, else a different configuration of agencies involved, with more large organizations, or lots more smaller organizations. Both options might introduce some healthy competition – or might increase the chances of duplication.

However, from another perspective a scaled up conservation sector is not immediately appealing. Critics of conservation organizations have found that they have been associated with diverse injustices, with too much proximity to industry and corporations, and that they are rarely accountable or fair. A scaled up sector would simply result in more problems and bigger fights. This is a literature that has tended to be journalistic (Bonner, 1993; Fairhead and Leach, 2000; Chapin, 2004; Goenewald and Macleod, 2004; Dowie, 2005; Pearce, 2005a). But it has strong academic manifestations (Brockington, 2002; Chatty and Colchester, 2002; Brechin et al, 2003; Fortwangler, 2003; Sullivan, 2003; Adams, 2004; Igoe, 2004b; Duffy, 2005; Shanahan, 2005; Garland, 2006; Stephenson and Chaves, 2006; Winer et al, 2007).

Before we examine these viewpoints we need to set them in the context of a much bigger set of writings about the work of development NGOs, of which work on conservation ought to be a part. Research on development NGOs has examined their work as vehicles of planned development and agents in the process of immanent development (Cowen and Shenton, 1996; Bebbington, 2004). Work here is pegged out by a series of important texts reflecting a variety of positions on NGOs. These writings variously contain hope and expectation of NGOs (Edwards and Hulme, 1992; Fisher, 1998); growing worries about its compromised position in relation to states and donors (Edwards and Hulme, 1995; Fisher, 1997; Hulme and Edwards, 1997); severe doubts as to the long-term consequences of intervention (de Waal, 1997); and studies of the struggles and contests inherent in any alternative sector's attempt to pursue and maintain distinctiveness and be accountable (Bebbington, 2004; Townsend and Townsend, 2004; Igoe and Kelsall, 2005; Bebbington et al, 2007).

Remarkably, knowledge about development NGOs and conservation NGOs rarely interacts. Work on conservation NGOs is generally not grounded in the broader literature on development NGOs. Writings on development NGOs are generally quiet about the work on, and of, conservation NGOs. The mutual ignoring is curious, and there is no obvious reason why this should be the case. It cannot be explained by any difference in their subject matters. There is little difference between 'conservation' and 'development', in the South or the North, and none that would demand separate treatment of their NGOs. Conservationists have long complained that they are doing too much 'development' (Oates, 1999; Sanderson and Redford, 2003). But more fundamentally, even 'pure' conservation is just a form of development, in both senses of the word – planned development and immanent development. As development, conservation controls natural resource use, protected area development and trade in timber and wildlife designed by states to promote prosperity. Conservation NGOs, which support protected areas (sometimes established in mitigation for development projects, e.g. Goldman, 2001b), undertake research or environmental education, are perpetrating forms of planned development. As development, conservation follows from the growth of eco-tourists demanding particular products or environments, or from demographic or market changes that induce changes in natural resource management. Conservation NGOs that facilitate and respond to eco-tourism, or help local groups form cooperatives to manufacture and sell curios or produce in new markets or manage fish stocks are part of the process of immanent development. Analyses of conservation NGOs logically belong with the analyses of development NGOs.

There is also overlap in the findings of critics of conservation NGOs and those in mainstream development. As with development NGOs, observers contend that conservation NGOs have lost their independent critical voice, and become too close to foundations, donor governments and their corporate influences, and to corporations themselves, and less accountable to their core constituencies (Chapin, 2004; Romero and Andrade, 2004; Dorsey, 2005; Stephenson and Chaves, 2006). Critics fear that they are ignoring local voices, and failing to support local environmentalisms against the incursions of big businesses. Others observe that they are implicated in the inadequate greening of large financial institutions, lending their support to major development projects that deserve tighter environmental scrutiny (Goldman, 2001b).

Both literatures deal with similar anxieties about the role of NGOs in promoting democracies. A vibrant civil society can be part of healthy democracies but many observers find that NGOs can also be associated with democratic deficits (Luckham et al, 2000). With respect to conservation, studies of the role of NGOs in devolution of natural resource management have questioned the democratic nature and functioning of NGOs. Ribot and colleagues' study of decentralization trends globally has found that NGOs are not sufficiently downwardly accountable to local electorates and so can distort effective devolution (Ribot 2002, 2004, 2006; Logo, 2003; Oyono, 2004a).

In both conservation and development observers note a number of unfortunate synergies between international NGOs and local civil society. When larger NGOs work with local counterparts this is no simple empowerment process. Rather they can transform the activities and structure of local NGOs in ways that re-orient them to donors and their priorities at the expense of the agendas and needs of the local communities that are ostensibly their constituents (Igoe, 2003b). International conservation NGOs can displace local NGOs and compete with them for funds. Where they register national chapters they then become competitors for the same sources of money, and tend to be much better at presenting funding cases (Rodriguez et al, 2007). Local NGOs will not simply roll over and become spineless clients of wealthier partners, they will pursue their own agendas. Nonetheless the presence of relatively plentiful dollars will still have powerful impacts and can distort local agendas separating civil society organizations from their popular roots (Duffy, 2006c; Igoe, 2003b).

Finally, and perhaps most importantly there have been powerful criticisms about the impacts of large-scale planned development projects on the livelihoods of the poor, so also the impacts of large-scale conservation planning has been roundly castigated for its severe negative impacts on local lives and livelihoods (Colchester, 1997; Ghimire and Pimbert, 1997; Colchester and Erni, 1999; Fairhead and Leach, 2000; Brockington, 2002; Nelson and Hossack, 2003; Brockington and Igoe, 2006). In particular, conservation NGOs have tended to be associated with the harsh treatment of people moved from protected areas. But the survey of eviction did not find such a pattern (Brockington and Igoe, 2006). Evictions tended to be driven by strong nationally based environmental movements. Where NGOs were involved they tended to be the smaller, less sophisticated organizations.

One recent example is the case of African Parks Foundation and Nechasar National Park in southern Ethiopia (also written as Nechisar and as Nech Sar). Nechasar draws in a range of interesting themes in current conservation debates: the role of philanthropic individuals, the powers of national governments and the costs and benefits to local communities. African Parks Foundation engages in collaborations with the public and private sector to develop conservation initiatives in Africa. The Foundation emphasizes the stimulation of responsible tourism and associated private enterprise as a mechanism for achieving financial sustainability of parks as well as providing a foundation for sustainable economic development and poverty reduction.

In the six years since its establishment, African Parks Foundation has taken on responsibility for the management of seven protected areas in five different countries, covering a total area in excess of 25,000km^2.[8] One of those parks is Nechasar National Park. Refugees International estimated that 2000 families were removed from Nechasar National Park when external funding was made available to fence the park and develop tourist facilities. The families were forced to relocate to areas outside the park boundary, creating problems in the surrounding areas that were already settled.[9] African Parks Foundation made the funding available to develop the park, but this led to evictions that the Ethiopian government claimed were undertaken 'voluntarily'; however, Refugees International reported that homes were burnt down by government operatives to force people to move.[10] African Parks Foundation claimed that the development of tourism in the area would provide hundreds of jobs for local communities; however, the NGO Conservation Refugees argued that 10,000 people were displaced in 2004[11] to enclose the park and open it up for tourists; but since African Parks Foundation took over management of the park in 2005 their own figures indicate that only 90 local people have been employed as guides, drivers and so on.[12]

The late Paul van Vlissigen, the Dutch billionaire who was behind African Parks Foundation, claimed that:

> The government had told us that it was going to resettle the Kore and Guji tribes (sic) outside the park. It was a political decision, and there was European Union support for it. We said that we could work with people in the park, as we do in Zambia, but they said no.

We didn't want to be involved in the resettlement, so I put a clause
in the contract that said we wouldn't take over the park until the
resettlement was completed. (Pearce, 2005b)

African Parks Foundation claims that extensive ecological pressure was caused by
communities living with their cattle in the heart of the protected area and this
was causing serious damage and preventing long-term development and
management of the park. African Parks Foundation states that it 'has not
participated in discussions between the Government and local communities over
the last two years because this is a matter for the people and their local and
national governments, not for a park management body'.[13] However, given that
there is a strained relationship between the Ethiopian government and ethnic
minorities in southern Ethiopia, it seems naive (at best) to assume that the central
government would not use the opportunity of enforcing the park's boundaries to
further repress potential pockets of opposition in the area. In part as a result of
international concern within the conservation community African Parks
Foundation has withdrawn from Nechasar.

We stress the common ground between work on development and conservation
NGOs partly because it is unsatisfactory to have two groups of scholars saying the
same things, when there is no good reason for them to be merely repeating each
other and when they are unaware of the other's presence. It is also important to
recognize that the problems that conservation NGOs experience are common to a
broader sector all of whose members are wrestling in different ways with their need
to be effective and deliver objectives, and the need to work fairly, democratically
and in ways that make meaningful, and welcome, differences.

Understanding the work of conservation NGOs is vital if we are to appreciate
how conservation and capitalism are remaking the world. International
conservation organizations are among the groups that are transforming the nature
and meaning of sovereignty. One of the distinguishing features of the way
international organizations (conservation or otherwise) operate is as part of larger
consortiums of actors, with state actors almost always at the forefront and
apparently in charge. Mbembe (2001, p67) writing on African states notes that
they are weak and highly dependent on external support. He argues that
sovereignty and control in such situations is fragmented and highly decentralized –
employed in different ways, by different state actors, in different contexts, with
very little centralized control. Following political and economic liberalization, it
became possible for state actors to enter into strategic alliances with private
investors and international NGOs.

Both state actors and outsiders bring important resources to the table, without
which these alliances could not operate effectively. Outsiders, in this case
conservation NGOs, bring money and other external resources, on which
officials from impoverished states are highly dependent. State actors bring
sovereignty – the means of coercion that make it possible gain advantage in

struggles over resources traditionally the exclusive purview of the state (Mbembe, 2001, p78). Outsiders wishing to directly control, or otherwise define the use of these resources, are highly dependent on state actors for this commodity.

This does not usually mean that state actors cede sovereignty to these outsiders – although this does sometimes happen. More often state actors are able to use sovereignty to leverage resources and other forms of support from their powerful, and usually foreign, allies. Although Mbembe applied this analysis specifically to African states, his title – *On the Post colony* – implies that it can be fruitfully applied to any post-colonial situation in which weak states and aid dependence gives external actors extraordinary influence over the policies and actions of state actors. The relationships that emerge from these dynamics are usually ones of mutual dependence, characterized by a great deal of strategic negotiation. Such negotiations are usually difficult to discern, obscured as they are by discourses of official prerogatives. But note that in these processes sovereignty is transformed to a type of commodity, which circulates and realizes value in the world of all commodities.

This situation presents a distinctive – perhaps paradoxical – challenge to conservation NGOs because privatized sovereignty is useful. It provides plausible deniability with respect to evictions and other forms of displacement. Consider again Paul van Vlissingen's claim that African Parks Foundation would not take over the park until the resettlement was completed. His statement may constitute plausible deniability, but with it comes great responsibility. There are now numerous calls for a conservation code of practice that would encourage a greater sense of social responsibility among conservation practitioners (Brockington and Schmidt-Soltau, 2004; Winer et al, 2007).

International conservation NGOs are also at work with a specific vision of good conservation practice and community-based natural resource management. Organizations like the WCS, AWF, WWF and CI transmit this vision to the wider donor community, and ultimately to national governments. For example, African Wildlife Foundation claims that the core sentiment of its mission statement is 'Together with the People of Africa' and that it engages with communities in 'conservation enterprise' where communities are encouraged to develop commercially viable enterprises that conserve wildlife while improving the livelihoods of people.[14] WWF-International also readily advertises its commitment to community conservation as an approach that recognizes the need to improve rural livelihoods.[15] Equally, while CI states that it puts 'science' at the centre of its strategy, it also points to the importance of partnerships with local communities to make conservation strategies work.[16] This apparent commitment to a community-based approach to conservation has also been taken up by the World Bank, for example in engaging communities with Fynbos conservation in South Africa.[17]

It seems, then, that global organizations are keen to demonstrate their community-friendly credentials as part of a justification for their support for conservation. This results in a counter-intuitive relationship between IFIs, donors, environmental NGOs and national governments that pushes forward economic liberalization, political liberalization and good governance agendas alongside specific forms of environmental conservation. The latter are often justified as socially acceptable through including a component of community-based natural resource management (Goldman, 2001b; Zimmerer, 2006). But while the influence of global environmental NGOs has assisted in expanding community-based natural resource management, they are also a potential threat to community-based approaches to conservation. They frame and define the terms of environmental policy making in ways that can leave little room for local groups. Global NGOs are vital knowledge brokers and set conservation trends. CI and WCS are prominent in the resurgence of the 'fortress conservation' narrative (Sanderson and Redford, 2003; Brockington and Schmidt-Soltau, 2004; Hutton et al, 2005).

CI developed out of WWF because it wanted to break away from WWF-US and WWF-International that had clearly embraced community conservation approaches as the way forward for the South. CI wanted to pursue conservation programmes that 'put the science first' and move away from community conservation that it regarded as not as effective (see Chapin, 2004, for further discussion). At bottom, despite years of proclamations to the contrary (Adams and McShane, 1992; Gomez-Pompa and Kaus, 1992), the vision of a human-free wilderness remains a powerful one. Consequently, for many donors, saving exotic environments means that they have to become people free (Kalamandeen and Gillson, 2007). As a result of this shift in thinking back towards separation of people and wildlife, justified through appeals to scientific rationality, the commitment to community-based natural resource management has been downplayed from being an *approach* to conservation to becoming a *component* to justify and legitimate interventions to create new protected areas or interventions to conserve specific species (for further discussion see Hutton et al, 2005).

Transnational public–private networks and transfrontier conservation areas

The role of public–private networks has become increasingly important in the post-Cold War era. The proliferation of organizations engaged in a range of conservation activities is indicative of the growing complexity in the arena of environmental management. National parks and conservation activities may once have been the responsibility of state agencies but more recently transnational networks of donors, NGOs and private companies have begun to get engaged in managing protected areas, defining national conservation policies and establishing and maintaining private parks (Igoe and Brockington, under review). This can be related to wider shifts in the global system that has witnessed a move away from the focus on nation-states towards a system characterized by multiple sites of power and authority including international institutions, multinational corporations (MNCs) and NGOs (Rosenau, 1990, pp10–12; McGrew, 1992, p13). In many ways national governments have become inextricably linked with transnational networks of actors (Harrison, 2004, pp23–26; 2005).

Public–private networks that operate at a global scale have been heavily involved in developing 'transnational ecosystem' approaches to environmental management, especially in the field of wildlife conservation. The engagement between global NGOs, national governments, the private sector and donors have worked together to produce a powerful force behind the development of 'ecoregional' or 'ecosystem' approaches to conservation. This ecosystem approach has prompted a shift in thinking about 'national parks' within particular states, to the development of protected areas that encompass entire ecosystems regardless of whether they cross international boundaries. Transboundary conservation schemes can be defined as 'any process of co-operation across boundaries that facilitates or improves the management of natural resources to the benefit of all parties in the area concerned' (Westing, 1993; Griffen, 1999; Ali, 2007).

Transfrontier Conservation Areas (TFCAs), especially those supported by the South African based NGO, Peace Parks Foundation, are particularly prominent conservation initiatives. The Great Limpopo Transfrontier Park, which draws in territory from Zimbabwe, Mozambique and South Africa, is the best example of a 'working' TFCA (Duffy, 2006c). The Peace Parks Foundation describes the Great Limpopo Transfrontier Park as a flagship project that currently covers 35,000km²; however, it is intended to provide the core initiative for the future development of a protected area that covers 100,000km².[18]

TFCAs are presented as following a neutral scientific rationale, which in turn justifies highly political interventions. However, Chapin (2004) points out that large conservation schemes demand large conservation organizations with the capacity to manage them. He argues that the increased prominence of large-scale approaches to conservation at the turn of the 1990s was directly linked to the increased control of conservation funding by a few large organizations as outlined above. Büscher and Dressler (2007) further argue that the growth of transfrontier conservation organizations is linked to conservation's growing role in providing mitigating services to offset the negative economic consequences of economic growth while ensuring that the benefit of that growth reaches a broader diversity of constituents. Ironically, in this scenario, the more destructive economic progress becomes, the larger the protected areas that will be necessary to offset this destruction.

The idea of TFCAs was introduced as early as the 1920s, with the first bi-national park, the Waterton-Glacier National Park, established on the US–Canadian border in 1926. By 1997, there were 136 existing and 85 planned TFCAs that crossed 112 international borders in 98 nations (Griffen, 1999, pp11–15). The growing field of conservation biology has provided a clear scientific rationale for transboundary environmental management, in particular in terms of justifying the expansion of conservation to include entire ecosystems rather than small parts of it in a single national park (Wolmer, 2003). The promoters of TFCAs have pointed to the biological reasons for large transfrontier protected areas. The increasing isolation of habitats in national protected areas has reduced the genetic diversity of key species in certain ecosystems. They argue it is critical to ensure that the range areas for key species are kept as large as possible, and preferably transnational, in order to secure their long-term survival (Ali, 2007). Since political frontiers are not the same as ecological boundaries, ecosystems may be divided between two or more countries, and be subject to a variety of often contradictory management and land-use practices (Griffen, 1999; Kliot, 2001).

TFCAs clearly draw together transnational networks that link local communities with international actors. The moves towards transfrontier conservation areas can be viewed as part of the broader process of decentralizing power to multiple stakeholders by shifting responsibility for conservation out of state hands and into the hands public–private transnational networks. One specific part of the Mesoamerican Biological Corridor is the Mesoamerican Barrier Reef System Project (MBRS). It is a prime example of the operation of public–private networks that operate to enclose terrestrial and marine ecosystems in large-scale transboundary protected areas.

The MBRS extends from the southern half of the Yucatan Peninsula to the Bay Islands of Honduras, drawing in Belize, Mexico, Honduras and Guatemala, and it includes the second longest barrier reef in the world. It is an important ecosystem, providing breeding grounds for manatees amongst other species; the area is also of socio-economic importance to the people who depend on the resources contained within it.[19] The MBRS project is funded by the Global Environment Facility (GEF) and the governments of Belize, Guatemala, Honduras and Mexico. MBRS has received US$10 million from the GEF. The project is implemented by the World Bank and four countries are involved through the Central American Commission on Environment and Development (CCAD) of the System for Central American Integration. The MBRS project has a Project Coordinating Unit that works on behalf of the CCAD, with its headquarters in Belize City, Belize; and the United Nations Development Programme has been contracted to provide specific 'procurement and disbursement services' for the project.[20] The announcement of World Bank funding brought further pledges from donors to assist the stakeholders in getting the transfrontier reef project up and running. For example, the Netherlands/World Bank Environmental Partnership Fund, the Canadian Trust, the Food and Agricultural Organization and the CCAD provided funds for a regional workshop on the MBRS.[21]

TFCAs are linked in with global rhetoric about devolving management of protected areas to local communities, as discussed in the chapter about tourism and conservation. The intention is that communities will constitute the key actors involved in directly managing transboundary conservation areas. In so doing, TFCAs represent a departure from conservation, traditionally in state hands, and is more in line with debates about decentralization of power and control over policy making and environmental management. The role of NGOs in particular has been criticized by other actors in the conservation sector. For example, Gregory Ch'oc of the Kekchi Council of Belize suggested that national and international environmental NGOs that were involved in shaping the Sarstoon-Temash transfrontier management plans in Belize did not take account of the perspectives of the local communities.[22] It is clear that on the one hand the bargaining power of communities can be significantly enhanced through their relationships with the international NGOs. On the other hand, the needs and political power of communities can be severely undermined through their participation in transboundary conservation schemes that incorporate a number of globally powerful actors.

Critics of TFCAs have also argued that they do not reduce state control over border areas; rather, TFCAs actually provide an opportunity for national governments to increase control and surveillance over borderland areas and communities that live there. Numerous conservation programmes emphasize neoliberal policy of land tenure reform and land registration as the key to stimulating conservation-oriented behaviour within local communities. In the end, the prescriptions for biodiversity conservation in protected areas and their buffer zones has meant that the state has encroached on local environmental resources (Neumann, 2000). Neumann suggests that the extension of state control through environmental policy making constitutes a major new development in the South. Global conservation organizations have assisted national governments in obtaining control over border areas through the demarcation of protected areas and their surrounding buffer zones (Sivaramakrishnan, 1999; Neumann, 2000). The growth of public–private networks has on the one hand meant a shift in location of power away from the state, but paradoxically increased the expectations amongst global actors about the capacities of states to implement globally defined and approved environmental schemes.

The powers of public–private partnerships in protected areas

Public–private partnerships have been very important in terms of creating new protected areas. One recent example comes from Madagascar, where a transnational public–private network has been engaged in lobbying for, establishing and managing a new network of protected areas. Madagascar has become a key site for donor and NGO activity, partly because it contains very high levels of biodiversity and high rates of endemic species and is well known to have severe environmental problems.[23] The idea of an environmental crisis in a highly biodiverse and extremely poor country means that Madagascar has been identified by bilateral donors, NGOs, international financial institutions (IFIs) and others as a place that demands global attention, and, more importantly, global action (Kull, 1996). In order to understand the influence of the donor and NGO community in environmental politics in Madagascar it is important to outline its main features. The key organizations are global environmental NGOs, such as the WWF, WCS and CI, as well as IFIs, especially the World Bank, and Northern governments through their aid and development departments (such as United States Agency for International Development (USAID), Cooperation Suisse and Cooperation Française). The high profile of international environmental NGOs as donors in Madagascar is unusual, since in most developing states bilateral donors and IFIs are the most important donors.

The framework of conditionalities in the economic, political and environmental arenas in the 1980 and 1990s led to the creation of a series of national structures in Madagascar that conformed to the prescriptions of external donors. For example, in 1991 the World Bank provided US$100 million for a National Environmental Action Plan (NEAP) and The Charter for the Environment. The Charter was expected to run for 15 years, divided into three five-year programmes called Environmental Programme Phases I, II and III, to be implemented through the Office National Pour l'Environnement.[24] Whilst the funding for the NEAP and the Charter was provided by the World Bank, the funding for the central organizations established to oversee and implement them was provided primarily by WWF.[25]

The development of the NEAP and the involvement of donors and NGOs paved the way for the development of co-management schemes between the public and private sectors. Donors and environmental NGOs have been involved in directly running state-owned national parks in Madagascar. For example, Association Nationale pour la Gestion des Aires Protégées (ANGAP), the national agency responsible for managing protected areas in Madagascar, is run and funded by a group of international NGOs and donors in conjunction with Malagasy state agencies. ANGAP is essentially a private organization that runs a public utility, and has received funding from CI, the World Bank, WWF, USAID, the German development agency, and the French and British governments. The board of directors is drawn from government ministries, such as the Ministry of Tourism and the Ministry of the Environment, but donors including the World Bank and WWF also have seats on the board.[26]

In Madagascar, the powers of public–private partnerships have gone one step further where a transnational alliance of public and private interest groups are heavily involved in defining, prescribing and implementing conservation policies, especially in the form of creating a network of new protected areas. The idea of the Donor Consortium developed in tandem with the creation of the NEAP and the Charter for the Environment, and arose from the interactions between bilateral donors, IFIs, international NGOs and the Malagasy state. The Donor Consortium is comprised of USAID, the German government, the Japanese government, the French government (Cooperation Française), the Swiss government (Cooperation Suisse), CI, the WWF, the WCS (the latter joined in 2004), but the lynchpin is the World Bank.[27] The Donor Consortium meets monthly to review the progress, and determine future funding priorities and policies for Madagascar. Its composition highlights the unique nature of politics in Madagascar, since nowhere else are three global environmental organizations (and specifically wildlife-oriented ones) directing national policy, including the new national poverty reduction strategy.[28]

The power of NGOs is especially important in terms of understanding how the Donor Consortium determines conservation practice. In particular, it is useful to examine the ways that a group of international NGOs (especially the WCS and CI) operated within the Donor Consortium to persuade the Malagasy government to increase the number of protected areas. The result of lobbying by CI and the WCS was that in 2003 President Ravalomanana committed Madagascar to tripling the amount of land with protected area status within six years to create a six million hectare network of terrestrial and marine reserves.[29] The commitment was named the 'Durban Vision Initiative', because it was a specific outcome of the 2003 World Parks Congress held in Durban, South Africa (the initiative was very publicly announced by President Ravlomanana at the Congress). Within Madagascar, it led to the creation of the 'Durban Vision Group', which includes donors, NGOs and Malagasy government agencies.[30] The WCS and CI argued strongly that the Initiative was agreed in consultation with Malagasy government, and that Malagasy organizations would be *partners* or *stakeholders* it.[31]

By 2007 CI reported that the new protected areas comprised three large tracts: the 499,598-hectare (1929-square-mile) Fandriana–Vondrozo Forest Corridor in the southeast; the 276,836-hectare (1069-square-mile) Mahavavy–Kinkony Wetlands Complex of lake, river and forest on the northwest coast; and the Menabe Central Forest, 125,000 hectares (483 square miles) of dry deciduous forest in the southwest; and a number of other smaller protected areas had been declared to, for example, create corridors for wildlife between existing national parks. CI had also set up the Global Conservation Fund (GCF), and thus far GCF had provided US$2.2 million to support protected area projects in Madagascar. GCF and the CI-administered Critical Ecosystem Partnership Fund have contributed significantly to the planning and design of new protected areas across the country.

A wide range of organizations is involved in supporting the new initiative either financially or through provision of training and expertise, including CI, Association Fanamby, the WCS, WWF, Durrell Wildlife Conservation Trust, Missouri Botanical Garden, USAID, Agence Française de Développement, Fonds Français pour l'Environnnement Mondial, Germany's KfW Development Bank, and the World Bank.[32] As a result it is difficult to determine exactly how much funding has been made available to implement the Durban Vision Initiative, and to establish which organizations provided the money in the first place compared with organizations that have received funds from donors and spent them on the Initiative.

Immediately after the Durban Vision Initiative was announced concerns were raised that the two wildlife-oriented conservation NGOs had pressured the new

Malagasy president into agreeing to it when they met with him at the World Parks Congress in 2003 (see Horning, 2008 for further discussion). Since Ravalomanana was a new president who was looking towards the US to replace France as the major external donor, critics suggested that he had felt obliged to agree because of threats from the NGOs that they could effectively lobby in Washington to reduce support to the new president; it was clear to their opponents that the environmental NGOs had a great deal of power in Malagasy politics, and especially within the Donor Consortium as a transnational governance mechanism.

However, the case is more complex than external actors 'producing' a policy commitment in consultation with partners in the developing world. The newly set up Durban Vision Group (which included global and local NGOs, donor and state agencies) dealt with this policy announcement in a complicated way. The group rapidly redefined the meaning of 'protected areas' in order to create a policy that was globally and locally acceptable. Under the Durban Vision Initiative, the new protected areas will now include numerous types of 'multi-use' areas rather than requiring the establishment of national parks; protected areas are costly in financial and social terms as well as being time-consuming and extremely difficult to establish and enforce.[33] CI and the Critical Ecosystems Project Fund have identified these Sites de Conservation as a key mechanism through which conservation can be achieved whilst also delivering benefits to local communities.[34]

A number of the other donors were concerned at the growing levels of power of environmental organizations in the Donor Consortium. In particular, criticisms levelled at the WCS and CI are particularly problematic. One representative on the Donor Consortium argued that the commitment of the WCS and CI to science-based conservation and its use in pushing through the Durban Vision Initiative had already led to forced evictions of poor communities from future protected areas. In particular there are concerns that the Durban Vision Initiative will send a message that wildlife and habitats are more important than people, and will result in a potentially destructive separation of people and environments possibly through forced evictions from the newly declared protected areas.[35]

Conclusion

The development of what has been called global environmental governance provides the international context for conservation. Understanding these global dynamics is vitally important for understanding the complex ways conservation plays out in particular locations, and especially the ways that international-scale decisions and networks can bring costs and benefits to particular places and communities. For example, the power and limitations of the international legal apparatus is clear in our discussion of CITES and the ivory trade. The international legal framework provided by such as the Convention on Biodiversity and CITES aims to deal with transboundary environmental issues that cannot be tackled at the national or local level. However, through their regulatory activities international conventions can have a substantial impact on defining what national governments and local communities can and cannot do. This in turn intersects with one of the core themes of this book: the ways that conservation unevenly distributes fortune and misfortune.

This chapter also explored the complexities associated with global conservation, especially the proliferation of public–private networks and their active participation in defining and implementing conservation practice at the local, national and global scales. This is especially important given that conservation funding has been increasingly funnelled into a narrower range of conservation NGOs. This in turn increases their powers in the international arena as fund-raisers and as key organizations for definition of what constitutes good conservation practice. Furthermore, their financial powers also provide them with a greater degree of influence over what local communities can and cannot do and how national governments can define their conservation policies. This is clear in the case of Madagascar, where the financial and lobbying power of a small number of conservation NGOs means that they have powers that extend into countries that are far removed from their fund-raising centres in the West. Limiting that power will depend upon conservation funders, be they private companies, donors or individual supporters, adopting a constructively critical and quizzical stance to the publicity that they receive from grantees. In our final chapter we will pay closer attention to the difficulties inherent in that task and the power of the image in conservation.

Notes

1   www.cbd.int/convention/guide.shtml (accessed 19 December 2007).
2   www.cbd.int/biosafety/articles.shtml?a=cpb-01 (accessed 19 December 2007).
3   However, southern African states' common position on the potential uses of ivory since the ban in 1989 has begun to break down because Botswana has now begun to favour a more preservationist stance.
4   'Money to Burn', *Mail and Guardian* (South Africa), 1 November 2002.
5   www.africanparks-conservation.com/apffoundation/index.php (accessed 16 November 2007).
6   www.cites.org (accessed 10 November 2007); and TRAFFIC Recommendations to CITES at COP12, Chile 2002, www.traffic.org/cop12/proposal3_14.html#pro6 (accessed 13 May 2004).
7   Species Survival Network (2002), *CITES 2002: African Elephant*, www.speciessurvivalnetwork.org (accessed 13 May 2004); 'Wildlife Officials Brace for 2004 Ivory Sale', *Mail and Guardian* (South Africa), 12 November 2003; 'All Clear for Ivory Trade', *Mail and Guardian*, 27 June 1997; 'Ivory Vote Sparks New Fears for Elephants', *Guardian* (UK), 13 November 2002.

8   www.africanparks-conservation.com/apffoundation/index.php (accessed
    16 November 2007).
9   www.refugeesinternational.org/content/photo/detail/4727/ (accessed 16 November
    2007).
10 www.refugeesinternational.org/content/article/detail/5639?PHPSESSID=5cfliegen
    3C (accessed 16 November 2007).
11 http://conservationrefugees.org/NechSar (accessed 16 November 2007).
12 www.african-parks.org/apffoundation/index.php?option=com_content&task=view
    &id=61& Itemid=99 (accessed 16 November 2007).
13 www.african-parks.org/apffoundation/index.php?option=com_content&task=view
    &id=62&Itemid=100 (accessed 16 November 2007).
14 www.awf.org/section/people (accessed 16 August 2007).
15 www.panda.org/about_wwf/where_we_work/africa/what_we_do/cbnrm/index.cfm
    (accessed 14 August 2007).
16 http://web.conservation.org/xp/CIWEB/strategies/ (accessed 14 August 2007).
17 http://web.worldbank.org/WBSITE/EXTERNAL/OPPORTUNITIES/GRANTS/
    DEVMARKETPLACE/0,,contentMDK:20215186~menuPK:214469~pagePK:
    180691~piPK:174492~theSitePK:205098,00.html (accessed 14 August 2007).
18 www.peaceparks.org/tfca.php?mid=147&pid=1 (accessed 19 October 2007).
19 www.mbrs.org.bz/english/en_index.htm (accessed 18 October 2007).
20 www.mbrs.org.bz/english/project_support.htm (accessed 18 October 2007).
21 Interview with Natalie Rosado, Conservation Division, Forestry Department,
    Belmopan, 17 May 2000; Amandala, 17 October 1999, *Regional Meso American
    Barrier Reef System Project planning workshop complete*. http://wbln0018.worldbank.
    org/MesoAm/UmbExtLib.nsf/(By+Title+Web)/47269E38BE4742BC8525671A00
    4ECDC9?OpenDocument (accessed 18 October 2007). The Mesoamerican
    Biological Corridors Project aims to re-establish wildlife migration corridors, and
    create unbroken bioregions that cover rainforests, mangroves and coral reefs that
    stretch from Mexico, through Belize and Guatemala, to Honduras.
22 Interview with Gregory Ch'oc, Kekchi Council of Belize, Punta Gorda, 23 May
    2000.
23 For further discussion of threats to biodiversity in Madagascar see www.bbc.co.uk
    'Madagascar Biodiversity Threatened', 16 January 2002 (accessed 8 February 2002);
    and *Financial Times*, 15 May 2001, 'Madagascar's jewels of nature under threat'.
24 Madagascar is currently in Phase III of the programme, which is running two
    years behind schedule because World Bank support was suspended during the
    presidential crisis of 2001/02.
25 Interview with Hery Zo Rakotondrainbe, Office National Pour l'Environnement,
    Antananarivo, 29 August 2001.
26 Interview with Parfait Randriamampianina, Director of Parks, ANGAP,
    Antananarivo, 21 August 2001.
27 Interview with Dr Helen Crowley, Country Director, Madagascar Programme,
    Wildlife Conservation Society, Antananarivo, 25 March 2004; and interview with
    Bienvenu Rajohnson, Senior Environmental Policy, Adviser, World Bank,
    Antananarivo, 26 March 2004. Also see http://wcs.org/sw-around_the_globe/
    Africa/Madagascar (accessed 16 November 2004).

28 Interview with Tiana Razarimahatrata, CARE Madagascar, Antananarivo, 21 April 2004.
29 'Madagascar to Triple Areas Under Protection' (16 September 2003)
30 Interview with Dr Helen Crowley, Country Director, Madagascar Programme, Wildlife Conservation Society, Antananarivo, 25 March 2004; interview with Dr Joanna Durbin, Director of the Madagascar Programme, Durrell Wildlife Conservation Trust, Antananarivo, 31 March 2004; and interview with Leon M. Rajaobelina, Senior Executive Director, Conservation International Madagascar, Antananarivo, 23 March 2004; also see www.conservation.org/xp/CIWEB/regions/africa/madagascar/ (accessed 17 November 2004).
31 Interview with Dr Helen Crowley, Country Director, Madagascar Programme, Wildlife Conservation Society, Antananarivo, 25 March 2004; interview with Dr Joanna Durbin, Director of the Madagascar Programme, Durrell Wildlife Conservation Trust, Antananarivo, 31 March 2004; and interview with Leon M. Rajaobelina, Senior Executive Director, Conservation International Madagascar, Antananarivo, 23 March 2004.
32 'Madagascar creates 1 million hectares of new protected areas', http://web.conservation.org/xp/news/press_releases/2007/043007a.xml (accessed 4 July 2007).
33 Interview with Dr Helen Crowley, Country Director, Madagascar Programme, Wildlife Conservation Society, Antananarivo, 25 March 2004; interview with Dr Joanna Durbin, Director of the Madagascar Programme, Durrell Wildlife Conservation Trust, Antananarivo, 31 March 2004; and interview with Lantoniaina Antriamampianina, Director of the Terrestrial Programme, Wildlife Conservation Society, Antananarivo, 24 March 2004.
34 See 'An Overview of CEPF's Portfolio in the Madagascar and Indian Ocean Islands Biodiversity Hotspot: Madagascar' www.cepf.net/ImageCache/cepf/content/pdfs/cepf_2emadagascar_2eoverview_5f3_2e05_2epdf/v1/cepf.madagascar.overview_5f3.05.pdf (accessed 4 July 2007).
35 Anonymous interviewee, Madagascar 2004.

9

Conservation and Capitalism

...the present age ... prefers the sign to the thing signified, the copy to the original, representation to reality, the appearance to essence ... only illusion is sacred, truth profane. Nay, sacredness is held to be enhanced in proportion as truth decreases and illusion increases, so the highest degree of illusion comes to the highest degree of sacredness.

Marx, Feuerbach

The spectacle manifests itself as an enormous positivity, out of reach and beyond dispute. All it says is: Everything that appears is good; whatever is good will appear. The attitude that is demanded in principle is the same passive acceptance that it has already secured by means of its seeming incontrovertibility, and indeed by its monopolization of the realm of appearances.

Guy Debord, 1995 [1967]

There will always be animal reserves and Indian reservations to hide the fact that they are dead and that we are all Indians.

Jean Baudrillard, 1993

At the start of this book we argued that a good way to begin to understand the changes in wildlife and landscape conservation in the last few years is by looking at trends in the establishment of protected areas. It is clear that the period of most dramatic growth of protected areas was between 1985 and 1995, which coincides with the global rise, expansion and deepening of neoliberalism. As we have shown, conservation and capitalism are intertwining in the spread of some protected areas and rise of conservation NGOs, the development of international regulations and conventions, the creation of community and market-based conservation programmes and the faith in tourism as a driver for sustainability. For us the pattern is clear: conservation is increasingly compatible with capitalism and, rather like capitalism itself, it unevenly distributes fortune and misfortune.

It is time now to examine some of the closest relationships that have developed and their repercussions for different sets of people, in order to highlight the ways that this compatibility is being expanded through new and increasingly market-oriented initiatives. We examine three areas – first the emergence of new markets for carbon credits and their role in conservation policy, second certification, and third private parks.

It is also time to provide a conceptual framework that can make adequate sense of these interactions. Thus far we have presented the issues and problems associated with neoliberal conservation as an important and interesting puzzle that needs to be figured out. We have provided some potential explanations for different aspects of this puzzle, but we now need a comprehensive conceptual framework that could account for the seemingly paradoxical processes and relationships that we have described in the body of this book.

Any framework that is going to engage with biodiversity conservation and the concept of nature will need to deal with the physical environment and especially the place of people in the physical environment. However, it must also deal with ideas, images and representations, and these have become increasingly important with the global spread and increasing sophistication of electronic media. These media are now playing an increasingly important role in how many people conceptualize the environment and their place in the environment. It is our belief that images used in conservation, what we could call 'the Spectacle of Nature' is fast becoming one of the important ways in which capitalism and conservation are interacting and cooperating. The framework should also examine the conditions preceding and leading up to our current context. Finally, such a framework should address potential for fostering an environmental ethic, especially amongst middle class people in wealthy countries who are likely to support transnational conservation.

The framework we present begins with the ideas of Karl Marx and his observations about industrialization and liberal capitalism as a predecessor to our current context of neoliberal capitalism. Next we turn to the ideas of Jean Baudrillard and Guy Debord, who were concerned with the central role of images and media in shaping people's understandings of reality. Finally, we conclude with the question of environmental ethics and how these relate to this conceptual framework.

Conservation and carbon

The challenges posed by carbon dioxide increases and climate change to conservation policies are legion. In the first instance there are the physical changes of shifting ranges of species and habitat. Iconic centres of biodiversity such as the Cape Floral Kingdom and numerous isolated mountain habitats are more threatened as they have little space left to move to (southwards or upwards respectively) as climate warms. The growth of sugar and oil plantations for biofuels is becoming a major source of forest conversion and loss of habitat. At the same time it is widely recognized that measures to combat climate change such as reafforestation have only limited value because trees, after a certain age, leak carbon copiously. But the complexities of conservation and policy responses are fascinating because they demonstrate that concerns about carbon dioxide and greenhouse gases are becoming yet another means for conservation and capitalism to work closely together.

The construction of carbon markets demonstrates clearly the alliances that Sklair (2001) described, wherein the policies of sustainable development have been subsumed within a wider set of capitalist policies centred on consumerist ideologies. The main mechanisms of the Kyoto Protocol allow companies producing greenhouse gases to offset those emissions by investing in projects that either sequester carbon (typically in forestry) else that result in reduced greenhouse gas emissions from development projects. The Kyoto Protocol has led to jointly implemented schemes, in countries that have a commitment to reduce greenhouse gas emissions and which award emission reduction units, and the Clean Development Mechanism, which allows projects in countries without a requirement to reduce emissions to qualify for certified emission reductions. Companies with no requirement to reduce emissions also trade in verified and non-verified emission reduction schemes. Advocates of these schemes insist that they are an efficient means of reducing greenhouse gas emissions. Critics such as George Monbiot insist that this is just business as usual, that it is not reducing oil dependence and that ultimately coal and oil are better just left in the ground.

Carbon offsetting is seen as a potential income earner by many conservation organizations. It is common practice for NGO websites to include carbon calculators and offset sponsorship schemes on their websites. But the market is nascent. These schemes vary dramatically according to complicated technical issues concerning the relative importance of carbon to other climatic changes planes introduce, and the time period over which afforestation projects were considered to sequester carbon. Gossling and colleagues have analysed 41 different voluntary carbon offset schemes offered by a mixture of carbon trading companies and conservation NGOs specifically to compensate for flights. The amount of carbon produced for a given flight varied by up to a factor of five (0.27 to 1.5 CO_2 equivalent). The price offered per ton varied between €2.38 and €37.13. Overall the cost of offsetting the same flight varied by a factor of nearly 11 (€1.92 and €20.33). Moreover it was not always clear how much of the offset payments went to the scheme and how much to the administration costs of the organizations promoting them. They concluded that 'for individual customers, it is currently next to impossible to judge the real value of the credits they buy' (Gossling et al, 2007, p239).

Gossling and colleagues (2007) noted that there was a clear preference in the offsetting schemes they analysed to invest in forestry projects. Consumers prefer trees. This could lead to all sorts of benefits for conservation strategies. But there are clear limits to this policy. Other authors have noted that aviation offsets alone would fill all the space available for afforestation by 2050 (Boon et al, 2006, cited in Gossling et al, 2007). Nearly 30,000km^2 of new land would have to be afforested every year to offset the emissions of leisure aviation travel. More forest could be good for some conservation objectives but monoculture plantations that can result are not good for biodiversity. There are clear limits to the power of the business-as-usual scenario to deliver in the long run.

The Clean Development Mechanism is also not a good means of protecting forest on unprotected lands owned by rural communities because it does not currently admit averted deforestation as a valid source of carbon credit. Rural peoples in poorer parts of the world are thus unable to benefit from the carbon stored up in the vegetation all around them. This could change, and be a significant money earner, a means of providing valuable resources to poor communities, just as we have seen that arrangements with safari companies can be a lucrative money earner. But we have also seen that the local distribution of any form of income from forests (or wildlife) will be highly contested. The welcome income will be accompanied by restrictions on forest use and access that will be detrimental to some groups (charcoal burners, wood cutters, grazers). It is not clear that the people who lose most locally are compensated most when the money comes in. The reverse can be true (Dzingirai, 2003). As Brockington has argued elsewhere (and we discussed in Chapter 5) 'Community conservation is likely to consist of a myriad of marginalisations and inequalities enforced on smaller and smaller scales' (Brockington, 2004, p428). We welcome the news that rural groups can earn carbon credits for forest that remains standing on their land but also insist that the task of examining how these policies distributed fortune and misfortune remains as strong as ever.

Although rural communities cannot be incentivized not to cut down their trees through the current provisions of the Clean Development Mechanism, there is general recognition that deforestation is a major source of greenhouse gases. Stern noted that:

> Without prompt action emissions from deforestation between 2008 and 2012 are expected to total 40GT CO_2, which alone will raise atmospheric levels of CO_2 by -2ppm, greater than the cumulative total of aviation emissions from the invention of the flying machine until at least 2025.
>
> (Stern, 2007, p547)

Stern (2007) advocates reducing deforestation as a quick win that would contribute significantly to reducing the increase in carbon dioxide in the atmosphere. He notes that a programme costing \$10–15 billion a year could halve deforestation.[1]

Those sorts of sums could make a significant input on conservation strategies. But we were concerned by the tone of the Stern report, which repeatedly viewed conservation measures in a simplistic light and did not examine how they distributed fortune and misfortune to different groups. We have reproduced Box 25.1 from the Stern report to demonstrate the sort of thing we mean (Box 9.1). Compare that to the sorts of concerns that we were discussing in Chapter 5. Jesse Ribot's extensive review of deforestation did not appear in Stern's references.

Box 9.1. Local and Community ownership of forests

Latin America and South Asia have increasingly involved local communities in the ownership and stewardship of forests, and communities have often opted for more sustainable long-term programmes as a result. Another example is the Joint Forest Management Programme in India. This has both improved forest regeneration and had a positive impact on livelihoods. Similarly in Guatemala 13 community concessions, almost all certified by the Forest Stewardship Council, have managed to combine highly profitable mahogany enterprise with deforestation rates lower than in protected or outside areas.[a] Other approaches have allowed local communities to benefit from timber revenues. This helps promote local support. In Cameroon, for example, forest concessions were allocated through transparent auctions, with 50 per cent of the royalties going to local communities.[a]

[a] World Bank (2006) 'At Loggerheads? Agricultural expansion, poverty reduction, and environment in the tropical forests', Washington DC: World Bank
Source: Stern (2007, p541)

But with the sort of attention Stern advocates, protected areas harbouring tropical forest are likely to become increasingly valuable, and therefore increasingly attractive to both private companies and NGOs. They are already seen as a vehicle by which large companies can privately be offsetting the carbon that they produce. The environmentally conscious American Electrical Power is perhaps ahead of the game here, but may well represent the beginning of an increasingly popular trend. As part of a number of activities of corporate environmental responsibility it is sponsoring the Noel Kempff Mercado Park in Bolivia and the 17,000 acres of Atlantic Forest in Brazil.[2]

A similar scheme was supported by the Co-operative Bank in the UK. The bank's carbon offset programme included supporting the work of a company called Climate Care who were investing in a reafforestation in the Kibale National Park in Uganda as part of a package of measures that include wind turbines in India, fuel efficient stoves in Madagascar and the promotion of household energy efficiency in Pakistan. The bank had begun support in 2000 as a means of offsetting the carbon that was produced in association with its mortgages. It estimated that it will have offset 250,000 tonnes of carbon at the cost of $1.25 million by the end of 2007.

The Kibale project formed a substantial component of the bank's offset scheme. The bank estimated it will have received £500,000, resulting in the reforestation of 214 hectares of rainforest, sequestering 80,000 tonnes of carbon dioxide. However, it was the subject of a critical review by the BBC, which claimed that the people were being paid poor wages and suffered as a result of exclusion from the forest.[3] They specifically alleged that 'local people have lost access to vital resources that the forest once provided, such as firewood and water'.

We do not think that the low wages paid is such as important problem. Wages are generally extremely low in this country and the rates cited (£15 a month) are not particularly unusual. Moreover they are an additional resource in a poor area. We were more struck by the fact that the social impacts caused by this protected area on its nearby residents – the lost access to resources – had not seemed to be an important part of the decision making. When Brockington contacted Paul Monaghan, who was Head of Ethics and Sustainability at the Co-operative Bank, he was told that the park had been established 75 years ago, and that there were agreements with the local communities in place that allowed them to collect fallen wood, cut invasive species and elephant grass, and keep bees in the park. Monaghan also noted that 'this project is not designed to tackle poverty as a primary objective' (pers. comm. January 2007). However, we received no response to our request for more information about the park's impact on local livelihoods. The Co-operative Bank portrayed the scheme as beneficial to local livelihoods. But it is not clear to us whether the nature of the impacts of the protected area had been properly investigated.

The case is a specific example of a much wider problem – what will the local social impacts of carbon offset policies be? Currently the main push is to sequester carbon in forests if possible, and reduce deforestation rates. However, the implications of these policies for forest residents and the neighbours of protected areas have simply not been considered. Participants of the International Community Forestry Workshop of the Canadian Environmental Network agreed a resolution that lobbied the participants of the United Nations Climate Change Conference in Bali. This noted that forest dwellers' rights and livelihoods were not sufficiently prominent in the discussion. In 2007 the Royal Society and the Global Biodiversity Sub-Committee of the UK Global Environmental Change Committee met to examine the associated problems of biodiversity, climate change and poverty alleviation. But the meeting was virtually silent on livelihoods, to the consternation of a number of participants (Willis and Homewood pers. comm. September 2007). The report of the workshop outlined research priorities that made no mention of the need to examine the local impacts of policies to cope with climate change. Just as local rights and livelihoods have been forgotten in past conservation imperatives that saw the establishment of protected areas, so the new impetus to conserve in order to cope with carbon and climate change could result in a new set of oversights.

Certification

One of the means by which market mechanisms cope with the confusing barrage of information that environmentally conscious consumers have to cope with if they are to make environmentally responsible choices is certification. Certification is one example of an aspect of neoliberalism: the increasing standardization and regulation of activities. This form of standardization fits perfectly with notions of governance as a technical project that seeks to create a fix that is 'one size fits all'. As will be made clear below, such forms of governance involve the creation of rules and standards that will inevitably rely on a process of inclusion and exclusion. Therefore, certification as a form of governance will result in the uneven distribution of fortune and misfortune.

Perhaps the best-known certification schemes, however, are the forest certification schemes that provide easily visible and identifiable labels reassuring consumers that their products are from environmentally responsible sources. Certification provides a means of applying consumer pressure to forest management. A group of 51 NGOs and institutions have pooled their skills to introduce certification of carbon offset schemes (The Gold Standard).[4] Certification has also been mooted for schemes that make payments to rural villages for hunting or wildlife viewing safaris (Child, pers. comm. 2004). This could make it possible for clients to know how the extra revenues that they are contributing towards local development are being spent.

The problem is that there are numerous certification schemes: Forest Stewardship Council (FSC); Canadian Standard Association's Sustainable Forest Management Standard; Sustainable Forestry Initiative; Pan European Forest Certification (PEFC) (Ozinga, 2001). The value of the system depends entirely on the standards that it uses and the rigour with which independent observers apply them. It is entirely possible for certification bodies to be subservient to groups who wish to gain the security of the label but not apply the rigours of management.

Ozinga (2001) compared the work of several certification schemes (Table 9.1). He noted substantial differences between them. Consider for example the FSC and PEFC. The former operates in 40 countries and had certified 221,657km^2 in 2001. The latter, set up to provide a certification scheme more appropriate to Europe, works in five countries and had certified 322,370km^2. The FSC was generally more rigorous in its criteria. It demanded assessment and compliance based on actual performance and site visits. In contrast he noted that PEFC had effectively lower standards, and sometimes did not require site visits. Instead certifiers relied on management plans.

In some ways the FSC represents one of the highest standards of conservation policy in existence. It has three chambers, environmental, economic and social, who examine different aspects of forest management plans, all of which have to be adequate for certification to be awarded. At the same time the transaction costs required to implement certification are considerable and effectively make the scheme inaccessible to poorer rural communities. There is also a problem of consumer awareness. Currently a significant proportion of the market in the UK is driven by the actions of large purchasers such as department stores such as B&Q – a do-it-yourself store that sells raw timber and processed products. There is still little wider public recognition of the brand and its meaning. The complexities of the supply lines also cause difficulties. Many products (especially things like chipboard) involve wood from all sorts of sources, some of which are certified and some not.

Table 9.1 *Comparing the FSC and PEFC*

Forestry Practice	FSC	PEFC
Indig. people's rights	Requires respect for Sami customary grazing rights	Requires dialogue but no respect for Sami customary grazing rights
Set aside areas	5% of productive forest land	0–5% of productive forest land
Harvesting in mountains	Restricted	No specific restrictions
Protection of key biotopes	Protected	Temporarily but not permanently restricted
Retention of eternity	10 trees per hectare	5–10 trees per hectare trees
Use of fertilisers	Restricted	Not restricted
Use of chemicals	Relatively strict	Less strict
Ecological landscape planning required	Yes (>5000ha)	No requirements

Private parks

One of the most important developments in conservation in the last two decades is the growth in privately owned protected areas. These differ from parks and conservation initiatives that are merely funded (partly or wholly) through donations from private individuals, foundations and corporations. As we have discussed elsewhere, philanthropists and corporate investment in state-owned protected areas have key roles to play in terms of funding and supporting existing initiatives. However, the growth of 'private parks' signifies something quite different from state-based approaches to parks, and their arrival on the conservation scene raises a series of very difficult questions about the long-term future of parks. The debates centre on the capacity for privatized wildlife conservation to provide a solution to a complex knot of issues: paying for conservation when the state cannot or will not fund it, securing genuine community participation and involvement, and ability to deal with issues surrounding questions about who has the right to own land. They also raise the ethical issues associated with enforcement and anti-poaching patrols carried out by private 'armies' of rangers, as discussed elsewhere in this book. Finally, private parks also raise questions about the nature and suitability of private investment in conservation for long-term conservation of species and habitats.

The debate over whether the state or the private sector is best able to manage the environment is divided. The market and the state can be characterized as two different sets of management principles. The state is usually preferred as a wildlife manager because it is widely perceived as a publicly accountable institution that can devise management plans and has the capacity to implement them. In contrast, supporters of private parks argue that individuals seek to promote their own welfare and so protect the resources on which their welfare depends, and also because economic values for resources provide the most efficient way of allocating resources. Nevertheless, private parks have raised some fears and concerns. For example, if we assume that the private sector will be interested in profit in the longer term, then we must consider what the implications are for conservation if a privately owned protected area fails to become financially viable. In the case of investment by philanthropic individuals and foundations where profit may not be as important, then the long-term future of conservation through private parks may still be problematic because foundations can decide to change the focus for funding, and individual endowments may run out.

Private parks have been enthusiastically taken up in southern Africa. In Zimbabwe for example, the creation of private conservancies was welcomed as significant innovation in conservation in the 1990s. From the 1960s wildlife conservation was increasingly transferred to the private sector through policies that encouraged the devolution of authority and responsibility for wildlife to the landholder, coupled with the definition of wildlife as an economic resource. This approach was further consolidated in the 1975 Parks and Wildlife Act, which defined the *appropriate authority* for wildlife management on private land and commercial farms as the owner or occupier of that land. This trend arose out of fears that wildlife was rapidly disappearing outside the state-based national parks and reserves system. Wildlife populations within protected areas were becoming increasingly isolated, some parks were overpopulated by certain species because traditional migration routes were cut off between national parks. The transfer of conservation to the private sector was also intended to serve two other purposes – to ease pressure on falling budgets for wildlife, and make wildlife less subject to personal interests and power struggles in the government (Duffy, 2000). Privatizing wildlife conservation in this way clearly intersected with viewing wildlife as a commercial resource, or commodity, to be exploited like any other.

In post-independence Zimbabwe, the notion of privatized wildlife was politically controversial in terms of domestic politics, given the centrality of the land question and the continued racial disparity in land ownership. This was especially acute because the conservancies were developed by grouping together former cattle ranches, removing fences between them and restocking with wildlife. The conservancies (or private parks) were to become financially viable and profitable through the development of wildlife tourism, including sport hunting. As Wolmer suggests, the notion that the south east lowveld in Zimbabwe is not suited to arable farming for subsistence or cash crop production persisted as a powerful vehicle for arguing that the area should be given over to wilderness and wildlife ranching (Wolmer, 2007). In addition, the conservancies became core members of the national strategy for black rhino conservation through their creation of 'Intensive Protection Zones' (IPZs) for rhinos. These were essentially 'parks within parks' – a small area of land in the centre of a conservancy or national park that had higher levels of security to protect the black rhino. Therefore, the conservancies could legitimately claim to be engaged in internationally vital conservation of rare species, as well as ensuring that the land (which remained in the hands of white farmers) was used in the most economically productive way possible through servicing the international tourism industry. One of the most well known was the Save Valley Conservancy in the south east lowveld, which developed an upscale luxury tourist lodge in the 1990s (Duffy, 2000; Wels, 2003; Wolmer, 2007, pp116–143).

Critics of the conversion of land to this form of 'wildlife ranching' (as it is often called) pointed out that initiative was really about sidestepping the post-independence government's stated commitment from 1990 to compulsory purchase of land that was defined as 'underutilized'. This meant that the large white-owned cattle ranches of the midlands and south east lowveld had to demonstrate that they were using their ranches to full effect, and one way of doing so was to take advantage of the global growth in wildlife-based tourism. Furthermore, the conservancies also faced the same problem with boundary demarcation as national parks. In order for conservancies/game ranches to survive as wildlife conservation areas they require game fences to prevent the movement of wildlife onto farmland. For example Wels' study of private parks in Zimbabwe effectively demonstrates how the designation of conservancies/game ranches still relied on fences so that the fence became the 'white signature on the land' (Wels, 2003). According to Wels, these fences constituted a barrier to developing genuine reciprocal relations between communities and conservancies in both physical and symbolic terms. The demarcation of the boundaries for these private parks then created a sense amongst local communities that fences had written the message 'white land only' onto the landscape.

These concerns about the development of private parks and their implications for land redistribution have also arisen in the growth of private reserves in South Africa. Rather like Zimbabwe, South Africa is still marked by racially unequal land distribution that was established during the apartheid era, and many former cattle ranches have been turned over into wildlife ranches to take advantage of international tourism. The issue has even been the subject of a Sunday evening 'feel good' soap/drama on British television (*Wild at Heart*) that featured a British family struggling to develop a wildlife ranch. The private parks of South Africa cover a range of different tourism markets ranging from sport hunting through to upscale luxury eco-lodges with golf courses and spas. Sabi Sabi Reserve and Singita private eco-lodge have also been promoted as a means by which the 'boundaries' of the Kruger National Park can be extended. Kruger is bordered by a series of private reserves, which increase the area available for wildlife. Overall the country has 13 per cent of its land mass inside private protected areas, and only 6 per cent in state protection. Each reserve offers a slightly different variation on the wildlife tourism theme. For example, Conservation Corporation Africa (CC Africa) operates Bongani Mountain Lodge, a mid-range eco-resort in a private reserve that borders Kruger. Its variation on the product is that, unlike in the national park, the safari vehicles can drive off-road and get very close to the animals; and its landscape is more suited to (and attractive to) leopards than many parts of the state-owned park. CC Africa claims that it has joined forces with the local communities to establish one of South Africa's pioneering conservation initiatives:

> Our project develops our vision of sustainable, community-based ecotourism. Bongani Mountain Lodge is committed to CC Africa's core principle: Care of the Land, Care of the Wildlife, Care of the People.[5]

Therefore, as this example demonstrates, private parks are able to resonate with many of the global debates about conservation practice, including community conservation and commitment to wildlife conservation, rather than articulating their project in terms of a profit motive. The private parks are clearly part of the global growth of 'super luxury' ecotourism, as discussed earlier in this book. In line with this, the luxury safari lodges have also linked with the growth of medical tourism to South Africa to offer 'surgery and safari' tours. The 'Surgeon and Safari Company' matches up clients for cosmetic, ophthalmic, orthopaedic and dental surgery with safaris where they can recuperate from surgery in privacy.[6] One of the private reserves recommended by Surgeon and Safari is Tswalu, owned and operated by the Oppenheimer family.[7]

However, the growth of private reserves is not without its problems. For example, in conservation terms a number of private reserves have been criticized for offering 'canned hunting' of big cats, or for converting large areas to golf courses. This is apart from the wider questions about their implication for land redistribution in South Africa, the (often dubious) authority used for enforcement and anti-poaching patrols, and the concerns about the long-term viability for conservation purposes should the reserves become unprofitable. Doubts have also been raised about the fate of former farm workers, although some studies show a dramatic rise in employment demands on game ranches (Luck, 2003; Connor, 2006; Langholz and Kerley, 2006)

Marx, liberal capitalism and seeing nature from inside the box

To provide a conceptual framework for the sorts of changes we have witnessed we must return to the writings of Marx. Marx's concern about industrialization was that it alienated objects from people, thereby alienating people from themselves

(Marx, 1976 (1867)). What he meant by this was that in the past, people used resources from their environment to create objects that would be useful to them. If a blacksmith made a cooking pot, or a carpenter created a cabinet, the producers felt innately connected to the objects they produced. Moreover, these objects were seen as an extension of the person. They were seen this way for two reasons: 1) social relations between people were mediated through the production and exchange of those objects; and 2) because there was a close association between the person's sense of self and the object, as the object was an expression of the person's creativity.

According to Marx (1978 (1865–1870)), this basic relationship between people and objects changed dramatically with the first industrial revolution, which occurred in the late 18th century in the UK, from where it quickly spread to the rest of Europe and North America. This revolution revolved around the creation of the machine. The machine allowed human beings to: 1) capture fuel from the environment; 2) use the fuel to do work; and 3) to mass produce objects that are always the same.

These transformations not only transformed objects, but the social relationships between people that were mediated by the production and exchange of those objects. To operate these machines it became necessary to find large numbers of unskilled labourers. Mass-produced objects could no longer be seen as an extension of people and their creativity and they no longer circulated according to social relationships and use value, but according to the demands of the market and exchange value, which was measured in wholly abstract terms. These transformations were closely associated with what Marx called 'commodity fetishism'. In an industrial context, the exchange value (price) of commodities became much more important than their use value. In fact, human labour became just another commodity, and by extension humans became just another commodity, in that people were now required to work for a wage and then buy the things that they needed. In this context, it became impossible to know anything about the origins of commodities. They appeared on the shelves of shops as though by magic. Commodity fetishism refers to this context, in which people purchase and consume commodities without any knowledge of their socio-historical context.

The use of certification and private parks for conservation purposes hinges on the fetishization of commodities. It is only because commodities appear as if by magic, concealing all the social interactions that produced them, and the ecological costs and exchanges, that we require certification to reassure us that some care has been taken in the production of these commodities. But note the irony here – the certification is itself a form of fetishization, a symbol stamped on a product guaranteeing its sanctity, but through processes largely invisible and not understood by most consumers. Similarly, conserving through private parks attempts to use the security of commodified land to promote conservation. The land taken from its previous social contexts, alienated and sold. Only it is precisely these processes that cause tension with former farm workers in South Africa.

Towards the end of his career, Marx also became concerned that commodities were being taken out of their ecological context as well (Marx, 1971 (1875); Marx, 1978 (1863–65)). The specific terminology that Marx applied to this phenomenon was what he called the metabolic rift – a term that he borrowed from Liebig (Foster, 1999). Marx observed that industrialization and urbanization were transforming agriculture in Europe and North America by disrupting nutrient cycles (Liebig, 1859). These problems intensified over time, as fertilizers came to be derived from petrochemicals, and more industrialized forms of agriculture not only mined nutrients from the soil but also depleted water tables. A second aspect of the metabolic rift concerned the growing divide between the rural and the urban context, as products from the farm increasingly had to be shipped to urban centres where they could be sold for consumption (Gever et al, 1986). Over time, therefore, the whole systems became increasingly dependent on fossil fuels and the global infrastructure that supported them (Robbins, 2004).

The metabolic rift suggests an extractive and linear conception of and relationship to nature. In this conceptualization, everything is measured in terms of its exchange value, which allows for total fungibility between circulating objects. In other words, there is assumed to be a single standard of value, whereby the value of one thing can be objectively and qualitatively measured against the value of anything else. Figure 9.1 illustrates how this way of thinking about nature can be conceptualized.

In this paradigm nature is conceived as a factory, or perhaps more accurately a magic black box. Inputs such as water, fertilizer, pesticides and seeds are put in one end. Outputs, such as corn, beef, coffee and the like come out the other end. Since everything is measured in money all that matters in this case is that the value of '$2' is greater than the value of '$1'. As long as more dollars come out of the magic black box than are put into the magic black box, then the system works. Furthermore as long as the demand for outputs remains high, then there will be an incentive to find more inputs, be they fossil fuels, water or whatever resource is required.

THE METABOLIC RIFT AND THE BLACK BOX OF PRODUCTIVE NATURE

Figure 9.1 *The metabolic rift and the black box of productive nature*

This paradigm ignores two aspects of the relationships it describes. First, it does not account for social or ecological costs. If the process of changing inputs into outputs should damage people and/or the environment, it will not be registered so long as this damage does not have to be paid for in dollars. Even when the damage does has to be paid for in dollars, it is usually devalued to such an extent that it remains profitable. Hence we see that profit can be derived at a great expense to people and the environment so long as such expenses are not calculated in dollars that must be paid by the people and/or firms who are realizing the profit.

Next this paradigm assumes an infinite planet. The idea being that as long as there is an economic incentive to find more oil, water or whatever, that someone will be innovative enough to find more of the resource in question. They may find oil in the tar shale of Alberta, or they may find an innovative way to pump water from the great lakes to the American south west. If these types of solutions are not possible then they will find a substitute that can do the same work as the resource in question (Simon, 1981).

There are two problems here. The first, simply stated, is that the earth does not take MasterCard®. If there is no oil or water in the ground, it does not matter how much someone is willing to pay for it, they simply will not be able to have it. Setting aside resources for which there are no substitutes, like clean air and water, the argument about substitution is more substantial. We can, for instance, substitute wind and solar power for fossil fuels. It is questionable, however, whether profit motive is an appropriate driver for this transition (Robbins, 2004). The development of alternative fuels and technologies will require an upfront investment of fossil fuels to get the job done, but so long as it is more profitable to sell fossil fuels for other types of consumption there will be little incentive to invest in developing alternative technologies. From this perspective, high demand for a commodity may actually be the undoing of the global economy.

These problems are part of what Marx called the contradictions of capitalism, which he believed would lead to an inevitable crisis in capitalism and hence to a socialist revolution. Ecological Marxists such as O'Connor (1988) hold out hope that the ecological crisis resulting from capitalist expansion will prompt the types of social transformations necessary to create an economy that is simultaneously green and socialist. What this would amount to basically is people becoming aware of the types of social and ecological exchanges that are occurring in the black box of nature and the types of damage they cause. More immediately for many people, another important question becomes, 'What is it costing me?' Bringing about this type of awareness is a special kind of challenge since it requires people not only to see the connections between their consumption and environmental problems, but also for them to conclude that it is in their own interest to voluntarily reduce their consumption.

Another area of hope is that people will develop new types of environmental sensibilities by identifying more strongly with nature and that these sensibilities will be successfully promoted by the global conservation movement. But we must appreciate the problems inherent here and the relationship of conservation and ecotourism to the concepts of fetishization and the metabolic rift. As we saw in Chapter 6, parks, as landscapes of consumption, operate according to similar logics as the black box of productive nature. In this case, however, we are dealing with the green box of consumptive nature (Figure 9.2). Like the black box of productive nature, the green box of consumptive nature is a magic box. It is also apparently disconnected from the rest of the world in terms of its social and ecological costs, as well as its ecology in general. Animals, landscapes and ecosystemic processes appear as though by magic, with no reference to the historical ecological processes that allowed them to appear. As opposed to the black box of productive nature, which is presented as having no ecological costs, the green box of consumptive nature is presented as being immune from the types of ecological impacts that capitalism is having on the wider world. As such, it can be set aside for the purposes of science, to monitor and measure the ways in which 'undisturbed' nature works. It is also set aside for profits, since people will pay to see this undisturbed nature. Increasingly, in doing so, they are led to believe that they are doing their bit to protect the environment. They are protecting nature through consumption; here again ecology is often conflated with a particular view.

Like the black box of productive nature, therefore, the green box of consumptive nature is a for-profit box. Dollars are put in one end, in terms of investment, and more dollars come out the other. Unlike the black box of productive nature, however, which forbids people from seeing inside, the green box of consumptive nature welcomes people in. Tourists enter the green box of nature along with money, and 'tourist prime' come out the other end. 'Tourist prime' is an individual who has been transformed by his or her passage through the green box of consumptive nature. This transformation depends heavily on what she or he has seen and experienced, which is in turn limited by the parameters of the box, what it makes visible, and what it renders invisible.

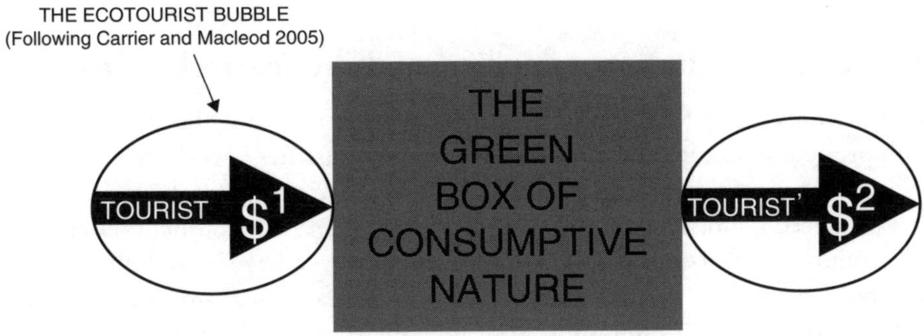

Figure 9.2 *The ecotourism bubble and the green box of consumptive nature*

Source: Following Carrier and Macleod, 2005.

Carrier and Macleod's idea of the ecotourism bubble, as outlined in Chapter 7, is also an essential element of the green box of consumptive nature. As we explained in Chapter 7, the tourist experience is an especially mediated experience. Tourists pay to have particular experiences of people and places, and tour companies and governments work hard to deliver those particular views and experiences. Therefore, it is not enough to imagine tourism as taking place inside a green magic box; the micro-management of tourists actually involves the constant creation and maintenance of these views and experiences. Tourists often do not connect their consumption of nature with the ecological costs of burning jet fuel, or if they do the black box of productive nature allows them to imagine that this problem can be resolved by paying a carbon offset. Tourists also remain for the most part unaware of the social costs of the views that they enjoy: what people were displaced to make this view possible and what were the costs of this displacement to them. People who they meet in 'cultural villages' or handicraft stands appear as though they were unproblematically waiting around for their culture to be consumed. Ecotourists are also presented with nature in ways that render invisible the temporal and spatial scopes of ecological processes.

This brief discussion suggests an alarming correspondence between the black box of productive nature and the green box of consumptive nature: both function to conceal the ecological connections of people's daily consumptive practices. Moreover, the green box of consumptive tourism also apparently absolves people of responsibility for their consumptive practices. Marxist concepts of alienation, fetishization and the metabolic rift are all useful for helping us to understand how conservation in the context of liberal capitalism ironically often contributes to the very types of relationships and processes that it seeks to mitigate. One of conservation's main challenges in this context, therefore, is to find innovative ways of helping people see the ecology of their consumptive practices through connections to the environment. This is a task that is rendered doubly difficult by the transformations that have recently occurred in global capitalism, which we will call 'the neoliberal turn'.

Neoliberalism, disaster capitalism and the spectacle of nature

Marxist concepts of fetishization helps us to understand how liberal regimes of both productive nature and consumptive nature construct a world of circulating objects that appear divorced from the historical, political and ecological contexts that produced them. The same is true of landscapes and environments consumed by ecotourists and ecocapitalists. Recent years, however, have been dominated by neoliberal capitalism. As the name suggests, neoliberal capitalism carries forward key elements of liberal capitalism, most notably its emphasis on small states and free markets. However, neoliberal capitalism also differs from liberal capitalism quantitatively and qualitatively. Quantitatively, neoliberalism revolves around an acceleration and proliferation of economic activity: a 24–7 business model, more money in circulation, increased numbers of exchanges and parties to exchanges, the proliferation of subcontracting and outsourcing, more commodities being created and destroyed in order to generate increased demand, more consumers being brought into the world economy, and more types of value being created and circulated as broadly as possible (Urry and Lash, 1987; Appadurai, 1996; Klein, 2007). These quantitative changes appear to have occurred, and continue to be occurring, in spite of the impending crises in liberal capitalism predicted by Marx and environmental Marxists (Menzies, 1989).

In order for these quantitative changes to be possible, qualitative changes also had to take place. Some of these were similar to the types of changes that accompanied the emergence of liberal capitalism in the late 19th century. These 19th-century changes revolved around the ascendancy of corporations and the deregulation of trade in order to facilitate the spread of free markets. According to Polanyi (2001 (1944)) the negative socio-economic consequences of these transformations became so acute with the world depression of the 1930s that they prompted the enlightened emergence of economic regulation, consumer protection and the rise of the welfare state. This 'great transformations', started to be 'rolled back' in the early 1980s. This is the period most commonly associated with the rise of neoliberalism.

Peck and Tickell argue that while neoliberalism began with 'rolling back' the welfare state and the regulation of corporations and commerce, it ultimately advanced to the 'rolling out' of new types of states and governance (Peck and Tickell, 2002). 'Roll back' neoliberalism of the 1980s is associated with the downsizing of state bureaucracies, the deregulation of trade and industry, and the restructuring of developing world economies by international financial institutions in order to facilitate the spread of free market capitalism. By the mid-1990s, however, most of this work had been effectively completed. Roll back neoliberalism gradually shifted to 'roll out' neoliberalism. While roll back neoliberalism revolved around the concept of deregulation, roll out neoliberalism revolved around re-regulation – the use of newly emerging forms of 'neoliberal states' to facilitate the transformation of previously untradable things and ideas into commodities that are visible and tradable in the world capitalist economy (McAfee, 1999; Castree, 2007a, b). As with liberal capitalism, these commodities include things like natural resources and labour. As will be addressed in detail below, however, they increasingly include new types of virtual commodities, which are far less tangible but no less valuable.

Unfortunately, these transformations appear to mitigate the kinds of social consciousness predicted by green Marxists like O'Connor by apparently resolving the contradictions between economic growth and the protection of nature. As Sklair has argued (2001), the job of resolving these contradictions has been undertaken by what he labelled 'the transnational capitalist class'. Members of this class, he argues, collectively act to promote global economic growth based on the 'cultural-ideology of consumerism', by colluding to offer solutions to the environmental crises inherent to global consumer capitalism, while strengthening an consumerist ideology. The central message that members of this class promote is that not only is consumption compatible with the conservation of natural resources, it is actually essential to it. As such, members of this transnational capitalist class direct the global spread of neoliberal processes, but they simultaneously work to resolve the types of crises that Marx and environmental Marxists believe to be inherent to global capitalism. As such, it thus far appears that neoliberalism has been impervious to the kinds of shocks and backlashes that plagued liberal capitalism in the mid-20th century.

In fact, Naomi Klein (2007) goes so far as to argue that the very crises created by neoliberal capitalism themselves become commodities and opportunities for profit. The political instability that has accompanied the spread of neoliberalism, along with 'natural disasters', allows corporations, NGOs and governments to pursue new types of revenues and profits. In a tragic contradiction to the optimistic predictions of environmental Marxists, it appears that the more politically and environmentally messed up the world becomes, the more that neoliberalism will continue to thrive. The phenomenon of disaster capitalism can be seen in both the day-to-day mundane and the more dramatic aspects of our current environmental crisis.

The mundane aspects can be seen in the increased prominence of the idea of 'mitigating services', the idea that conservation can offset the ecological impacts of economic growth, as we have seen in the discussion above of carbon offsetting. A dramatic example of disaster capitalism can be seen in the destruction that Hurricane Katrina wrought on the gulf coast of the US, which has meant boom times for Home Depot, construction firms and private security companies (Giroux, 2006). Perhaps most ironically, the suffering and displacement of local people has been commoditized in the context of New Orleans' tourist economy, as 'devastation tours' have become an increasingly popular part of the tourist experience (Neves and Igoe, in production).

The value of these types of commodities depends a great deal on sophisticated and deceptive representations of the world. This is the final major difference between liberal capitalism and neoliberal capitalism. The hyper acceleration of the world economy and the rise of disaster capitalism have been accompanied by what Baudrillard (1981, 1993) calls the emergence of hyperreality. On a most basic level hyperreality refers to the inability to distinguish imagination from reality, in fact it involves the possibility of 'knowing' experience that one has never had. In a world dominated by media and images we are presented with what appears to be a coherent and neatly bound reality. Baudrillard takes this argument even further, arguing that hyperreality is powerful because of the resemblances that it bears to actual reality. The essential difference, however, is that hyperreality presents a simulation of the world that is coherent and bounded in ways that the real world could never be. People then view the real world through the filter of these simulations, which has the effect of selectively bringing forth the things in the real world that fit the logic of these simulations, while concealing those aspects of the real world that do not fit. From this perspective, actual reality appears as just another simulation, indistinguishable from all the other simulations of it. As such, hyperreality begins to remake the world according to its own logic.

In the realm of conservation, the effects of these hyperreal processes are visible in new types of virtual consumption that actually transform the material world. Authors such as Duffy (2002, 2004) and West and Carrier (2004) have shown how tourists' desires and expectations change the places they visit, reforming them according to their visitors' imaginations. They act, in other words as virtualisms, which Carrier (1998) defines as models of reality that are 'prescriptive not descriptive'. When reality differs from the model, it is reality – not the model – that is expected to change. More concretely, we can think of virtualisms as collections of images, ideas, discourses and values that reproduce the material world according to ways that they imagine it to be. West and Carrier (2004, p485) observe that the image of natural environments that western ecotourists expect to see is that of a nature 'separate from and prior to humanity', from which people should be kept separate. Accordingly, meeting tourists' needs often requires removing people from nature or at least disciplining their activities vis-à-vis natural resources and their interactions with tourists.

The power of international tour companies is such that they can effect transformations in landscapes and the everyday lives of remote communities. As we discussed previously, beaches are built, wildernesses are produced and wildlife populations are actively managed to satisfy tourist imaginings of a truly 'natural' experience. Some examples of the power of tourism to delimit, define and discipline everyday life and landscapes are quite extreme. Consider for example an eco-lodge in the Chiang Mai area of northern Thailand. Lisu Lodge[8] runs a profit sharing scheme with the local Lisu community and has begun a reforestation project, Himmapaan, which will allow tourists to care for and plant seedlings as part of their vacation experience. These activities are to be promoted as a means by which tourists can offset the carbon footprint of their holiday, but will obviously change the landscape of the area earmarked for reforestation. Furthermore, the power of the international tour companies in transforming the landscapes and lives of communities around the lodge came into sharp focus during bird flu scares. The tour operators needed to respond to queries and concerns of their customers about what steps would be taken by their hotels and lodges to prevent the spread of bird flu. The local communities, like many rural communities, had over 2000 chickens running freely around the village. To satisfy the concerns of the international tour operators the lodge asked the community to kill all the chickens, which they (understandably) refused to do. A compromise was reached after discussions between the lodge and community and the lodge paid to build three chicken coops one kilometre from the village. All the chickens were caught and placed in the coops for five months until Thailand was declared safe from bird flu.

We take this argument further: virtualisms remake the environment even in the absence of tourists. In turning their expectant gaze on protected areas, conservation NGOs, donors and their corporate sponsors apply similar virtualisms of nature to the places they seek to protect, and with similar results. Protected areas and their associated virtualisms are part of a global economy of images, which extends far beyond the reach of mere tourist receipts and specific tracts of land.

Sometimes the images are commodities in themselves (Ansel Adams prints, costing $225 individually) or in coffee table books and postcards.[9] But more pervasively, they are produced or purchased by other organizations as part of larger projects. Images of conserved nature on credit cards, or company calendars, in television adverts, in posters and glossy brochures all proclaim individuals', companies' and organizations' stewardship over nature. This is not a new thing. Edward Abbey commented on it in his fictional account *The Monkey Wrench Gang* (1975):

> He watched the news. Same as yesterday's. The General Crisis
> coming along nicely. Nothing new except the commercials full of sly
> art and eco-porn. Scenes of the Louisiana bayous, strange birds in
> slow-motion flight, cypress trees bearded with Spanish moss. Above
> the primeval scene the voice of Power spoke, reeking with sincerity,
> in praise of itself, the Exxon Oil Company – its tidiness, its
> fastidious care for all things wild, its concern for human needs.

But since Abbey wrote, the economy of images has proliferated through the multiplication of magazines, cable and satellite television and the growth of the internet and the emergence and expansion of markets for these media globally.

Protected areas and conservation work therefore are not just consumed when tourists visit them. Rather, they become part of what Debord (1995 (1967)) referred to as Spectacle. Guy Debord, who in turn influenced Baudrillard, applied Marx's ideas of alienation and fetishization to images and imagination. Accordingly, he argued that Spectacle was alienated experience achieved through the fetishization of images. Through mass media, people were presented with collections of images removed from the social and political context of their production, such that they mistook these imaginary images for the real. Significantly, Debord argued that Spectacle encouraged the consumption of commodities, but was also a commodity in and of itself, which people would pay to consume.

The commodification of nature as virtualism and Spectacle has profound socio-ecological implications. Spectacle, as defined by Debord, is self-referential; in Gregory Bateson terms, it is a 'closed dialectic loop'. In such a loop, two ideas and or processes are in dialogue with little or no reference to external information (Bateson and Bateson, 1988). In our case, virtualisms of wilderness inform the creation of protected areas (cf. West and Carrier, 2004). As this occurs, an iterative process develops. The images and ideas of these landscapes become the source for the production of more virtualisms. These virtualisms in turn become the source for the production of more 'wilderness' landscapes. The dialogues occurring between these landscapes and the virtualisms that informed their production become increasingly impervious to ideas and arguments that are not derived from the realities they describe and prescribe. In this context, protected areas become hyperreal spaces, in which the lines between western fantasies about nature and actual experiences of nature become dangerously blurred (Baudrillard, 1993).[10] They simultaneously facilitate the production of a 'Spectacle of Nature' that circulates in the global consumer economy.

These processes have effects that are more insidious and potentially devastating than the black box and green box of liberal capitalism. Increasingly, the ascendancy of images and virtual consumption has facilitated what Tsing (2004) calls spectacular accumulation, in which images and ideas are used to mobilize resources through transnational networks of people, most of whom are not even aware of each other's existence. These resources may be mobilized for profit or other causes. Specifically she shows how the idea of frontiers and rugged individualism were used to fire the imagination of Canadian investors to invest in gold prospecting in Indonesia. The mining company was successful in mobilizing significant investment, though the no gold was ever found.

Spectacular accumulation is also visible in the ways in which mainstream conservation operates in the context of global neoliberalism by inviting people to identify with particular environments and to associate those environments with particular products, experiences and celebrities. For instance, The 2004 newsletter of the African Wildlife Fund (AWF) features a photograph of CEO Patrick Bergin with Burton Robbins of the popular 'reality' show SURVIVOR Pearl Islands. A banner at the bottom of the same page proclaims: 'the AWF and Starbucks Team Up for Africa!' Text in the box below encourages readers to visit a website where they can sign up for the Starbucks Duetto Visa Card. With their first purchase on the card, $5 is donated to the AWF.[11] Conversely, consumers can sign up for an AWF platinum visa card, featuring 'a magnificent elephant with ears extended, a giraffe with spectacular Mt. Kilimanjaro as its backdrop, or a pensive mountain gorilla looking right at you'.[12] When the cardholder makes a purchase – of a Starbuck's latte for instance – a percentage of that purchase goes to the AWF. Meanwhile the AWF and Starbucks are 'blending coffee with conservation' in Kenya's Samburu heartland to help bring small-scale coffee farmers into the market and out of elephant corridors.[13]

As the name suggests, spectacular accumulation revolves centrally around spectacle as both a commodity and a means of selling other commodities. In this way, as Debord (1995 (1967)) argued, it conditions people to be passive, while teaching them that the only viable path to action and efficacy is through consumption. People can consume 'the Spectacle of Nature' from a hot air balloon above the Serengeti, at Disney's Animal Kingdom Lodge, at the Rainforest Café, in an IMAX theatre, or sitting in their living room watching 'Critter Cam' on *Wild*

Chronicles sponsored by *National Geographic* and the World Wildlife Fund.[14] All of these experiences are commodities in themselves. Through the spread of ecotourism and protected areas they facilitate an ever widening flow of money, images and values and bring more and more of the planet's surface into the ambit of consumptive experiences and the production of more valuable spectacle. As we have already seen above, these spectacular commodities can be used to sell lots of other commodities such as coffee, Disney merchandise, compact discs, SUVs, gasoline and jet fuel. They can also be used for green public image enhancement for corporations such as Exxon, following the Valdez oil spill (Dowie, 1996) and Dow Chemicals, experiencing renewed pressure for the methyl isocyanate spill that killed over 3000 people in Bhopal India in 1984 (Fortun, 2001).[15]

The Spectacle of Nature also teaches consumers that their only course of ethical environmental action is through consumption that supports the work of more qualified people to save the world. Sting and Mike Fay will save the rainforest. Oprah and Bono will save the people of Africa. Sean Penn will save the people of New Orleans. As part of their purchased experience, visitors to Disney's Animal Kingdom can enjoy the spectacle of 'the vet team on stage'. Visitors are able to watch through glass and ask questions, while Disney vets perform examinations on exotic animals using high-tech equipment and educating viewers about the importance of their efforts to the future of global ecosystems (Stevens, 2005, p16). Animal Kingdom 'cast members' also travel to different parts of the world as part of conservation expeditions.[16] When visitors stay at the Animal Kingdom Lodge, simulacra of luxury lodges in African parks, they are encouraged to make a contribution to the Disney Wildlife Conservation Fund, which funds expert wildlife researchers and organizations like the AWF to continue protecting nature and wildlife on their behalf.[17]

Helping people and the environment in this context becomes a simple proposition. The AWF's 'engaging you' web page presents a variety of ways that individuals can help, all of which involve giving money so experts can fix the problem. Through images they can connect special people in their lives, living and deceased, to people and wildlife in Africa who are the putative beneficiaries of their largesse and who most of them will never see in real life. They can choose between protecting wild animals, protecting wild lands or empowering African people. At the 'adopt an animal' website they are presented with a gallery of African animals with names and personalities like the characters in Disney's Lion King. Auntie Botha is a lioness who 'adopted' two cubs when their parents were killed by poison. 'Charles, a wise mountain gorilla' is devoted to the safety of his family. To adopt one of these virtual animals, a person puts it into her/his virtual shopping cart, enters a series of numbers representing virtual value into a website, and then s/he presses a virtual button. A short time later the person receives a certificate of adoption, a fact sheet about her/his adopted animal, and a plush toy representing the adopted animal. The donation, minus the value of the plush toy, is tax deductible.[18]

The problem with this 'spectacular' approach to fundraising is that the same images and distances that make it seem easy to save the world without compromising one's standard of living work to conceal the complicated relationships and problems that are part of global neoliberalism. As Baudrillard (1993) argues about the first Gulf War, it becomes impossible for the consumer to evaluate whether the images that s/he sees on the AWF website really correspond to actual people, places and animals. Even if they do, they present such a limited representation of those people, places and animals without reference to the social and ecological complexity in which they exist. Moreover, it is equally impossible for them to know what happens to their money and whether or not it actually goes to protect Auntie Botha and her cubs, improve the lives of Maasai women, preserve a particular landscape. The fantasy of conservation in this context becomes as much of a commodity as any other, as the person's donation or purchase bears no clearly verifiable relationship to the nature that the consumer believes that she or he is saving.

These emerging forms of commercially mediated relationships and experiences are exemplary of the ways in which Sklair's 'sustainable development historical bloc' relies on and facilitates the circulation of images, ideas and value. This ideally unfettered circulation depends on and reproduces a worldview in which conservation and consumption are not only seen as compatible but mutually dependent on one another. The global economy of images and signs, of which it is a part, is essential to both hyper-consumption on a global scale, the consolidation of mainstream conservation by a handful of mega-conservation NGOs, and the recent and rapid proliferation of the global protected area estate. This global economy of images and signs, as it is circulated through the Spectacle of Nature and the hyperrealities it produces, conceals the production and reproduction of global inequalities, while failing to address the root causes of the environmental problems with which the conservation movement is so justifiably concerned. Finally, and most importantly, this makes it exceedingly difficult to imagine and execute solutions to these problems that are simultaneously effective and equitable.

Conclusion

We believe that Marx was correct that liberal capitalism alienated people from the environment in ways that ecological connections were no longer evident to them. We further agree that these disconnections have been greatly exacerbated and intensified in the context of neoliberalism. While environmental crises may still have the potential to spark environmental movements as predicted by ecological Marxists, in the neoliberal context they have also become commodities and opportunity for profit. Unfortunately, mainstream conservation is also implicated in these processes, which has profound implications for the protection of nature and biodiversity conservation into the future.

A counter argument to this position is that conservationists did not create these conditions, but must still contend with them and so creatively engage with corporations to raise money to protect nature and to help encourage corporations to be green. The problem with this argument, as we have seen in this conclusion, is that it assumes a separation that does not really exist. Mainstream conservation has never stood outside of these processes.

As the anthropologist Gregory Bateson (1979) frequently opined, what really matters are not objects but relationships between living entities. As all good ecologists understand, relationships are essential to the functioning of healthy ecosystems. Furthermore, if we consider humans as part of these systems, integrated at different spatial and temporal scale (Neves-Graca, 2004), then debates over the relative primacy of politics versus ecology (Peet and Watts, 1996; Vayda and Walters, 1999), people versus the environment, poverty alleviation versus biodiversity conservation, become less compelling if not counterproductive. In fact the lines between the social sciences and the environmental sciences appear increasingly artificial (Neves-Graca, 2003).

The intensified circulation of ideas and images over ever greater distances, which we have described in this article, makes the patterns of our interactions with nature even more difficult to discern. For example Neves-Graca's work (2004, 2006, 2007b) compares the aesthetics of attachment necessary to Bateson's holistic ecology with a prevailing aesthetic of detachment. She highlights the processes that contribute to the 'iconification' of ecosystems by presenting them as things instead of complex flows of information. From this perspective, the current proliferation of protected areas and their associated virtualisms contribute to this 'iconification' by presenting ecosystems as fragmented snapshots of the environments at stake. These snapshots are literally created through the physical enclosures and human displacements that the creation of protected areas entails, but they are also virtually created by the conceptual enclosures of nature and natural systems. These enclosures are represented in maps, fund-raising literature, ecotourist experiences, and all the kinds of spectacular virtualisms outlined in the previous section. True to the Marxist concept of fetishization, the resulting knowledge is presented as an object, rather than as a process. It is bracketed in time and in space and therefore does not account for the temporal and spatial complexity of living ecosystems (Neves-Graca, 2004, 2007a).

The aesthetic of the Spectacle of Nature dissects reality into autonomous units such that relationships between cause and effect are lost or at least radically simplified (Neves-Graca 2007b, 2009). In this mental mapping of the world it is normal for people to have 'green sensibilities' and a strong commitment to social justice, while consistently doing things that are bad for the environment and that perpetuate inequality and human suffering on a global scale. Here 'the patterns that connect' are rendered invisible (Neves-Graca, 2006). Individuals may feel connected to the environment by pushing a virtual button to 'adopt' a lion on the other side of the world, but they will have a much more difficult time seeing the ways in which their lives are implicated in the problems they are trying to solve by pushing that button, and the types of patterns and relationships that are rendered invisible by the positivist spin of mainstream conservation.

We are not arguing that an aesthetic of attachment is more 'authentic' than an aesthetic of detachment. We are mindful of Carrier's (2003, p20) argument that people are able to think in creative ways about their place in the world, even the absence of 'direct, practical engagement' with their surroundings, and that a broad 'diversity of understandings of and engagements with the surrounding (can) exist within a single social group and even a single individual'. In spite of this diversity, however, there is nevertheless a disturbing pattern of socio-ecological relationships that are emerging in the context of mainstream conservation's continued convergence with global neoliberal consumer capitalism. The pattern revolves around an aesthetic of detachment in which ecosystems are being fragmented (both literally and figuratively) and consumed as material and virtual commodities. In these circumstances it is not surprising that trends of visits to national parks and other activities involving engaging with nature outdoors shows a steady decline in advanced economies over the last few years (Pergams and Zaradic, 2008). Nor is it at all surprising that this decline is well correlated with videophilia, a sedentary lifestyle based on consuming images (Pergams and Zaradic, 2006; Zaradic and Pergams, 2007).

How we are to realize this vision of more holistic and diverse approaches to conservation is a challenge to which there is no simple solution. The types of connections and relationships we are talking about have been disrupted by the global emergence of liberal capitalism and later neoliberal capitalism. At the same time, these approaches to running the world have proven themselves harmful to both the environment and human livelihoods. In short, we are in need of alternatives, but because of the extent and influence of capitalist systems there are few alternatives to draw from. Marx's vision of a world society of utopian communism is, at best, naive. Even O'Connor's hope that the ecological crises of late capitalism will spark social movements leading us to ecological socialism appears overly optimistic in the context of neoliberalism and disaster capitalism.

Considering these apparently overwhelming difficulties, it may be that mainstream conservation is the best bet that we have for the future of our planet. And yet as Dowie (forthcoming) and Adams (2004) point out, our greatest losses in terms of species extinction and biodiversity are occurring at a time when mainstream conservation has been making monumental strides in funding, influence and extending the world's protected area estate to over 12 per cent of the planet's surface, an area roughly equivalent to the continent of Africa. It is not clear to what extent more resources for the conservation mainstream will help it to become more effective.

Fortunately, there are many solutions out there. They just need to be discovered, illuminated and built upon in creative and innovative ways. In writing about the ongoing positive alliances between Conservation International (CI) and the

Kayapo Indians of Brazil for instance, Mark Dowie (forthcoming) explains that this alliance is unique because it is based on relationships of affection and affinity that are direct and personal. Barbara Zimmerman, the mediator between CI and the Kayapo, has worked among the Kayapo for ten years, speaks their language fluently, and maintains fictive familial relationships within Kayapo society. As a result of her influence, CI invited a Kayapo chief to join its board as the first ever indigenous representative on the board of a conservation BINGO.

In the course of our collective fieldwork we have all encountered many such examples of individuals building such connections and relationships to produce workable conservation solutions in defiance of the general trend. Many cases such as these exist throughout the realm of international conservation and international development. They also exist in myriad other contexts such as indigenous societies, social movements, private enterprise and the like. What they will all share in common is an emphasis on connections and relationships between human beings, as well as between humans and non-humans, rather than a focus on objects. These relationships and connections are flexible and specific, as opposed to rigid and universalizing, while also being pragmatic and effective. They also involve people creating new types of values and aesthetics and accepting direct and personal responsibility for socio-environmental problems.

The outcomes of these types of engagements and processes and relationships are unpredictable, and therefore never uniform or universalizing. They foster what Dowie (forthcoming) calls 'vital diversities', multitude ways of seeing and interacting with the planet and each other, which could stand in direct contrast to the types of homogenizing and alienating processes that have so alarmed theorists like Marx, Debord and Baudrillard.

We are still a long way from making these types of solutions visible and acceptable. However, we hope that this book has shown both some possibilities for fostering these types of solutions, as well as the potential costs of not doing so. While this sort of perspective, and the agendas for research and action that it implies, is frequently portrayed as hostile to conservation and romanticizing of local people, it is actually neither of these things. Rather it is inspired by a broader vision of seeking to understand 'patterns that connect' in ways that might contribute to new types of human–environmental relational aesthetics that foster new types of ecological and ethical sensitivity that, in turn, may promote increased commitment to ecosystems and to the people who live within them.

Notes

1   www.lse.ac.uk/collections/pressAndInformationOffice/newsAndEvents/archives/
2007/NickSternLectures.htm (accessed 4 January 2008).
2   www.aep.com/environmental/conservation/reforestation/rainforest.htm (accessed
4 January 2008).
3   www.bbc.co.uk/london/content/articles/2006/12/29/insideout_100107_feature.
shtml (accessed 4 January 2008).

4   www.cdmgoldstandard.org/about_goldstandard.php?id=16 (accessed 4 January 2008).
5   www.ccafrica.com/reserve-1-id-2-5 (accessed 29 December 2007).
6   www.surgeon-and-safari.co.za/safaris/safaris_bush.html (accessed 29 December 2007).
7   www.tswalu.com/ (accessed 29 December 2007).
8   www.lisulodge.com (accessed 16 March 2008).
9   www.anseladams.com/index.asp?PageAction=VIEWCATS&Category=9 (accessed 18 March 2008).
10 Western visions of nature are not monolithic. Nevertheless, the wilderness ideal has been exported to much of the world to create what Nugent (1994) has termed 'ecodomains': putative a-social landscapes that loom large in the Western imagination such as the Amazon Rainforest, the Serengeti Plain and the Himalayas. As lucrative tourist resorts, these landscapes have become hyperreal in the manner outlined above.
11 www.awf.org/documents/SUMMER04.pdf (accessed 28 June 2007).
12 www.awf.org/section/engaging_you/getcc (accessed 28 June 2007).
13 www.awf.org/content/solution/detail/3372 (accessed 28 June 2007). A recent report from the Kenya *Daily Standard* indicates that coffee farmers are not happy with this arrangement www.eastandard.net/archives/cl/hm_news/news.php?articleid=1143961897 (accessed 28 June 2007).
14 www.worldwildlife.org/wildchronicles/ (accessed 28 June 2007).
15 This is clearly illustrated in Dow's Human Element Campaign, which can be viewed at www.dow.com/Hu/ (accessed 18 February 2008). Human element adverts ran on national television in the US during major sporting events, although Dow sells no retail consumer products.
16 www.wdwpublicaffairs.com/ContentDrillDown.aspx?DisplayItem=6bcc53c7-f43d-48d0-8049-ccdccb2775fe (accessed 28 June 2007).
17 www.wdwnews.com/ViewPressRelease.aspx?PressReleaseID=99937 (accessed 28 June 2007). www.awf.org/content/headline/detail/1171 (accessed 28 June 2007).
18 www.eastandard.net/archives/cl/hm_news/news.php?articleid=1143961897 (accessed 28 June 2007).

References

Abbey, E. (1975) *The Monkey Wrench Gang*. New York: Avon Books, Harper Collins

Abbott-Cone, C. (1995) 'Crafting selves: The lives of two Mayan women'. *Annals of Tourism Research* 22: 314–327

Adams, J. S. and McShane, T. O. (1992) *The Myth of Wild Africa. Conservation Without Illusion*. Berkeley, CA: University of California Press

Adams, W. M. (1986) *Nature's Place. Conservation Sites and Countryside Change*. London: Allen & Unwin

Adams, W. M. (1996) *Future Nature: A Vision for Conservation*. London: Earthscan

Adams, W. M. (2004) *Against Extinction: The Story of Conservation*. London: Earthscan

Adams, W. M., Aveling, R., Brockington, D., Dickson, B., Elliott, J., Hutton, J., Roe, R., Vira, B. and Wolmer, W. (2004) 'Biodiversity conservation and the eradication of poverty'. *Science* 306: 1146–1149

Agrawal, A. (2001) 'Common property institutions and sustainable governance of resources'. *World Development* 29(10): 1648–1672

Agrawal, A. (2003) 'Sustainable governance of common-pool resources: Context, methods, and politics'. *Annual Review of Anthropology* 32: 243–262

Agrawal, A. (2005) 'Environmentality. Community, intimate government, and the making of environmental subjects in Kumaon, India'. *Current Anthropology* 46(5): 161–190

Agrawal, A. and Gibson, C. C. (1999) 'Enchantment and disenchantment: The role of community in natural resource conservation'. *World Development* 27(4): 629–649

Agrawal, A. and Ostrom, E. (2001) 'Collective action, property rights, and decentralization in resource use in India and Nepal'. *Politics and Society* 29: 485–514

Agrawal, A. and Redford, K. (2007) 'Conservation and displacement: An overview'. In K. H. Redford and E. Fearn (eds) *Protected Areas and Human Displacement: A Conservation Perspective*. New York: Wildlife Conservation Society

Alcorn, J. B. (1993) 'Indigenous peoples and conservation'. *Conservation Biology* 7(2): 424–426

Alexander, J. and McGregor, J. (2000) 'Wildlife and politics: CAMPFIRE in Zimbabwe'. *Development and Change* 31: 605–627

Ali, S. (2007) *Peace Parks Conservation and Conflict Resolution*. Cambridge, MA: The MIT Press

Allen, H. (1981) 'Against waking the rainbow serpent'. *Arena* 59(2): 25–42

Alvard, M. S. (1993) 'Testing the "ecologically noble savage" hypothesis: Interspecific prey choice by Piro hunters of Amazonian Peru'. *Human Ecology* 21(4): 355–387

Alvard, M. S. (1995) 'Intraspecific prey choice by Amazonian hunters'. *Current Anthropology* 36(5): 789–818

Alvard, M. S., Robinson, J. G., Redford, K. H. and Kaplan, H. (1997) 'The sustainability of subsistence hunting in the neotropics'. *Conservation Biology* 11(4): 977–982

Amend, S. and Amend, T. (1995) *National Parks Without People? The South American Experience*. Gland: IUCN

Amsden, A. (1990) 'Third world industrialization: Global Fordism or a new model?'. *New Left Review* 182: 5–32

Anderson, D.G. (2001) 'Hunting caribou and hunting tradition: Aboriginal identity and economy in Canada and Siberia'. In D. G. Anderson and K. Ikeya (eds) *Parks, Property and Power: Managing Hunting Practice and Identity within State Policy Regimes Senri Ethnological Studies no 59.* pp7–25. Osaka: National Museum of Ethnology

Anderson, D. G. and Berglund, E. (2003) *Ethnographies of Conservation. Environmentalism and the Distribution of Privilege.* New York: Bergahn Books

Anderson, D. M. and Grove, R. (1987) *Conservation in Africa. People, Policies and Practice.* Cambridge: Cambridge University Press

Anderson, J., Rowcliffe, J. M. and Cowlishaw, G. (2007) 'Does the matrix matter? A forest primate in a complex agricultural landscape'. *Biological Conservation* 135(2): 212–222

Appadurai, A. (1996) *Modernity at Large: Cultural Dimensions of Globalization.* Minneapolis, MN: University of Minnesota Press

Appadurai, A. (2004) 'The capacity to aspire. Culture and the terms of recognition'. In V. Rao and M. Walton (eds) *Culture and Public Action.* pp59–84. California: Stanford University Press

Ashenafi, Z., Coulson, T., Sillero-Zubiri, C. and Leader-Williams, N. (2005) 'Behaviour and ecology of the Ethiopian wolf (*Canis simensis*) in a human-dominated landscape outside protected areas'. *Animal Conservation* 8: 113–121

Austral Foundation, The (2007) *Review and Analysis of Fiji's Conservation Sector.* Waitakere City: The Austral Foundation

Azcarate, M. C. (2007) 'Between local and global discourses and practices rethinking ecotourism development in Celestún Yucatán México'. *Journal of Ecotourism* 5(1,2): 97–111

Baillie, J. E. M., Hilton-Taylor, C. and Stuart, S. N. (2004) *2004 IUCN Red List of Threatened Species (TM). A Global Species Assessment.* Gland: IUCN

Baland, J. M. and Platteau, J. P. (1996) *Halting Degradation of Natural Resources: Is There a Role for Local Communities?.* Oxford: Clarendon Press

Ballantine, J. L. and Eagles, P. F. J. (1994) 'Defining Canadian ecotourists'. *Journal of Sustainable Tourism* 2: 210–214

Balmford, A. (1996) 'Extinction filters and current resilience: The significance of past selection pressures for conservation biology'. *Trends in Ecology & Evolution* 11(5): 193–196

Balmford, A., Green, R. E. and Jenkins, M. (2003a) 'Measuring the changing state of nature'. *Trends in Ecology & Evolution* 18(7): 326–330

Balmford, A., Gaston, K. J., Blyth, S., James, A. and Kapos, V. (2003b) 'Global variation in terrestrial conservation costs, conservation benefits, and unmet conservation needs'. *Proceedings of the National Academy of Sciences of the United States of America* 100(3): 1046–1050

Balmford, A., Crane, P., Dobson, A., Green, R. E. and Mace, G. (2005a) 'The 2010 challenge: Data availability, information needs and extraterrestrial insights'. *Philosophical Transactions of the Royal Society* B 360: 221–228

Balmford, A, Green, R. E. and Scharlemann, J. P. W. (2005b) 'Sparing land for nature: Exploring the potential impact of changes in agricultural yield on the area needed for crop production'. *Global Change Biology* 11: 1594–1605

Balmford, A. and Whitten, T. (2003) 'Who should pay for tropical conservation, and how could these costs be met?'. *Oryx* 37(2): 238–250

Barnes, J. I., MacGregor, J. and Weaver, L. C. (2002) 'Economic efficiency and incentives for change with Namibia's community wildlife use initiatives'. *World Development* 30(4): 667–681

Barnosky, A. D., Koch, P. L., Feranec, R. S., Wing, S. L. and Shabel, A. B. (2004) 'Assessing the causes of Late Pleistocene extinctions on the continents'. *Science* 306(5693): 70–75

Barrett, C. B. and Arcese, P. (1995) 'Are integrated conservation–development projects (IDCPs) sustainable? On the conservation of large mammals in Sub-Saharan Africa'. *World Development* 23: 1073–1084

Barrow, E. and Fabricius, C. (2002) 'Do rural people really benefit from protected areas – rhetoric or reality?' *Parks* 12: 67–79

Barrow, E. and Murphree, M. (2002) 'Community conservation from concept to practice: A practical framework'. Community Conservation Research in Africa Principles and Comparative Practice Working Paper No. 8. Manchester: IDPM

Barthes, R. (2000 (1957)) *Mythologies*. London: Vintage

Bateson, G. (1979) *Mind and Nature: A Necessary Unity*. Dutton: New York

Bateson, G. and Bateson, M. (1988) *Angels Fear: Towards an Epistemology of the Sacred*. New York: Bantam Books

Baudrillard, J. (1981) *Simulacra and Simulation*. Ann Arbor, MI: University of Michigan Press

Baudrillard, J. (1993) *Symbolic Exchange and Death*. London: Sage Publications

Bebbington, A. J. (2004) 'NGOs and uneven development: Geographies of development intervention'. *Progress in Human Geography* 28(6): 725–745

Bebbington, A. J., Hickey, S. and Mitlin, D. C. (2007) *Can NGOs Make a Difference? The Challenge of Development Alternatives*. London: ZED

Bedunah, D. J. and Schmidt, S. M. (2004) 'Pastoralism and protected area management in Mongolia's Gobi Gurvansaikhan National Park'. *Development and Change* 35(1): 167–191

Bennett, E. L. (2002) 'Is there a link between wild meat and food security?'. *Conservation Biology* 16(3): 590–592

Bennett, E. L., Blencowe, E., Brandon, K., Brown, D., Burn, R. W., Cowlishaw, G., Davies, G., Dublin, H., Fa, J. E., Milner-Gulland, E. J., Robinson, J. G., Rowcliffe, J. M., Underwood, F. M. and Wilkie, D. S. (2007) 'Hunting for consensus: Reconciling bushmeat harvest, conservation, and development policy in west and central Africa'. *Conservation Biology* 21(3): 884–887

Benton, T. (2006) *Bumblebees*. London: Harper Collins

Berkes, F. (1989) *Common Property Resources. Ecology and Community-based Sustainable Development*. London: Belhaven Press

Berkes, F. (1999) *Sacred Ecology. Traditional Ecological Knowledge and Resource Management*. London: Taylor and Francis

Beteille, A. (1998) 'The idea of indigenous people'. *Current Anthropology* 39(2): 187–191

Bhomia, R. K. and Brockington, D. (2006) 'Conservation: pride or prejudice? An analysis of the protected areas of India'. *Policy Matters* 14: 142–154

Bianchi, R. (2004) 'Tourism restructuring and the politics of sustainability. A critical view from the European periphery: The Canary Islands'. *Journal of Sustainable Tourism* 126: 495–529

Bianco, M. and Alder, S. (2001) 'The politics of implimentation: The corporatist paradigm applied to the implementation of Oregon's statewide transportation planning rule'. *Journal of Planning Education and Research* 21(1): 5–16

Bishop, K., Dudley, N., Phillips, A. and Stolton, S. (2004) *Speaking a Common Language. The Uses and Performance of the IUCN System of Management Categories for Protected Areas.* Cardiff: Cardiff University; IUCN; UNEP-WCMC

Blomely, T. and Ramadhani, H. (2006) 'Going to scale with participatory forest management: Early lessons from Tanzania'. *International Forestry Review* 8(1): 93–100

Bodmer, R. E., Eisenberg, J. F. and Redford, K. H. (1997) 'Hunting and the likelihood of extinction of Amazonian mammals'. *Conservation Biology* 11(2): 460–466

Bodmer, R. E. and Lozano, E. P. (2001) 'Rural development and sustainable wildlife use in Peru'. *Conservation Biology* 15(4): 1163–1170

Bolaane, M. (2004a) 'The impact of game reserve policy on the River BaSarwa/Bushmen of Botswana'. *Social Policy and Administration* 38(4): 399–417

Bolaane, M. (2004b) 'Wildlife conservation and local management: The establishment of the Moremi Park, Okavango, Botswana in the 1950s–1960s'. D.Phil, Oxford University

Bolaane, M. (2005) 'Chiefs, hunters and adventurers: The foundation of the Okavango/Moremi National Park, Botswana'. *Journal of Historical Geography* 31: 241–259

Bonner, R. (1993) *At the Hand of Man. Peril and Hope for Africa's Wildlife.* London: Simon and Schuster

Boo, E. (1990) *Ecotourism: The Potentials and the Pitfalls Vols 1 and 2.* Washington DC: WWF

Borgerhoff Mulder, M. and Coppolillo, P. (2005) *Conservation. Linking Ecology, Economics and Culture.* Princeton: Princeton University Press

Borner, M. (1985) 'The increasing isolation of Tarangire National Park'. *Oryx* 19: 91–96

Borrini-Feyerabend, G., Banuri, T., Farvar, T., Miller, K. and Phillips, A. (2002) 'Indigenous and local communities and protected areas: Rethinking the relationship'. *Parks* 12: 5–15

Bottrill, C. G. (1995) 'Ecotourism: Towards a key elements approach to operationalising the concept'. *Journal of Sustainable Tourism* 3: 45–54

Boza, M. A. (1993) 'Conservation in action: Past, present and future of the national park system of Costa Rica'. *Conservation Biology* 7(2): 239–247

Bramwell, B. and Lane, B. (2001) Editorial. *Journal of Sustainable Tourism* 9(1): 1–3

Bramwell, B. and Lane, B. (2005) 'From niche to general relevance? Sustainable tourism research and the role of tourism journals'. *The Journal of Tourism Studies* 16(2): 52–62

Brandon, K. (1998) 'Perils to parks: The social context of threats'. In K. Brandon, K. H. Redford and S. E. Sanderson (eds) *Parks in Peril. People, Politics and Protected Areas.* Washington DC: The Nature Conservancy

Brandon, K., Redford, K. H. and Sanderson, S. E. (1998) *Parks in Peril. People, Politics and Protected Areas.* Washington DC: The Nature Conservancy

Brashares, J. S., Arcese, P., Sam, M. K., Coppolillo, P. B., Sinclair, A. R. E. and Balmford, A. (2004) 'Bushmeat hunting, wildlife declines, and fish supply in West Africa'. *Science* 306(5699): 1180–1183

Brechin, S. R., Wilshusen, P. R., Fortwangler, C. L. and West, P. C. (2003) *Contested Nature. Promoting International Biodiversity with Social Justice in the Twenty-first Century*. Albany, NY: State University of New York Press

Brockington, D. (2002) *Fortress Conservation. The Preservation of the Mkomazi Game Reserve, Tanzania*. Oxford: James Currey

Brockington, D. (2003) 'Myths of sceptical environmentalism'. *Environmental Science and Policy* 6: 543–546

Brockington, D. (2004) 'Community conservation, inequality and injustice. Myths of power in protected area management'. *Conservation and Society* 2(2): 411–432

Brockington, D. (2006) 'The politics and ethnography of environmentalisms in Tanzania'. *African Affairs* 105(418): 97–116

Brockington, D. (2007) 'Devolution, community conservation and forests. On local government performance and village forest reserves in Tanzania'. *Society and Natural Resources* 20: 835–848

Brockington, D. (2008) 'Corruption, taxation, democracy and natural resource management in Tanzania'. *Journal of Development Studies* 44(1): 103–126

Brockington, D. and Igoe, J. (2006) 'Eviction for conservation. A global overview'. *Conservation and Society* 4(3): 424–470

Brockington, D. and Schmidt-Soltau, K. (2004) 'The social and environmental impacts of wilderness and development'. *Oryx* 38(2): 140–142

Brohman, J. (1996) 'New directions in tourism for Third World development'. *Annals of Tourism Research* 23: 48–70

Bromely, D. W. and Cernea, M. M. (1989) *The Management of Common Property Resources. Some Conceptual and Operational Fallacies*. Washington DC: The World Bank

Brook, B. W., Burney, D. A., Flannery, T. F., Gagan, M. K., Gillespie, R., Johnson, C. N., Kershaw, P., Magee, J. W., Martin, P. S., Miller, G. H., Peiser, B. and Roberts, R. G. (2007) 'Would the Australian megafauna have become extinct if humans had never colonized the continent? Comments on "A review of the evidence of a human role in the extinction of Australian megafauna and an alternative explanation", by S. Wroe and F. Field'. *Quaternary Science Reviews* 26(3–4): 560–564

Brooks, S. (2005) 'Images of "Wild Africa": Nature tourism and the (re)creation of Hluhluwe game reserve, 1930–1945'. *Journal of Historical Geography* 31: 220–240

Brooks, T. and Balmford, A. (1996) 'Atlantic forest extinctions'. *Nature* 380(6570): 115

Brooks, T. M., Mittermeier, R. A., Mittermeier, C. G., da Fonseca, G. A. B., Rylands, A. B., Konstant, W. R., Flick, P., Pilgrim, J., Oldfield, S., Magin, G. and Hilton-Taylor, C. (2002) 'Habitat loss and extinction in the hotspots of biodiversity'. *Conservation Biology* 16(4): 909–923

Brooks, T. M., Mittermeier, R. A., da Fonseca, G. A. B., Gerlach, J., Hoffmann, M., Lamoreux, J. F., Mittermeier, C. G., Pilgrim, J. D. and Rodrigues, A. S. L. (2006) 'Global biodiversity conservation priorities'. *Science* 313(5783): 58–61

Brooks, T. M., Pimm, S. L. and Collar, N. J. (1997) 'Deforestation predicts the number of threatened birds in insular southeast Asia'. *Conservation Biology* 11(2): 382–394

Brooks, T. M., Pimm, S. L. and Oyugi, J. O. (1999) 'Time lag between deforestation and bird extinction in tropical forest fragments'. *Conservation Biology* 13(5): 1140–1150

Brosius, J. P. (2006) 'Common round between anthropology and conservation biology'. *Conservation Biology* 20(3): 683–685

Brown, J. H. (1995) *Macroecology*. Chicago: University of Chicago Press

Brummitt, N. and Lughadha, E. N. (2003) 'Biodiversity: Where's hot and where's not'. *Conservation Biology* 17(5): 1442–1448

Bruner, A. G., Gullison, E., Rice, R. E. and da Fonseca, G. A. B. (2001a) 'Effectiveness of parks in protecting tropical biodiversity'. *Science* 291(5501): 125–128

Bruner, A. G., Gullison, E., Rice, R. E. and da Fonseca, G. A. B. (2001b) 'Response to Vanclay'. *Science* 293: 1007a

Bryant, D., Nielsen, D. and Tangley, L. (1997) *Last Frontier Forests*. Washington DC: World Resources Institute

Bryman, A. (2002) 'McDonalds as a Disneyfied institution'. In G. Ritzer (ed) *McDonaldization: The Reader*. Thousand Oaks, CA: Pine Forge Press, pp54–69

Buergin, R. (2003) 'Shifting frames for local people and forests in a global heritage: The Thung Yai Naresuan Wildlife Sanctuary in the context of Thailand's globalization and modernization'. *Geoforum* 24: 375–393

Buergin, R. and Kessler, Chr. (2000) 'Intrusions and exclusions: Democratization in Thailand in the context of environmental discourses and resource conflicts'. *Geojournal* 52(1): 71–80

Bulbeck, C. (2005) *Facing the Wild Ecotourism Conservation and Animal Encounters*. London: Earthscan

Burger, J. (1987) *Report From the Frontier: The State of the World's Indigenous Peoples*. London: Zed Books

Burgman, M. A. (2002) 'Are listed threatened plant species actually at risk?'. *Australian Journal of Botany* 50(1): 1–13

Burnham, P. (2000) *Indian Country God's Country: Native Americans and National Parks*. Washington DC: Island Press

Büscher, B. and Dressler, W. (2007) 'Linking neoprotectionism and environmental governance: On the rapidly increasing tensions between actors in environment–development nexus'. *Conservation and Society* 5(4): 596–611

Butchart, S. H. M., Stattersfield, A. J., Bennun, L. A., Shutes, S. M., Akcakaya, H. R., Baillie, J. E. M., Stuart, S. N., Hilton-Taylor, C. and Mace, G. M. (2004) 'Measuring global trends in the status of biodiversity: Red list indices for birds'. *PLoS Biology* 2(12): 2294–2304

Butchart, S. H. M., Stattersfield, A. J., Baillie, J., Bennun, L. A., Stuart, S. N., Akcakaya, H. R., Hilton-Taylor, C. and Mace, G. M. (2005) 'Using Red List Indices to measure progress towards the 2010 target and beyond'. *Philosophical Transactions of the Royal Society B-Biological Sciences* 360(1454): 255–268

Butchart, S. H. M., Stattersfield, A. J. and Collar, N. J. (2006a) 'Biodiversity indicators based on trends in conservation status: Strengths of the IUCN Red List Index'. *Conservation Biology* 20(2): 579–581

Butchart, S. H. M., Stattersfield, A. J. and Collar, N. J. (2006b) 'How many bird extinctions have we prevented?'. *Oryx* 40(3): 266–278

Butcher, J. (2003) *The Moralisation of Tourism Sun Sand ... and Saving the World?* London: Routledge

Campbell, B., Mandondo, A., Nemarundwe, N., Sithole, B., De Jong, W., Luckert, M. and Matose, F. (2001) 'Challenges to proponents of common property resource systems: Despairing voices from the social forests of Zimbabwe'. *World Development* 29(4): 589–600

Caro, T. and Scholte, P. (2007) 'When protection falters'. *African Journal of Ecology* 45: 233–235

Carrier, J. G. (1998) 'Introduction'. In J. G. Carrier and D. Miller (eds) *Virtualism. A New Political Economy*. pp1–24. Oxford: Berg

Carrier, J. G. (2003) 'Mind, gaze, and engagement: Understanding the environment'. *Journal of Material Culture* 8(1): 5–23

Carrier, J. G. and Macleod, D. V. L. (2005) 'Bursting the bubble: The socio-cultural context of eco-tourism'. *Journal of the Royal Anthropological Institute* 11: 315–334

Carruthers, J. (1989) 'Creating a National Park, 1910–26'. *Journal of Southern African Studies* 15(2): 188–216

Carruthers, J. (1995) *The Kruger National Park. A Social and Political History*. Pietermaritzburg: University of Natal Press

Castillo, A. R. (2004) *Sustainable Inequalities? Community-based Conservation in an 'Inequitable Society'. The Case of Il Ngwesi Group Ranch, Kenya*. Oxford: University of Oxford.

Castree, N. (2007a) 'Neoliberalizing nature: Processes, effects and evaluations'. *Environment and Planning. A* 40: 153–171

Castree, N. (2007b) 'Neoliberalizing nature: The logics of de- and re-regulation'. *Environment and Planning. A* 40: 131–152

Castro, G. and Locker, I. (2000) *Mapping Conservation Investments: An Assessment of Biodiversity Funding in Latin America and the Caribbean*. Washington DC: Biodiversity Support Program

Cater, E. (1994) 'Ecotourism in the Third World – problems and prospects for sustainability'. In E. Cater and G. Lowman (eds) *Ecotourism. A Sustainable Option*. pp69–86. London: John Wiley and Sons

Cater, E. (2006) 'Ecotourism as a western construct'. *Journal of Ecotourism* 5(1, 2): 23–39

Catton, T. (1997) *Inhabited Wilderness: Indians, Eskimos, and National Parks in Alaska*. Albuquerque: University of New Mexico Press

Caughley, G. (1994) 'Directions in conservation biology'. *Journal of Animal Ecology* 63: 215–244

Ceballos-Lascuráin, H. (2003) 'Preface'. In M. Lück and T. Kirstges (eds) *Global Ecotourism Policies and Case Studies Perspectives and Constraints*. ppviii–xii. Clevedon: Channel View Publications

Cernea, M. M. and Schmidt-Soltau, K. (2006) 'Poverty risks and national parks: Policy issues in conservation and resettlement'. *World Development* 34: 1808–1830

Chan, K. M. A., Pringle, R. M., Ranganatran, J., Boggs, C. L., Chan, Y. L., Ehrlich, P. R., Haff, P. K., Heller, N. E., Al-Krafaji, K. and Macmynowski, D. P. (2007) 'When agendas collide: Human welfare and biological conservation'. *Conservation Biology* 21(1): 59–68

Chape, S., Spalding, M. and Lysenko, I. (2005) 'Measuring the extent and effectiveness of protected areas as an indicator for meeting global biodiversity targets'. *Philosophical Transactions of the Royal Society B* 360: 443–455

Chapin, M. (2000) *Defending Kuna Yala*. Washington DC: USAID Biodiversity Support Program

Chapin, M. (2004) 'A challenge to conservationists'. *World Watch Magazine* Nov/Dec: 17–31

Chatty, D. and Colchester, M. (eds) (2002) *Conservation and Mobile Indigenous Peoples: Displacement, Forced Settlement and Sustainable Development*. Oxford: Berghan.

Chernlea, J. (2005) 'The politics of mediation: Local–global interactions in the central Amazon'. *American Anthropologist* 107(4): 620–631

Child, B. (2000a) 'Application of the southern African experience to wildlife utlisation'. In H. H. T. Prins, J. G. Grootenuis and T. T. Dolan (eds) *Wildlife Conservation by Sustainable Use*. pp218–245. Boston: Kluwer Academic Publishers

Child, B. (2000b) 'Making wildife pay: Converting wildlife's comparative advantage onto real incentives for having wildlife in African savannas. Case studies from Zimbabwe and Zambia'. In H. H. T. Prins, J. G. Grootenuis and T. T. Dolan (eds) *Wildlife Conservation by Sustainable Use*. pp218–245. Boston: Kluwer Academic Publishers

Child, B. and Dalal-Clayton, B. (2001) 'Transforming approaches to CBNRM: Learning from the Luangwa experience'. MS: Synopsis of a review for the IIED, London

Cinner, J. E. and Aswani, S. (2007) 'Integrating customary management into marine conservation'. *Biological Conservation* 140: 201–216

Clapham, C. (1996) *Africa and the International System. The Politics of State Survival*. Cambridge: Cambridge University Press

Colchester, M. (1997) 'Salvaging nature: Indigenous peoples and protected areas'. In K. B. Ghimire and M. P. Pimbert (eds) *Social Change and Conservation*. London: Earthscan

Colchester, M. (2002) 'Indigenous rights and the collective conscious'. *Anthropology Today* 18(1): 1–3

Colchester, M. (2003) *Salvaging Nature: Indigenous Peoples, Protected Areas and Biodiversity Conservation*. Moreton-in-Marsh: World Rainforest Movement; Forest Peoples Programme

Colchester, M. and Erni, C. (1999) *Indigenous Peoples and Protected Areas in South and Southeast Asia. From Principles to Practice*. Copenhagen: IWGIA

Conklin, B. and Graham, L. (1995) 'The shifting middle ground: Amazonian Indians and eco-politics'. *American Anthropologist* 974: 695–710

Connor, T. K. (2006) 'Opportunity and constraint: Historicity, hybridity and notions of cultural identity in the Sundays River Valley (Eastern Cape) and Pafuri (Mozambique)'. PhD, Rhodes University

Cook, L. (2002) 'Operators eyeing European markets'. *Business Day*. Johannesburg, 14 January 2002

Coombes, B. L. and Hill, S. (2005) 'Na whenua, na Tuhoe. Ko D.o.C. te partner' – Prospects for co-management of Te Urewera National Park. *Society & Natural Resources* 18: 135–152.

Cooney, R. and Jepson, P. (2006) 'The international wild bird trade: What's wrong with blanket bans?'. *Oryx* 40(1): 18–23

Corlett, R. T. (2007) 'The impact of hunting on the mammalian fauna of tropical Asian forests'. *Biotropica* 39(3): 292–303

Cosgrove, D. E. (1984) *Social Formation and Symbolic Landscape*. London: Croom Helm

Cowen, M. and Shenton, R. (1996) *Doctrines of Development*. London: Routledge

Cowlishaw, G. (1999) 'Predicting the pattern of decline of African primate diversity: An extinction debt from historical deforestation'. *Conservation Biology* 13(5): 1183–1193

Cronon, W. (1995) 'The trouble with wilderness; or getting back to the wrong nature'. In W. Cronon (ed) *Uncommon Ground. Rethinking the Human Place in Nature*. New York: W. W. Norton

Cuaron, A. D. (1993) 'Extinction rate estimates'. *Nature* 366(6451): 118

Cumming, D. and Jones, B. (2005) 'Elephants in southern Africa: Management issues and options'. WWF-SAPIRO Occasional Paper 11

da Fonseca, G. A. B. (2003) 'Conservation science and NGOs'. *Conservation Biology* 17: 345–347

Daily, G. C. and Walker, B. H. (2000) 'Seeking the great transition'. *Nature* 403(6767): 243–245

Daniels, S. (1993) *Fields of Vision. Landscape Imagery and National Identity in England and the United States*. Oxford: Polity Press

Daniels, S. and Cosgrove, D. (1988) 'Introduction: Iconography and landscape'. In D. Cosgrove and S. Daniels (eds) *The Iconography of Landscape. Essays on the Symbolic Representation, Design and Use of Past Environments*. Cambridge: Cambridge University Press

Dann, G. (1996) *The Language of Tourism. A Sociolinguistic Perspective*. Oxon: CABI

Darlington, S. M. (1998) 'The ordination of a tree: The Buddhist ecology movement in Thailand'. *Ethnology* 37(1): 1–15

Davies, R. (2000) 'Madikwe Game Reserve: A partnership in conservation'. In H. H. T. Prins, J. G. Grootenuis and T. T. Dolan (eds) *Wildlife Conservation by Sustainable Use*. pp218–245. Boston: Kluwer Academic Publishers

de Merode, E. and Cowlishaw, G. (2006) 'Species protection, the changing informal economy, and the politics of access to the bushmeat trade in the Democratic Republic of Congo'. *Conservation Biology* 20(4): 1262–1271

de Merode, E., Homewood, K. and Cowlishaw, G. (2004) 'The value of bushmeat and other wild foods to rural households living in extreme poverty in Democratic Republic of Congo'. *Biological Conservation* 118: 573–581

de Souza, M. and de Leeuw, P. N. (1984) 'Smallstock use of reserved grazing areas on Merushi Group Ranch'. *Proceedings CSRP Workshop on Small Ruminants*. Nairobi, 1984

De Waal, A. (1997) *Famine Crimes. Politics and the Disaster Relief Industry in Africa*. Oxford: James Currey

Debord, G. (1995 (1967)) *Society of the Spectacle*. New York: Zone Books

DeFries, R., Hansen, A., Newton, A. C. and Hansen, M. C. (2005) 'Increasing isolation of protected areas in tropical forests over the past twenty years'. *Ecological Applications* 15(1): 19–26

Denevan, W. M. (1992) 'The Pristine Myth: The landscape of the Americas in 1492'. *Annals of the Association of American Geographers* 82(3): 269–285

Denman, R. (2001) *Guidelines for Community Based Ecotourism Development*. Ledbury: The Tourism Company; Geneva: WWF-International

Diamond, J. M. (1972) 'Biogeographic kinetics: Estimation of relaxation times for avifaunas of southwest Pacific islands'. *Proceedings of the National Academy of Sciences of the United States of America* 69(11): 3199–3203

Dirzo, R. and Raven, P. H. (2003) 'Global state of biodiversity and loss'. *Annual Review of Environment and Resources* 28: 137–167

Dombrowski, K. (2002) 'The praxis of indigenism and native Alaskan timber politics'. *American Anthropologist* 104: 1067–1072

Donald, P. F. (2004) 'Biodiversity impacts of some agricultural commodity production systems'. *Conservation Biology* 18(1): 17–37

Dorsey, M. (2005) 'Conservation, collusion and capital'. *Anthropology News* October: 45–46

Dove, M. (2006) 'Indigenous people and environmental politics'. *Annual Review of Anthropology* 35: 191–208

Dowie, M. (1996) *Losing Ground: American Environmentalism at the Close of the 20th Century*. Cambridge, MA: MIT Press

Dowie, M. (2005) 'Conservation refugees. When protecting nature means kicking people out'. *Orion* Nov/Dec (www.oriononline.org/pages/om/06-06om/Dowie.html): 16–27

Dowie, M. (2006) 'Problems in paradise. How making new parks and wildlife preserves creates millions of conservation refugees around the world'. *San Francisco Chronicle* 11 June

Dowie, M. (forthcoming) *Vital Natures: Balancing the Protection of Nature and Culture*. Cambridge, MA: MIT Press

Duffy, R. (2000) *Killing for Conservation. Wildlife Policy in Zimbabwe*. Oxford: James Currey

Duffy, R. (2002) *A Trip Too Far: Ecotourism, Politics and Exploitation*. London: Earthscan

Duffy, R. (2004) 'Ecotourists on the beach'. In J. Urry and M. Sheller (eds) *Tourism Mobilities: Places to Play, Places in Play*. pp32–43. London: Routledge

Duffy, R. (2005) 'The politics of global environmental governance: The powers and limitations of transfrontier conservation areas in central America'. *Review of International Studies* 31(1): 307–323

Duffy, R. (2006a) 'Global environmental governance and the politics of ecotourism in Madagascar'. *Journal of Ecotourism* 5(1,2): 128–144

Duffy, R. (2006b) 'Global governance and environmental management: The politics of transfrontier conservation areas in southern Africa'. *Political Geography* 25(1): 89–112

Duffy, R. (2006c) 'NGOs and governance states: The impact of transnational environmental management networks in Madagascar'. *Environmental Politics* 15(5): 731–749

Duffy, R. (2008a) 'Ivory trade: Enforceability, effectiveness and ethical concerns'. In C. Wemmer and K. Christen (eds) *Elephants and Ethics: The Morality of Coexistence*. Baltimore, MA: Johns Hopkins Press

Duffy, R. (2008b) 'Neoliberalising nature global networks and ecotourism development in Madagascar'. *Journal of Sustainable Tourism*, in press

Dunn, K. (2003) 'National parks and human security in East Africa'. In *Proceedings of the Conference: Beyond the Arch: Community Conservation in Greater Yellowstone and East Africa*. pp103–122. Mammoth Spring, WY: US National Park Service

Dunn, R. R., Gavin, M. C., Sanchez, M. C. and Solomon, J. N. (2006) 'The pigeon paradox: Dependence of global conservation on urban nature'. *Conservation Biology* 20(6): 1814–1816

Dzingirai, V. (2003) 'The new scramble for the African countryside'. *Development and Change* 34(2): 243–263

Edwards, E. (1996) 'Postcards – greetings from another world'. In T. Selwyn (ed) *The Tourist Image Myths and Myth Making in Tourism*. pp197–221. New York: John Wiley and Sons

Edwards, M. and Hulme, D. (1992) *Making a Difference: NGOs and Development in a Changing World*. London: Earthscan

Edwards, M. and Hulme, D. (1995) *Non-Governmental Organisations: Performance and Accountability. Beyond the Magic Bullet*. London: Earthscan

Egloff, B. J. (1979) 'Mumballa Mountain. An anthropological and archeological investigation'. Aboriginal and Historical Resources, National Parks and Wildlife Services

Egloff, B. J. (2004) *Biamanga and Gulaga. Aboriginal Cultural Association with Biamanga and Gulaga National Parks*. Canberra: Cultural Heritage Research Centre, University of Canberra, Australia.

Ehrlich, P. R. and Wilson, E. O. (1991) 'Biodiversity studies: Science and policy'. *Science* 253: 758–762

Ellis, S. (1994) 'Of elephants and men. Politics and nature conservation in South Africa'. *Journal of Southern African Studies* 20: 53–69

Environmental-Investigation-Agency (1994) *CITES Enforcement Not Extinction*. London: EIA

Fa, J. E., Peres, C. A. and Meeuwig, J. (2002) 'Bushmeat exploitation in tropical forests: An intercontinental comparison'. *Conservation Biology* 16(1): 232–237

Fabricius, C. and de Wet, C. (2002) 'The influence of forced removals and land restitution on conservation in South Africa'. In D. Chatty and M. Colchester (eds) *Conservation and Mobile Indigenous Peoples. Displacement, Forced Settlement, and Sustainable Development*. New York: Berghahn Books

Fairhead, J. and Leach, M. (2000) 'The nature lords: After desolation, conservation – and eviction. The future of West African forests and their peoples. *Times Literary Supplement*. 5 May (5066): 3–4

Fay, D. (2007) 'Struggles over resources and community formation in Dwesa-Cwebe, South Africa. *International Journal of Biodiversity Science and Management* 3(2): 88–102

Feeny, D., Berkes, F., McCay, B. J. and Acheson, J. M. (1990) 'The tragedy of the commons twenty-two years later'. *Human Ecology* 18: 1–19

Fennell, D. (1999) *Ecotourism, An Introduction*. London: Routledge

Ferguson, J. (1990) *The Anti-politics Machine: 'Development', Depoliticisation and Bureaucratic State Power in Lesotho*. Cambridge: Cambridge University Press

Ferguson, J. (2006) *Global Shadows. Africa in the Neoliberal World Order*. Durham: Duke University Press

Fiedel, S. and Haynes, G. (2004) 'A premature burial: Comments on Grayson and Meltzer's "Requiem for overkill"'. *Journal of Archaeological Science* 31(1): 121–131

Fisher, J. (1998) *Nongovernments. NGOs and the Political Development of the Third World*. West Hartford: Kumarion

Fisher, R. J., Maginnis, S. W., Jackson, J., Barrow, E. and S. Jeanrenaud, S. (2005) *Poverty and Conservation. Landscapes, People and Power*. Gland: IUCN

Fisher, W. F. (1997) 'Doing good? The politics and anti-politics of NGO practices'. *Annual Review of Anthropology* 26: 439–464

Fjeldstad, O.-H. (2001) 'Taxation, coercion and donors: Local government tax enforcement in Tanzania'. *The Journal of Modern African Studies* 39(2): 289–306

Fjeldstad, O.-H. and Semboja, J. (2000) 'Dilemmas of fiscal decentralisation: A study of local government taxation in Tanzania'. *Forum for Development Studies* 27(1): 7–41

Fjeldstad, O.-H. and Semboja, J. (2001) 'Why people pay taxes: The case of the development levy in Tanzania'. *World Development* 29(12): 2059–2074

Fortmann, L. (1997) 'Voices from communities managing wildlife in southern Africa'. *Society and Natural Resources* 10: 403–422

Fortmann, L. (2005) 'What we need is a community Bambi: The perils and possibilities of powerful symbols'. In J. P. Brosius, A. L. Tsing and C. Zerner (eds) *Communities and Conservation. Histories and Politics of Community-based Natural Resource Management*. pp195–205. Walnut Creek, CA: Altamira

Fortun, K. (2001) *Advocacy after Bhopal*. Chicago: University of Chicago Press

Fortwangler, C. (2003) 'The winding road. Incorporating social justice and human rights into protected area policies'. In S. R. Brechin, P. R. Wilchusen, C. L. Fortwrangler and P. C. West (eds) *Contested Nature. Promoting International Biodiversity Conservaton with Social Justice in the Twenty-first Century*. New York: State University of New York Press

Fortwangler, C. (2007) 'Friends with money: Private support for national parks in the U.S. Virgin Islands'. *Conservation and Society* 5(4): 504–533

Foster, J. (1999) 'Marx's Theory of the Metabolic Rift: Classical foundations for environmental sociology'. *American Journal of Sociology* 105(2): 366–405

Frank, D. J., Hironaka, A. and Schofer, E. (2000) 'The Nation-state and the Natural Environment over the Twentieth Century'. *American Sociological Review* 65: 96–116

Frynas, J. G. (2000) *Oil in Nigeria: Conflict and Litigation Between Oil Companies and Village Communities*. Hamburg: LIT Verlag/Transaction Publishers

Gadgil, M. and Guha, R. (1993) *This Fissured Land. An Ecological History of India*. Delhi: Oxford University Press

Galbreath, R. (2002) 'Displacement, conservation and customary use of native plants and animals in New Zealand'. *New Zealand Journal of History* 36(1): 36–47

Gamburd, M. R. (2000) 'Relocated lives: Displacement and resettlement in the Mahaweli Project, Sri Lanka'. *American Anthropologist* 102(4): 951–954

Garland, E. (2006) 'State of nature: Colonial power, neoliberal capital and wildlife management in Tanzania'. Unpublished PhD Thesis. University of Chicago

Geisler, C. (2003) 'A new kind of trouble: Evictions in Eden'. *International Social Science Journal* 55(1): 69–78

Geisler, C. and de Sousa, R. (2001) 'From refuge to refugee: The African case'. *Public Administration and Development* 21: 159–170

Gever, J, Kaufman, R., Skole, D. and Vorosmarty, C. (1986) *Beyond Oil: The Threat to Food and Fuel in the Coming Decades*. Cambridge, MA: Ballinger

Ghimire, K. B. (1994) 'Parks and people: Livelihood issues in national parks management in Thailand and Madagascar'. *Development and Change* 25: 195–229

Ghimire, K. B. and Pimbert, M. P. (1997) *Social Change and Conservation*. London: Earthscan

Gilardi, J. D. (2006) 'Captured for conservation: Will cages save wild birds? A response to Cooney & Jepson'. *Oryx* 40(1): 24–26

Gillies, C. A., Leach, M. R., Coad, N. B., Theobald, S. W., Campbell, J., Herbert, T., Graham, P. J. and Pierce, R. J. (2003) 'Six years of intensive pest mammal control at Trounson Kauri Park, a Department of Conservation "mainland island", June 1996 to July 2002'. *New Zealand Journal of Zoology* 30(4): 399–420

Giroux, H. (2006) *Stormy Weather: Katrina and the Politics of Disposability*. Boulder, CO: Paradigm Publishers

Goldman, M. (2001a) 'The birth of a discipline. Producing authoritative green knowledge, World Bank-style'. *Ethnography* 2(2): 191–217

Goldman, M. (2001b) 'Constructing an environmental state: Eco-governmentality and other transnational practices of a "green" World Bank'. *Social Problems* 48(4): 499–523

Gomez-Pompa, A. and Kaus, A. (1992) 'Taming the wilderness myth'. *Bioscience* 42(4): 271–279

Gossling, S., Broderick, J., Upham, P., Ceron, J.-P., Dubois, G., Peeters, P. and Strasdas, W. (2007) 'Voluntary carbon offsetting schemes for aviation: Efficiency, credibility and sustainable tourism'. *Journal of Sustainable Tourism* 15(3): 223–248

Gray, A., Parellada, A. and Newing, H. (1998) 'From principles to practice. Indigenous peoples and biodiversity conservation in Latin America'. *Proceedings of the Puscallpa Conference*. Copenhagen: IWGIA

Gray, T. N. E., Chamnan, H., Borey, R., Collar, N. J. and Dolman, P. M. (2007) 'Habitat preferences of a globally threatened bustard provide support for community-based conservation in Cambodia'. *Biological Conservation* 138: 341–350

Grayson, D. K. and Meltzer, D. J. (2003) 'A requiem for North American overkill'. *Journal of Archaeological Sciences* 30: 585–593

Grayson, D. K. and Meltzer, D. J. (2004) 'North American overkill continued?'. *Journal of Archaeological Science* 31(1): 133–136

Green, R. E., Cornell, S. J., Scharlemann, J. P. W. and Balmford, A. (2005a) 'Farming and the fate of wild nature'. *Science* 307(5709): 550–555

Green, R. E., Cornell, S. J., Scharlemann, J. P. W. and Balmford, A. (2005b) 'The future of farming and conservation: Response'. *Science* 308(5726): 1257–1258

Greenberg, R., Bichier, P., Angon, A. C. and Reitsma, R. (1997) 'Bird populations in shade and sun coffee plantations in central Guatemala'. *Conservation Biology* 11(2): 448–459

Griffen, J. (1999) *Study on the Development and Management of Transboundary Conservation Areas in Southern Africa*. Lilongwe Malawi: USAID Regional Centre for Southern Africa

Groenewald, Y. and Macleod, F. (2004) 'Park plans bring grief'. *Weekly Mail and Guardian*. 25 June 2004

Hafild, E. (2005) 'Social movements, community-based natural resource management, and the struggle for democracy; experiences from Indonesia'. In J. P. Brosius, A. L. Tsing and C. Zerner (eds) *Communities and Conservation. Histories and Politics of Community-Based Natural Resource Management*. Walnut Creek, CA: Altamira

Hall, C. M. (1994) *Tourism and Politics Policy Power and Place*. New York: John Wiley and Sons

Halpern, B. S., Pyke, C. R., Fox, H. E., Haney, J. C., Schlaepfer, M. A. and Zaradic P. (2006) 'Gaps and mismatches between global conservation priorities and spending'. *Conservation Biology* 20(1): 56–64

Hardin, G. (1968) 'The tragedy of the commons'. *Science* 162: 1243–1248

Harkness, J. (1998) 'Recent trends in forestry and conservation of biodiversity in China'. *The China Quarterly* 156: 911–934

Harrison, D. (1992) *Tourism and the Less Developed Countries*. London: Belhaven Press

Harrison, G. (2004) *The World Bank and Africa. The Construction of Governance States*. London: Routledge

Harrison, G. (2005) 'The World Bank governance and theories of political action in Africa'. *British Journal of Politics and International Relations* 72: 240–260

Hart, K. (1982) *The Political Economy of West African Agriculture*. Cambridge: Cambridge University Press

Hayes, T. M. (2006) 'Parks, people, and forest protection: An institutional assessment of the effectiveness of protected areas'. *World Development* 34(12): 2064–2075

Hayes, T. M. and Ostrom, E. (2005) 'Conserving the world's forests. Are protected areas the only way?'. *Indiana Law Review* 38: 595–617

Heaney, L. R. (1986) 'Biogeography of mammals in SE Asia: Estimates of rates of colonisation, extinction and speciation'. *Biological Journal of the Linnaean Society* 28: 127–165

Heywood, V. H., Mace, G. M., May, R. M. and Stuart, S. N. (1994) 'Uncertainties in extinction rates'. *Nature* 368(6467): 105

Hitchcock, M. and Teague, K. (2000) *Souvenirs, The Material Culture of Tourism*. Aldershot: Ashgate

Hodgson, D. (2002a) 'Introduction: Comparative perspectives on the indigenous rights movement in Africa and the Americas'. *American Anthropologist* 104(4): 1037–1049

Hodgson, D. (2002b) 'Precarious alliances: The cultural politics and structural predicaments of the indigenous rights movement in Tanzania'. *American Anthropologist* 104(4): 1086–1097

Hoekstra, J. M., Boucher, T. M., Ricketts, T. H. and Roberts, C. (2005) 'Confronting a biome crisis: Global disparities of habitat loss and protection'. *Ecology Letters* 8(1): 23–29

Hofer, D. (2002) 'The lion's share of the hunt: Trophy hunting and conservation – a review of the Eurasian tourist hunting market and trophy trade under CITES'. Brussels: TRAFFIC Europe Regional Report

Homewood, K. M. and Rodgers, W. A. (1991) *Maasailand Ecology. Pastoralist Development and Wildlife Conservation in Ngorongoro, Tanzania*. Cambridge: Cambridge University Press

Honey, M. (1999) *Ecotourism and Sustainable Development. Who Owns Paradise?*. Washington DC: Island Press

Horning, A. J. (2004) *In the Shadow of Ragged Mountain: Historical Archaeology of Nicholson, Corbin, & Weakley Hollows*. Luray, VA: Shenandoah National Park Association

Horning, N. R. (2005) 'The cost of ignoring rules: Forest conservation and rural livelihood outcomes in Madagascar'. *Forests Trees and Livelihoods* 15: 149–166

Horning, N. R. (2008) 'Strong support for weak performance: Donor competition in Madagascar'. *African Affairs* 107(428): 405–431

Hulme, D. and Edwards, M. (1997) *NGOs, States and Donors: Too Close for Comfort?.* London: Macmillan

Hulme, D. and Infield, M. (2001) 'Community conservation, reciprocity and park–people relationships. Lake Mburo National Park, Uganda'. In D. Hulme and M. Murphree (eds) *African Wildlife and Livelihoods.* Portsmouth: Heinemann

Hulme, D. and Murphree, M. (1999) 'Communities, wildlife and the new conservation in Africa'. *Journal of International Development* 11(3): 277–285

Hulme, D. and Murphee, M. (2001) *African Wildlife and Livelihoods. The Promise and Performance of Community Conservation.* Portsmouth: Heinemann

Hunn, E. S., Johnson, D. R., Russell, P. N. and Thornton, T. F. (2003) 'Huna Tlingit traditional environmental knowledge, conservation and the management of a "wilderness" park'. *Current Anthropology* 44(Supplement): S79–S103

Hurt, R. and Ravan, P. (2000) 'Hunting and its benefits: An overview of hunting in Africa with special reference to Tanzania'. In H. H. T. Prins, J. G. Grootenuis and T. T. Dolan (eds) *Wildlife Conservation by Sustainable Use.* Boston: Kluwer Academic Publishers

Hutton, J. and Dickson, B. (2000) *Endangered Species Threatened Convention. The Past, Present and Future of CITES.* London: Earthscan

Hutton, J. and Leader-Williams, N. (2003) 'Sustainable use and incentive-driven conservation: Realigning human and conservation interests'. *Oryx* 37(2): 215–226

Hutton, J., Adams, W. M. and Murombedzi, J. C. (2005) 'Back to the barriers? Changing narratives in biodiversity conservation'. *Forum for Development Studies* NUPI 2005(2): 341–370

Igoe, J. (2000) 'Ethnicity, civil society, and the Tanzanian pastoral NGO movement: The continuities and discontinuities of liberalized development'. PhD., Boston University

Igoe, J. (2003a) 'Decentralised hegemony and the displacement of the political in Tanzanian civil society: The story of the Barabaig NGOs'. The Hanang Community Development Project

Igoe, J. (2003b) 'Scaling up civil society: Donor money, NGOs and the pastoralist land rights movement in Tanzania'. *Development and Change* 34: 863–885

Igoe, J. (2004a) 'Becoming indigenous in Africa: The globalization of Maasai and Barabaig ethnic identities'. Boston University, African Studies Working Paper 248

Igoe, J. (2004b) *Conservation and Globalisation: A Study of National Parks and Indigenous Communties from East Africa to South Dakota.* Belmont, CA: Wadsworth/Thomson Learning

Igoe, J. (2004c) 'History, culture, and conservation: In search of more informed guesses about whether "community-based conservation" has a chance to work'. *Policy Matters* 13: 174–185

Igoe, J. (2005) 'Global indigenism and spaceship Earth: Convergence, space, and re-entry friction'. *Globalizations* 2(3): 1–13

Igoe, J. (2006a) 'Becoming indigenous peoples: Difference, inequality, and the globalisation of East African identity politics'. *African Affairs* 105(420): 399–420

Igoe, J. (2006b) 'Measuring the costs and benefits of conservation to local communities'. *Ecological Anthropology* 10: 72–77

Igoe, J. (2008) 'Global indigenism and spaceship Earth: Convergence, space, and re-entry friction'. In J. Oosthoek and B. Gills (eds) *The Globalization of the Environmental Crisis.* pp95–106. London: Routledge

Igoe, J. and Brockington, D. (2007) 'Neoliberal conservation: A brief introduction'. *Conservation and Society* 5(4): 432–449

Igoe, I. and Brockington, D. (under review) 'Saving a dead world? Wildlife conservation, virtualisms and the consumption of spectacle'. *Current Anthropology.*

Igoe, J. and Croucher, B. (2007) 'Poverty alleviation meets the spectacle of nature: Does reality matter?'. *Conservation and Society* 5(4): 534–561

Igoe, J. and Fortwangler, C. (2007) 'Whither communities and conservation?'. *International Journal of Biodiversity Science and Management* 3: 65–76

Igoe, J. and Kelsall, T. (2005) *African NGOs, Donors, and the State: Between a Rock and a Hard Place.* Durham, NC: Carolina Academic Press

Ikeya, K. (2001) 'Some changes among the San under the influence of relocation plan in Botswana'. In D. G. Anderson and K. Ikeya (eds) *Parks, Property and Power: Managing Hunting Practice and Identity within State Policy Regimes.* Senri Ethnological Studies no. 59. pp183–198. Osaka: National Museum of Ethnology

Ingram, J. C. (2004) 'Questioning simplistic representations of environmental change in southeastern Madagascar: An assessment of forest change, condition and diversity of littoral forests'. Conference paper presented at 'Trees, Rain and Politics in Africa. The dynamics and politics of climatic and environmental change'. Oxford

Ingram, J. C., Whittaker, R. J. and Dawson, T. P. (2005) 'Tree structure and diversity in human-impacted littoral forests, Madagascar'. *Environmental Management* 35(6): 779–798

IUCN (2003) Fifth World Parks Congress 2003: Recommendation 12 'Tourism as a Vehicle for Conservation and Support of Protected Areas' www.iucn.org/themes/wcpa/wpc2003/pdfs/outputs/recommendations/approved/english/html/r12.htm (accessed 16 July 2007)

Ives, J. D. and Messerli, B. (1989) *The Himalayan Dilemma. Reconciling Development and Conservation.* London: Routledge

Jackson, J. (1999) 'The politics of ethnographic practice in Columbian Vaupes'. *Identities* 6(2–3): 281–317

Jacoby, K. (2001) *Crimes against Nature. Squatters, Poachers, Thieves and the Hidden History of American Conservation.* Berkeley: University of California Press

James, A., Gaston, K. J. and Balmford, A. (2001) 'Can we afford to conserve biodiversity?'. *Bioscience* 51(1): 43–52

Jeanrenaud, S. (2002) *People-Orientated Approaches in Global Conservation. Is the Leopard Changing its Spots?.* London: IIED

Jenkins, M., Green, R. E. and Madden, J. (2003) 'The challenge of measuring global change in wild nature: Are things getting better or worse?'. *Conservation Biology* 17(1): 20–23

Jepson, P. and Whittaker, R. J. (2002) 'Histories of protected areas: Internationalisation of conservationist values and their adoption in the Netherlands Indies (Indonesia)'. *Environment and History* 8: 129–172

Jepson, P., Momberg, F. and van Noord, H. (2002) 'A review of the efficacy of the protected area system of East Kalimantan Province, Indonesia'. *Natural Areas Journal* 22(1): 28–42

Johnson, C. (2001) 'Community formation and fisheries conservation in southern Thailand'. *Development and Change* 32(5): 951–974

Jones, B. and Murphree, M. (2001) 'The evolution of policy on community conservation in Namibia and Zimbabwe'. In D. Hulme and M. Murphree (eds) *African Wildlife and Livelihoods*. Portsmouth: Heinemann

Kalamandeen, M. L. Gillson, L. (2007) 'Demything "wilderness": Implications for protected area designation and management'. *Biodiversity and Conservation* 16: 165–182

Karanth, K. K. (2007) 'Making resettlement work: The case of India's Bhadra wildlife sanctuary'. *Biological Conservation* 139(3–4): 315–324

Keck, M. E. and Sikkink, K. (1998) *Activists Beyond Borders. Advocacy Networks in International Politics*. Ithaca, NY: Cornell University Press

Keller, R. and Turek, M. (1998) *American Indians & National Parks*. Tuscon: University of Arizona Press

Khan, S. A. and bin Talal, H. (1987) 'Introduction'. In S. A. Khan and H. B. Talal (eds) *Indigenous Peoples: A Global Quest for Justice*. London: Zed Books

Khare, A. and Bray, D. B. (2004) 'Study of critical new forest conservation issues in the global South'. Final report submitted to the Ford Foundation.

King, D. A. and Stewart, W. P. (1996) 'Ecotourism and commodification: Protecting people and places'. *Biodiversity and Conservation* 5(3): 293–305

Kitson, J. C. (2002) 'What limits the number of TiTi (*Puffinus griseus*) harvested by Rakiura Maori?'. *Human Ecology* 30(4): 503–521

Kiwasila, H. (1997) 'Not just a Maasai Garden of Eden'. *The Observer*, 13 April 1997

Klein, N. (2007) *The Shock Doctrine: The Rise of Disaster Capitalism*. New York: Metropolitan Books

Kliot, N. (2001) 'The political geography of cooperation and conflict in borderlands'. In D. Newman, C. Schofield and D. Alasdair (eds) *The Razors Edge International Boundaries Geopolitics and Political Geography Essays in Honour of Professor Gerald Blake*. London: Kluwer Academic

Klooster, D. (2000) 'Community forestry and tree theft in Mexico: Resistance or complicity in conservation'. *Development and Change* 31: 281–305

Koch, E. (1997) 'Ecotourism and rural reconstruction in South Africa: Reality or rhetoric?'. In K. B. Ghimire and M. P. Pimbert (eds) *Social Change and Conservation*. London: Earthscan

Koch, P. L. and Barnosky, A. D. (2006) 'Late quaternary extinctions: State of the debate'. *Annual Review of Ecology Evolution and Systematics* 37: 215–250

Kothari, A., Pande, P., Singh, S. and Variava, D. (1989) *Management of National Parks and Sancturies in India. A Status Report*. New Delhi: Indian Institute of Public Administration

Kothari, A., Pathak, N., Anurdha, R. V. and Taneja, B. (1998) *Communities and Conservation. Natural Resource Management in South and Central Asia*. New Delhi: Sage

Kothari, A., Pathak, N. and Vania, F. (2000) *Where Communities Care. Community-based Wildlife and Ecosystem Management in South Asia*. Pune and London: Kalpavriksh and IIED

Kramer, R., von Schaik, C. and Johnson, J. (1997) *Last Stand. Protected Areas and the Defense of Tropical Biodiversity*. Oxford: Oxford University Press

Kull, C. A. (1996) 'The evolution of conservation efforts in Madagascar'. *International Environmental Affairs* 8(1): 50–86

Kumar, S. (2002) 'Does "participation" in common pool resource management help the poor? A social cost–benefit analysis of joint forest management in Jharkhand, India'. *World Development* 30(5): 763–782

Kuper, A. (2003) 'The return of the native'. *Current Anthropology* 44(3): 389–402

Lamoreux, J., Akcakaya, H. R., Bennun, L., Collar, N. J., Boitani, L., Brackett, D., Brautigam, A., Brooks, T. M., de Fonseca, G. A. B., Mittermeier, R. A., Rylands, A. B., Gardenfors, U., Hilton-Taylor, C., Mace, G., Stein, B. A. and Stuart, S. (2003) 'Value of the IUCN Red List'. *Trends in Ecology & Evolution* 18(5): 214–215

Lane, M. (2003) 'Decentralization or privatization of environmental governance? Forest conflict and bioregional assessment in Australia'. *Journal of Rural Studies* 19: 283–294

Langholz, J. and Kerley, G. H. (2006) *Combining Conservation and Development on Private Lands: An Assessment of Eco-tourism Based Private Game Reserves in the Eastern Cape*. Port Elizabeth: Centre for African Conservation Ecology, NMMU

Langton, M., Ma Rhea, Z. and Palmer, L. (2005) 'Community-orientated protected areas for indigenous peoples and local communities'. *Journal of Political Ecology* 12: 23–50

Laungaramsri, P. (1999) 'The ambiguity of "watershed": The politics of people and conservation in northern Thailand. A case study of the Chom Thong conflict'. In M. Colchester and C. Erni (eds) *Indigenous Peoples and Protected Areas in South and Southeast Asia. From Principles to Practice*. Copenhagen: IWGIA

Laurance, W. F., Croes, B. M., Tchignoumba, L., Lahm, S. A., Alonso, A., Lee, M. E., Campbell, P. and Ondzeano, C. (2006) 'Impacts of roads and hunting on central African rainforest mammals'. *Conservation Biology* 20(4): 1251–1261

Lawrence, D. (2000) *Kakadu: The Making of a National Park*. Melbourne: Melbourne University Press

Lawton, J. (1997) 'The science and non-science of conservation biology'. *Oikos* 79(1): 3–5

Leakey, R. (2003) 'Science, sentiment, and advocacy (an interview)'. *Yellowstone Science* 10(3): 8–12

Lemos, M. C. and Agrawal, A. (2006) 'Environmental governance'. *Annual Review of Environment and Resources* 31: 297–325

Levi-Strauss, C. (1969 (1964)) *The Raw and the Cooked. Introduction to a Science of Mythology*. New York: Harper and Row

Levy, B. (1989) 'Foreign aid in the making of economic policy in Sri Lanka, 1977–1983'. *Policy Sciences* 22(3–4): 437–461

Li, T. M. (2000) 'Articulating indigenous identity in Indonesia: Resource politics and the tribal slot'. *Comparative Studies in Society and History* 421: 149–179

Liebig, J. von (1859) *Letters on Modern Agriculture*. London: Walton & Maberly

Lindberg, K., Enriquez, J. and Sproule, K. (1996) 'Ecotourism questioned: Case studies from Belize'. *Annals of Tourism Research* 23: 543–562

Lindsey, P. A., Roulet, P. A. and Romanach, S. S. (2007) 'Economic and conservation significance of the trophy hunting industry in sub-Saharan Africa'. *Biological Conservation* 134: 455–469

Litfin, K. (1994) *Ozone Discourses: Science and Politics in Global Environmental Co-Operation*. New York: Columbia University Press

Locke, H. and Dearden, P. (2005) 'Rethinking protected area categories and the new paradigm'. *Environmental Conservation* 32(1): 1–10

Logo, P. B. (2003) 'The decentralised forestry taxation system in Cameroon: Local management and state logic'. In J. C. Ribot and P. G. Veit (eds) *Environmental Governance in Africa*. Washington DC: World Resources Institute

Lomborg, B. (2001) *The Skeptical Environmentalist. Measuring the Real State of the World*. Cambridge: Cambridge University Press

Lovecraft, A. (2007) 'Interest groups and science rhetoric in legislative testimony framing the Arctic National Wildlife Refuge'. Paper presented at the Western Political Science Association Conference Las Vegas 7–10 March 2007

Loveridge, A. J., Searle, A. W., Murindagomo, F. and Macdonald, D. W. (2007) 'The impact of sport-hunting on the population dynamics of an African lion population in a protected area'. *Biological Conservation* 134(4): 548–558

Luck, G. W., Ricketts, T. H., Daily, G. C. and Imhoff, M. (2004) 'Alleviating spatial conflict between people and biodiversity'. *Proceedings of the National Academy of Sciences of the United States of America* 101(1): 182–186

Luck, K. (2003) 'Contested Rights: The impact of game farming on farm workers in the Bushman's river area'. MA, Rhodes University

Luckham, R., Goetz, A-M. and Kaldor, M. (2000) 'Democratic institutions and politics in contexts of inequality, poverty and conflict'. IDS Working Paper 104

Lund, J. F. and Nielsen, O. J. (2006) 'The promises of participatory forest management is forest conservation and poverty alleviation: The case of Tanzania'. In H. Charton and C. Médard (eds) *L'Afrique Orientale*. Annuaire 2005. Paris: L'Harmattan

MacDonald, K. (2004) 'Developing "nature": Global ecology and the politics of conservation in northern Pakistan'. In J. Carrier (ed) *Confronting Environments: Local Environmental Understanding In a Globalising World*. Lantham: AltaMira Press

MacDonald, K. (2005) 'Global hunting grounds: Power, scale and ecology in the negotiation of conservation'. *Cultural Geographies* 12: 259–291

Mace, G. M. (1994) 'An investigation into methods for categorising the conservation status of species'. In P. J. Edwards, R. M. May and N. R. Webb (eds) *Large-scale Ecology and Conservation Biology*. Oxford: Blackwell Scientific Publications

Mace, G. M. (2004) 'The role of taxonomy in species conservation'. *Philosophical Transactions of the Royal Society B* 359: 711–719

Mace, G. M., Balmford, A., Boitani, L., Cowlishaw, G., Dobson, A. P., Faith, D. P., Gaston, K. J., Humphries, C. J., Vane-Wright, R. I., Williams, P. H., Lawton, J. H., Margules, C. R., May, R. M., Nicholls, A. O., Possingham, H. P., Rahbek, C. and van Jaarsveld, A. S. (2000) 'It's time to work together and stop duplicating conservation efforts'. *Nature* 405(6785): 393–393

Mackenzie, J. (1988) *The Empire of Nature: Hunting, Conservation and British Imperialism*. Manchester: Manchester University Press

Mann, C. C. (1991) 'Extinction: Are ecologists crying wolf?'. *Science* 253: 736–738

Mann, C. C. (1993) 'The high cost of biodiversity'. *Science* 260: 1868–1871

Margules, C. R. and Pressey, R. L. (2000) 'Systematic conservation planning'. *Nature* 405: 243–253

Mark, A. F. (1989) 'Responses of indigenous vegetation to contrasting trends in utilization by red deer in 2 southwestern New Zealand national parks'. *New Zealand Journal of Ecology* 12: 103–114

Marx, K. (1971 (1875)) *Critique of the Gotha Program*. Moscow: Progress

Marx, K. (1976 (1867)) *Capital* vol 1. London: Penguin

Marx, K. (1978 (1863–65)) *Capital* vol 3. New York: Vintage

Marx, K. (1978 (1865–70)) *Capital* vol 2. New York: Vintage

Mbembe, A. (2001) *On the Postcolony*. Berkeley: University of California Press

McAfee, K. (1999) 'Selling nature to save it? Biodiversity and green developmentalism'. *Environment and Planning D: Society and Space* 17: 133–154

McAlpine, C. A., Spies, T. A., Norman, P. and Peterson, A. (2007) 'Conserving forest biodiversity across multiple land ownerships: Lessons from the Northwest Forest Plan and the Southeast Queensland regional forests agreement (Australia)'. *Biological Conservation* 134(4): 580–592

McGrew, A. G. (1992) 'Conceptualising global politics'. In A. G. McGrew and P. G. Lewis (eds) *Global Politics*. pp1–28. Cambridge: Polity Press

McLean, J. and Straede, S. (2003) 'Conservation, relocation and the paradigms of park and people management: A case study of Padampur villages and the Royal Chitwan National Park, Nepal'. *Society and Natural Resources* 16: 509–526

McNeely, J. A. and Scherr, S. J. (2003) *Ecoagriculture. Strategies to Feed the World and Save Wild Biodiversity*. Washington DC: Island Press

Meir, E., Andelman, S. and Possingham, H. P. (2004) 'Does conservation planning matter in a dynamic and uncertain world?'. *Ecology Letters* 7: 615–622

Mendelson, J. R., Lips, K. R., Gagliardo, R. W., Rabb, G. B., Collins, J. P., Diffendorfer, J. E., Daszak, P., Ibanez, R., Zippel, K. C., Lawson, D. P., Wright, K. M., Stuart, S. N., Gascon, C., da Silva, H. R., Burrowes, P. A., Joglar, R. L., La Marca, E., Lotters, S., du Preez, L. H., Weldon, C., Hyatt, A., Rodriguez-Mahecha, J. V., Hunt, H., Robertson, S., Lock, B., Raxworthy, C. J., Frost, D. R., Lacy, R. C., Alford, R. A., Campbell, J. A., Parra-Olea, G., Bolanos, F., Domingo, J. J. C., Halliday, T., Murphy, J. B., Wake, M. H., Coloma, L. A., Kuzmin, S. L., Price, M. S., Howell, K. M., Lau, M., Pethiyagoda, R., Boone, M., Lannoo, M. J., Blaustein, A. R., Dobson, A., Griffiths, R. A., Crump, M. L., Wake, D. B. and Brodie, E. D. (2006) 'Biodiversity: Confronting amphibian declines and extinctions'. *Science* 313(5783): 48–48

Menzies, H. (1989) *Fast Forward and Out of Control: How Technology is Changing Your Life*. Toronto, ON: Macmillan Publishers

Mgumia, F. H. and Oba, G. (2003) 'Potential role of sacred groves in biodiversity conservation in Tanzania'. *Environmental Conservation* 30(3): 259–265

Middleton, B. (2003) 'Ecology and objective based management: A study of the Keoladeo National Park, Bharatpur, Rajasthan'. In V. Saberwal and M. Rangarajan (eds) *Battles over Nature. Science and the Politics of Conservation*. Delhi: Permanent Black

Milliken, T. (2002) *The Worlds Unregulated Domestic Ivory Markets*. Cambridge: TRAFFIC International

Milner-Gulland, E. J. (2004) 'Against extinction: The story of conservation'. *Nature* 429(6990): 346–347

Milner-Gulland, E. J., Bennett, E. L. and SCB 2002 Annual Meeting Wild Meat Group (2003) 'Wild meat: The bigger picture'. *Trends in Ecology and Evolution* 18(7): 351–357

Mintz, S. (1985) *Sweetness and Power: The Place of Sugar in Modern History*. New York: Penguin Books

Mishra, H. R. (1994) 'South and southeast Asia'. In J. A. McNeely, J. Harrision and P. Dingwall (eds) *Protecting Nature: Regional Reviews of Protected Areas*. Gland: IUCN

Mittermeier, R. A., Mittermeier, C. G., Brooks, T. M., Pilgrim, J. D., Konstant, W. R., da Fonseca, G. A. B. and Kormos, C. (2003) 'Wilderness and biodiversity conservation'. *Proceedings of the National Academy of Sciences of the United States of America* 100(18): 10309–10313

Mittermeier, R. A., Robles-Gil, P. and Mittermeier, C. G. (1997) *Megadiversity*. Mexico City: CEMEX.

Molnar, A., Scherr, S. J. and Khare, A. (2004a) *Who Conserves the World's Forests? A New Assessment of Conservation and Investment Trends*. Washington DC: Forest Trends; Ecoagriculture partners

Molnar, A., Scherr, S. J. and Khare, A. (2004b) *Who Conserves the World's Forests? Community-driven Strategies to Protect Forests and Respect Rights*. Washington DC: Forest Trends.

Monela, G. C., Chanshana, S. A. O., Mwaipopo, R. and Gamassa, D. M. (2004) *A Study of the Social, Economic and Environmental Impacts of Forest Landscape Restoration in Shinyanga Region, Tanzania*. Nairobi: IUCN, Eastern Africa Regional Office

Mosse, D. (2004) 'Is good policy unimplementable? Reflections on the ethnography of aid policy and practice'. *Development and Change* 35(4): 639–671

Mowforth, R. and Munt, I. (1998) *Tourism and Sustainability Dilemmas in Third World Tourism*. London: Routledge

Muchnick, B. (2007) '9/10 of the law: Vigilante conservation in the American West'. Paper presented to 106th American Anthropological Association Annual Meeting. Washington DC

Muehlebach, A. (2001) '"Making Place" at the United Nations: Indigenous cultural politics at the UN working group on indigenous populations'. *Cultural Anthropology* 163: 415–448

Murdoch, W., Polasky, S., Wilson, K. A., Possingham, H. P., Kareiva, P. and Shaw, R. (2007) 'Maximizing return on investment in conservation'. *Biological Conservation* 139: 375–388

Murombedzi, J. (2001) 'Committees, rights, costs & benefits. Natural resource stewardship & community benefits in Zimbabwe's CAMPFIRE programme'. In D. Hulme and M. Murphree (eds) *African Wildlife and Livelihoods. The Promise and Performance of Community Conservation*. Oxford: James Currey

Murombedzi, J. (2003) 'Devolving the expropriation of nature: The devolution of wildlife management in southern Africa'. In W. M. Adams and M. Mulligan (eds) *Decolonizing Nature. Strategies for Conservation in a Post-colonial Era*. London: Earthscan

Murphree, M. (1995) 'Optimal principles and pragmatic strategies: Creating an enabling politico-legal environment for community based natural resource management (CBNRM)'. In Keynote Address to the Conference of the Natural Resources Management Programme (SADC Technical Coordination Unit, Malawi, USAID-NRMP Regional) Chobe, Botswana 3 April 1995

Murphree, M. W. (1996) 'Approaches to community participation'. In ODA (ed) *African Wildlife Policy Consultation, Final Report*. London: Jay Printers

Murphree, M. (2001) 'Community, council and client. A case study in ecotourism development from Mahenye, Zimbabwe'. In D. Hulme and M. Murphree (eds) *African Wildlife and Livelihoods*. Portsmouth: Heinemann

Murphree, M. (2005) 'Congruent objectives, competing interests, and strategic compromise: Concept and process in the evolution of Zimbabwe's CAMPFIRE, 1984–1996'. In J. P. Brosius, A. L. Tsing and C. Zerner (eds) *Communities and Conservation. Histories and Politics of Community-Based Natural Resource Management*. pp105–147. Walnut Creek, CA: Altamira

Mutchler, J. C. (2007) 'The failure of wilderness: Bureaucracy, bovine, and bullets'. Paper presented to 106th American Anthropological Association Annual Meeting. Washington DC

Mutwira, R. (1989) 'Southern Rhodesian wildlife policy 1890–1953. A question of condoning game slaughter?'. *Journal of Southern African Studies* 15: 250–262

Myers, N. (2003) 'Biodiversity hotspots revisted'. *Bioscience* 53(10): 916–917

Myers, N. and Lanting, F. (1999) 'What we must do to counter the biotic holocaust'. *International Wildlife* 29(2): 30–39

Myers, N., Mittermeier, R. A., Mittermeier, C. G., da Fonseca, G. A. B. and Kent, J. (2000) 'Biodiversity hotspots for conservation priorities'. *Nature* 403: 853–858

Myers, N. and Mittermeier, R. A. (2003) 'Impact and acceptance of the hotspots strategy: Response to Ovadia and to Brummitt and Lughadha'. *Conservation Biology* 17(5): 1449–1450

Nabakov, P. and Lawrence, L. (2004) *Restoring a Presence: A Documentary Overview of Native Americans and Yellowstone National Park*. Norman, OK: University of Oklahoma Press

Nadelman, E. A. (1990) 'Global prohibition regimes. The evolution of norms in international society'. *International Organisation* 44: 479–526

Nash, R. (2001) *Wilderness and the American Mind*. New Haven: Yale Nota Bene

Naughton-Treves, L., Holland, M. B. and Brandon, K. (2005) 'The role of protected areas in conserving biodiversity and sustaining local livelihoods'. *Annual Review of Environment and Resources* 30: 219–252

Nelson, F. (2004) 'The evolution and impacts of community-based ecotourism in northern Tanzania'. IIED Drylands Programme Issue Paper 131

Nelson, F. and Makko, S. O. (2003) 'Communities, conservation and conflicts in the Tanzanian Serengeti'. Third Annual Community-based conservation network seminar: Turning Natural Resources into Assets, Savannah Georgia, 2003

Nelson, J. and Hossack, L. (2003) *Indigenous Peoples and Protected Areas in Africa*. Moreton-in-Marsh: Forest Peoples Programme

Nepstad, D., Schwartzman, S., Bamberger, B., Santilli, M., Ray, D., Schlesinger, P., Lefebvre, P., Alencar, A., Prinz, E., Fiske, G. and Rolla, A. (2006) 'Inhibition of Amazon deforestation and fire by parks and indigenous lands'. *Conservation Biology* 20(1): 65–73

Netting, D. (1981) *Balancing on an Alp: Ecological Change and Continuity in a Swiss Mountain Community*. Cambridge: Cambridge University Press

Neumann, R. (2004) 'Moral and discursive geographies in the war for biodiversity in Africa'. *Political Geography* 23: 813–837

Neumann, R. (2005) *Making Political Ecology*. London: Hodder Books

Neumann, R. P. (1997) 'Primitive ideas: Protected area buffer zones and the politics of land in Africa'. *Development and Change* 28: 559–582

Neumann, R. P. (1998) *Imposing Wilderness. Struggles over Livelihood and Nature Preservation in Africa*. Berkeley: University of California Press

Neumann, R. P. (2000) *Primitive Ideas: Protected Area Buffer Zones and the Politics of Land in Africa?* Uppsala: Nordiska Afrikainstitutet

Neves, K. and Igoe, J. (in production) 'Disneyfied disaster: Neoliberal recovery and parreality in post-Katrina New Orleans'. Under production for submission to *American Anthropologist*.

Neves-Graca, K. (2003) 'Investigating ecology: Cognition in human–environmental relationships'. In P. Meusburger and T. Schwan (eds) *Humanökologie: Ansätze zur Überwindung der Natur-Kultur-Dichotomie*. (Human Ecology: Towards Overcoming the Nature–Culture Dichotomy.) pp287–307. Stuttgart, Germany: Steiner Verlag

Neves-Graca, K. (2004) 'Revisiting the tragedy of the commons: Whale watching in the Azores and its ecological dilemmas'. *Human Organisation* 63(3): 289–300

Neves-Graca, K. (2006) 'Politics of environmentalism and ecological knowledge at the intersection of local and global processes'. *Journal of Ecological Anthropology* 10: 19–32

Neves-Graca, K. (2007a) 'Animals and global warming'. In M. Siano (ed) *The Encyclopedia of Global Warming and Climate Change*. Thousand Oaks, CA: Sage Publications

Neves-Graca, K. (2007b) 'Elementary methodological tools for a recursive approach to human–environmental relations'. In J. Wassmann and K. Stockhaus (eds) *Person, Space, and Memory in the Contemporary Pacific: The Experience of New Worlds*. Oxford: Berghahn Books

Neves-Graca, K. (2009) 'The aesthetics of ecological learning at Montreal's Botanical Garden'. *Anthropologica*, Special Issue edited by S. Aprahiman, K. Neves-Graca and N. Rapport

Nielsen, M. R. (2006) 'Importance, cause and effect of bushmeat hunting in the Udzungwa Mountains, Tanzania: Implications for community based wildlife management'. *Biological Conservation* 128(4): 509–516

Niezen, R. (2003) *The Origins of Indigenism: Human Rights and the Politics of Identity.* Berkeley, California: University of California Press

Nikol'skii, A. A. (1994) 'North Eurasia'. In J. A. McNeely, J. Harrision and P. Dingwall (eds) *Protecting Nature: Regional Reviews of Protected Areas*. Gland: IUCN

Norton, D. (2004) 'Echoes of Timberlands in high country debate: Are more decisions being made on the basis of political ideology rather than principles of ecological sustainability?'. *New Zealand Journal of Forestry* November: 39–41.

Novelli, M., Barnes, J. and Humavindu, M. (2006) 'The other side of the ecotourism coin: Consumptive tourism in southern Africa'. *Journal of Ecotourism* 5(1, 2): 62–79

Novelli, M. and Humavindu, M. (2005) 'Wildlife tourism: Wildlife use vs local gain trophy hunting in Namibia'. In M. Novelli (ed) *Niche Tourism: Current Issues Trend and Cases*. Oxford: Elsevier

Nugent, S. (1994) *Big Mouth: The Amazon Speaks*. San Francisco: Brown Trout Press

Nygren, A. (2000) 'Environmental narratives on protection and production: Nature-based conflicts in Rio SanJuan, Nicaragua'. *Development and Change* 31: 807–830

Oates, J. F. (1999) *Myth and Reality in the Rain Forest: How Conservation Strategies are Failing in West Africa.* Berkeley: University of California Press

O'Brien, R., Goetz, A.-M., Scholte, J. A. and Williams, M. (2000) *Contesting Global Governance, Multilateral Economic Institutions and Global Social Movements.* Cambridge: Cambridge University Press

O'Connor, J. (1988) 'Capitalism, nature, and socialism: A theoretical introduction'. *Capitalism, Nature, and Socialism* 1: 11–38

Oldfield, S. (2002) *The Trade in Wildlife: Regulation for Conservation.* London, Earthscan

Olson, D. M. and Dinerstein, E. (2002) 'The global 200: Priority ecoregions for global conservation'. *Annals of the Missouri Botanical Garden* 89(2): 199–224

Olwig, K. F. and Olwig, K. (1979) 'Underdevelopment and the development of "natural" park ideology'. *Antipode* 11(21): 16–25

Onneweer, M. (2005) 'New nature: On the topography and temporality of a paradox'. Paper for the conference People Protecting Nature: Social Dimensions of Environmental Conservation: 20–21 October 2005. Oxford, Brookes

Ostrom, E. (1990) *Governing the Commons. The Evolution of Institutions for Collective Action.* Cambridge: Cambridge University Press

Ostrom, E., Burger, J., Field, C. B., Norgaard, R. B. and Policansky, D. (1999) 'Revisiting the commons: Local lessons, global challenges'. *Science* 284: 278–282

Ostrom, E., Dietz, T., Dolsak, N., Stern, P. C., Stonich, S. and Weber, E. U. (2002) *The Drama of the Commons.* Washington DC: National Academy Press

Ostrom, E. and Nagendra, H. (2006) 'Insights on linking forests, trees and people from the air, on the ground, and in the laboratory'. *Proceedings of the National Academy of Sciences of the United States of America* 103(51): 19224–19231

Ovadia, O. (2003) 'Ranking hotspots of varying sizes: A lesson from the nonlinearity of the species–area relationship'. *Conservation Biology* 17(5): 1440–1441

Oyono, P. R. (2004a) 'Institutional deficit, representation, and decentralized forest management in Cameroon'. In J. C. Ribot and P. G. Veit (eds) *Environmental Governance in Africa.* Washington DC: World Resources Institute

Oyono, P. R. (2004b) 'One step forward, two steps backward? Paradoxes of natural resources management decentralisation in Cameroon'. *Journal of Modern African Studies* 42(1): 91–111

Oyono, P. R. (2004c) 'The social and organisation roots of ecological uncertainties in Cameroon's forest management decentralisation model'. *European Journal of Development Research* 16(1): 174–191

Ozinga, S. (2001) *Behind the Logo. An Environmental and Social Assessment of Forest Conservation Schemes.* Moreton-in-Marsh: FERN

Palmer, R., Timmermans, H. and Fay, D. (2002) *From Conflict to Negotiation. Nature-based Development of the South African Wild Coast.* Pretoria: Human Sciences Research Council

Pardo, C. (1994) 'South America'. In J. A. McNeely, J. Harrison and P. Dingwall (eds) *Protecting Nature: Regional Reviews of Protected Areas.* Gland: IUCN

Pathak, N., Bhatt, S., Tasneem, B., Kothari, A. and Borrini-Feyerabend, G. (2004) *Community Conservation Areas. A Bold Frontier for Conservation.* Tehran: TILCEPA, IUCN, CENESTA, CMWG and WAMIP

Pattullo, P. (1996) *Last Resorts: The Cost of Tourism in the Caribbean*. London: Cassell

Pawson, E. (2002) 'The meanings of mountains'. In E. Pawson and T. Brooking (eds) *Environmental Histories of New Zealand*. pp136–150. Melbourne: Oxford University Press

Peacock, C. P. (1987) 'Herd movement on a Maasai Group Ranch in relation to traditional organisation and livestock development'. *Agricultural Administration and Extension* 27: 61–74

Pearce, F. (2005a) 'Big game losers'. *New Scientist* 16 April 2005: 21

Pearce, F. (2005b) 'Laird of Africa'. *New Scientist* 13 August 2005: 48–50

Peck, J. and Tickell, A. (2002) 'Neoliberalizing space'. *Antipode* 34(3): 381–404

Peet, R. and Watts, M. (1996) 'Liberation ecology. Development, sustainability and environment in an age of market triumphalism'. In R. Peet and M. Watts (eds) *Liberation Ecologies. Environment, Development and Social Movements*. London and New York: Routledge

Peluso, N. L. (1993) 'Coercing conservation? The politics of state resource control'. *Global Environmental Change* June: 199–217

Pergams, O. R. W. and Zaradic, P. (2006) 'Is love of nature in the US becoming love of electronic media? 16 year down trend in national park visits explained by watching movies, playing video games, internet use and oil price'. *Journal of Environmental Management* 80: 387–393

Pergams, O. R. W. and Zaradic, P. (2008) 'Evidence for a fundamental and pervasive shift away from nature-based recreation'. *Proceedings of the National Academy of Sciences of the United States of America* 105(7): 2295–2300

Perry, D. (2004) 'Animal rights and environmental wrongs: The case of the Grey Squirrel in northern Italy'. *Essays in Philosophy* 5(2)

Petersen, L. and Sandhovel, A. (2001) 'Forestry policy reform and the role of incentives in Tanzania'. *Forest Policy and Economics* 2(1): 39–55

Philpott, S. M. and Dietsch, T. (2003) 'Coffee and conservation: A global context and the value of farmer involvement'. *Conservation Biology* 17(6): 1844–1846

Pimenta, B. V. S., Haddad, C. F. B., Nascimento, L. B., Cruz, C. A. G. and Pombal, J. P. (2005) 'Comment on "Status and trends of amphibian declines and extinctions worldwide"'. *Science* 309:1999b

Pimm, S. L. (1991) *The Balance of Nature? Ecological Issues in the Conservation of Species and Communities*. Chicago: University of Chicago Press

Pimm, S. L. and Askins, R. A. (1995) 'Forest losses predict bird extinctions in eastern North America'. *Proceedings of the National Academy of Sciences of the United States of America* 92(20): 9343–9347

Pimm, S. L. and Brooks, T. M. (1997) 'The sixth extinction. How large, where, and when?'. In P. H. Raven and T. Williams (eds) *Nature and Human Society. The Quest for a Sustainable World*. Washington DC: National Academy Press

Pimm, S. L. and Raven, P. (2000) 'Extinction by numbers'. *Nature* 403: 843–845

Pimm, S. L., Russell, G. J., Gittleman, J. L. and Brooks, T. M. (1995) 'The future of biodiversity'. *Science* 269: 347–350

228 | NATURE UNBOUND

Poirier, R. and Ostergren, D. (2002) 'Evicting people from nature: Indigenous land rights and national parks in Australia, Russia and the United States'. *Natural Resources Journal* 42: 331–351

Polanyi, K. (2001 (1944)) *The Great Transformation. The Political and Economic Origins of Our Time.* Boston: Beacon Press Books

Porter, M. (1990) *The Competitive Advantage of Nations.* London: Macmillan

Possingham, H. P., Andelman, S. J., Burgman, M. A., Medellin, R. A., Master, L. L. and Keith, D. A. (2002) 'Limits to the use of threatened species lists'. *Trends in Ecology & Evolution* 17(11): 503–507

Potkanski, T. (1997) 'Pastoral economy, property rights and traditional mutual assistance mechanisms among the Ngorongoro and Salei Maasai of Tanzania'. IIED Pastoral Land Tenure Series Monograph 2

Princen, T. and Finger, M. (1994) *Environmental NGOs in World Politics, Linking the Global and the Local.* London: Routledge

Pringle, T. R. (1988) 'The privation of history: Landseer, Victoria and the Highland myth'. In D. Cosgrove and S. Daniels (eds) *The Iconography of Landscape. Essays on the Symbolic Representation, Design and Use of Past Environments.* Cambridge: Cambridge University Press

Proctor, J. D. and Pincetl, S. (1996) 'Nature and the reproduction of endangered space: The spotted owl in the Pacific northwest and southern California'. *Environment and Planning D: Society and Space* 14: 683–708

Ramphal, S. (1993) 'Para nosotros la patria es el planeta tierra'. In J. McNeely (ed) *Parks for Life: Report of the IVth World Congress on National Parks and Protected Areas.* Gland: IUCN

Ramutsindela, M. (2007) *Transfrontier Conservation in Africa at the Confluence of Capital Politics and Nature.* Oxford: Oxford University Press

Rangan, H. (1992) 'Romanticizing the environment: Popular environmental action in Garhwal Himalayas'. In J. Friedman and H. Rangan (eds) *Defense of Livelihoods: Comparative Studies in Environmental Action.* pp155–181. West Hartford, CN: Kumarian

Ranganathan, J., Chan, K. M. A., Karanth, K. U. and Smith, J. L. D. (2008) 'Where can tigers persist in the future? A landscape-scale density-based population model for the Indian subcontinent'. *Biological Conservation* 141: 67–77

Rangarajan, M. (2001) *India's Wildlife History.* Delhi: Permanent Black

Rangarajan, M. and Shahabuddin, G. (2006) 'Displacement and relocation from protected areas: Towards a biological and historical synthesis'. *Conservation and Society* 4(3): 359–378

Ranger, T. (1999) *Voices from the Rocks. Nature, Culture and History in the Matapos Hills of Zimbabwe.* Oxford: James Currey

Rao, M., Rabinowitz, A. and Khaing, S. T. (2002) 'Status review of the protected-area system in Myanmar, with recommendations for conservation planning'. *Conservation Biology* 16(2): 360–368

Rappole, J. H., King, D. I. and Rivera, J. V. H. (2002a) 'Coffee and conservation'. *Conservation Biology* 17(1): 334–336

Rappole, J. H., King, D. I. and Rivera, J. V. H. (2002b) 'Coffee and conservation III: Reply to Philpott and Dietsch'. *Conservation Biology* 17(6): 1847–1849

Redford, K. H. (1990) 'The ecologically noble savage'. *Orion* 9: 25–29

Redford, K. H. (1992) 'The empty forest'. *Bioscience* 42(6): 412–422

Redford, K. H., Coppolillo, P., Sanderson, E. W., Da Fonseca, G. A. B., Dinerstein, E., Groves, C., Mace, G., Maginnis, S., Mittermeier, R. A., Noss, R., Olson, D., Robinson, J. G., Vedder, A. and Wright, M. (2003) 'Mapping the conservation landscape'. *Conservation Biology* 17(1): 116–131

Redford, K. H. and Fearn, E. (eds) (2007) *Protected Areas and Human Displacement: A Conservation Perspective*. New York: Wildlife Conservation Society

Redford, K. H., Robinson, J. G. and Adams, W. M. (2006) 'Parks as shibboleths'. *Conservation Biology* 20(1): 1–2

Redford, K. H. and Sanderson, S. E. (2000) 'Extracting humans from nature'. *Conservation Biology* 14(5): 1362–1364

Redford, K. H. and Stearman, A. M. (1993a) 'Forest-dwelling native Amazonians and the conservation of biodiversity: Interests in common or in collision?'. *Conservation Biology* 7(2): 248–255

Redford, K. H. and Stearman, A. M. (1993b) 'On common ground: Response'. *Conservation Biology* 7(2): 427–428

Reeve, R. (2002) *Policing the International Trade in Endangered Species: The CITES Treaty and Compliance*. London: Royal Institute of International Affairs/Earthscan

Reeve, R. and Ellis, S. (1995) 'An insider's account of the South African security forces' role in the ivory trade'. *Journal of Contemporary African Studies* 13: 222–243

Reid, D. G. (2003) *Tourism, Globalisation and Development: Responsible Tourism Planning*. London: Pluto Press

Reid, H. (2001) 'Contractual national parks and the Makuleke community'. *Human Ecology* 29(2): 135–155

Reid, H. (2006) 'Culture, conservation and co-management: Lessons from Australia and South Africa'. *Policy Matters* 14: 255–268

Reid, H., Fig, D., Magome, H. and Leader-Williams, N. (2004) 'Co-management of contractual national parks in South Africa: Lessons from Australia'. *Conservation and Society* 2(2): 377–409

Reid, H. and Turner, S. (2004) 'The Richtersveld and Makuleke contractual parks in South Africa: Win–win for communities and conservation?'. In C. Fabricius, E. Koch, H. Magome and S. Turner (eds) *Rights, Resources and Rural Development. Community-based Natural Resource Management in Southern Africa*. pp93–111. London: Earthscan

Ribot, J. C. (2002) *Democratic Decentralisation of Natural Resources: Institutionalizing Popular Participation*. New York: World Resources Institute

Ribot, J. C. (2004) *Waiting for Democracy. The Politics of Choice in Natural Resource Decentralisation*. Washington DC: World Resources Institute

Ribot, J. C. (2006) 'Choose democracy: Environmentalists' socio-political responsibility'. *Global Environmental Change – Human and Policy Dimensions* 16(2): 115–119

Ricketts, T. H., Dinerstein, E., Boucher, T., Brooks, T. M., Butchart, S. H. M., Hoffmann, M., Lamoreux, J. F., Morrison, J., Parr, M., Pilgrim, J. D., Rodrigues, A. S. L., Sechrest, W., Wallace, G. E., Berlin, K., Bielby, J., Burgess, N. D., Church, D. R., Cox, N., Knox, D., Loucks, C., Luck, G. W., Master, L. L., Moore, R., Naidoo, R., Ridgely, R., Schatz, G. E., Shire, G., Strand, H., Wettengel, W. and Wikramanayake, E. (2005) 'Pinpointing and preventing imminent extinctions'.

Proceedings of the National Academy of Sciences of the United States of America 102(51): 18497–18501

Robbins, P. (2004) *Political Ecology: A Critical Introduction*. Oxford: Blackwell

Robbins, P. and Luginbuhl, A. (2005) 'The last enclosures: Resisting privatization of wildlife in the western United States'. *Capitalism Nature Socialism* 16(1): 45–61

Roberts, M., Norman, W., Minhinnick, N., Wihongi, D. and Kirkwood, C. (1995) 'Kaitiakitanga: Maori perspectives on conservation'. *Pacific Conservation Biology* 2: 7–20

Rodrigues, A. S. L. (2006) 'Are global conservation efforts successful?'. *Science* 313: 1051–1052

Rodrigues, A. S. L., Andelman, S. J., Bakarr, M. I., Boitani, L., Brooks, T. M., Cowling, R. M., Fishpool, L. D. C., da Fonseca, G. A. B., Gaston, K. J., Hoffmann, M., Long, J. S., Marquet, P. A., Pilgrim, J. D., Pressey, R. L., Schipper, J., Sechrest, W., Stuart, S. N., Underhill, L. G., Waller, R. W., Watts, M. E. J. and Yan, X. (2004) 'Effectiveness of the global protected area network in representing species diversity'. *Nature* 428: 640–643

Rodriguez, J. P., Taber, A. B., Daszak, P., Sukumar, R., Valladares-Padua, C., Padua, S., Aguirre, L. F., Medellin, R. A., Acosta, M., Aguirre, A. A., Bonacic, C., Bordino, P., Bruschini, J., Buchori, D., Gonzalez, S., Mathew, T., Mendez, M., Mugica, L., Pacheco, L. F., Dobson, A. P. and Pearl, M. (2007) 'Globalization of conservation: A view from the south'. *Science* 317: 755–756

Roe, D. (2006) 'Blanket bans: conservation or imperialism? A response to Cooney & Jepson'. *Oryx* 40(1): 27–28

Roe, D., Hutton, J., Elliot, J., Saruchera, M. and Chitepo, K. (2003) 'In pursuit of pro-poor conservation – changing narratives . . . or more?'. *Policy Matters* 12: 87–91

Romero, C. and Andrade, G. I. (2004) 'International conservation organisations and the fate of local tropical forest conservation initiatives'. *Conservation Biology* 18(2): 578–580

Rose, D. B. (1996) *Nourishing Terrains. Australian Aboriginal Views of Landscape and Wilderness*. Canberra: Australian Heritage Commission

Rosenau, J. N. (1990) *Turbulence in World Politics. A Theory of Change and Continuity*. New York: Harvester Wheatsheaf

Rosenweig, M. L. (2003) 'Reconciliation ecology and the future of species diversity'. *Oryx* 37(2): 194–205

Ross, E. (1998) *The Malthus Factor: Population, Politics, and Poverty in Capitalist Development*. London: Zed Books

Runte, A. (1979) *National Parks. The American Experience*. Lincoln: University of Nebraska Press

Saberwal, V., Rangarajan, M. and Kothari, A. (2001) *People, Parks and Wildlife. Towards Coexistence*. Hyderabad: Orient Longman

Salafsky, N., Margoluis, R., Redford, K. H. and Robinson, J. G. (2002) 'Improving the practice of conservation: A conceptual framework and research agenda for conservation science'. *Conservation Biology* 16(6): 1469–1479

Sanders, D. (1980) *Background Information on the World Council of Indigenous Peoples*. Lethbridge, Alberta: Fourth World Documentation Project

Sanderson, E. W., Jaiteh, M., Levy, M. A., Redford, K. H., Wannebo, A. V. and Woolmer, G. (2002) 'The human footprint and the last of the wild'. *Bioscience* 52(10): 891–904

Sanderson, S. (2004) 'Conservation in an era of poverty'. *Yellowstone Science* 12(2): 5–12

Sanderson, S. E. and Redford, K. H. (2003) 'Contested relationships between biodiversity conservation and poverty alleviation'. *Oryx* 37: 1–2

Sandoval, C. (2000) *Methodology of the Oppressed*. Minneapolis, MN: University of Minnesota Press

Sarkar, S. (1999) 'Wilderness preservation and biodiversity conservation: Keeping divergent goals distinct'. *Bioscience* 49(5): 405–412

Sarkar, S., Pressey, R. L., Faith, D. P., Margules, C. R., Fuller, T., Stoms, D. M., Moffett, A., Wilson, K. A., Williams, K. J., Williams, P. H. and Andelman, S. (2006) 'Biodiversity conservation planning tools: Present status and challenges for the future'. *Annual Review of Environment and Resources* 31: 123–159

Sato, J. (2000) 'People in between: Conversion and conservation of forest lands in Thailand'. *Development and Change* 31: 155–177

Sato, J. (2002) 'Karen and the land in between: Public and private enclosure of forests in Thailand'. In D. Chatty and M. Colchester (eds) *Conservation and Mobile Indigenous Peoples. Displacement, Forced Settlement and Sustainable Development.* pp277–295. New York: Berghahn Books

Saunders, A. and Norton, D. A. (2001) 'Ecological restoration at Mainland Islands in New Zealand'. *Biological Conservation* 99(1): 109–119

Schama, S. (1996) *Landscape and Memory*. London: Fontana Press

Scheyvens, R. (1999) 'Ecotourism and the empowerment of local communities'. *Tourism Management* 20: 245–249

Schmidt-Soltau, K. and Brockington, D. (2007) 'Protected areas and resettlement: What scope for voluntary relocation'. *World Development* 35(12): 2182–2202

Scholfield, K. and Brockington, D. (2008) *Non-governmental Organisations and African Wildlife Conservation: A Preliminary Analysis*. Manchester: University of Manchester

Scott, G. A. J. (1989) 'Environmental politics and place: A political geography of the South Westland Native Forests controversy'. Masters, University of Canterbury

Seligmann, P., Supriatna, J., Ampadu-Agyei, O., Roberts, C. S., Hails, C. and McCormick, S. J. (2005) 'A challenge to conservationists: Phase II – Letters'. *World Watch Magazine* Jan/Feb: 5–20

Shanahan, C. L. (2005) '"(No) Mercy" Nary Patrols: A controversial, last-ditch effort to salvage the Central African Republic's Chinko Basin'. *Thomas Jefferson Law Review* 27: 223–254

Sharpley, R. (2006) 'Ecotourism: A consumption perspective'. *Journal of Ecotourism* 5(1, 2): 7–22

Sheridan, M. and Nyamweru, C. (2008) *African Sacred Groves. Ecological Dynamics and Social Change*. Oxford: James Currey

Shi, Hua, Singh, A., Kant, S., Zhu, Z. and Waller, E. (2005) 'Integrating habitat status, human population pressure and protection status into biodiversity conservation priority setting'. *Conservation Biology* 19(4): 1273–1285

Simberloff, D. (1986) 'Are we on the verge of a mass extinction in tropical rain forests?'. In D. K. Elliot (ed) *Dynamics of Extinction*. pp165–180. New York: John Wiley and Sons

Simberloff, D. (1998) 'Small and declining populations'. In W. Sutherland (ed) *Conservation Science and Action*. pp116–134. Oxford: Blackwell

Simon, J. (1981) *The Ultimate Resource*. Princeton, NJ: Princeton University Press

Sivaramakrishnan, K. (1999) *Modern Forests: Statemaking and Environmental Change in Colonial Eastern India*. Oxford: Oxford University Press

Sjoholm, H. and Wily, L. (1995) 'Finding a way forward in natural forest management in Tanzania: The emergence of village forest reserves'. *IRDC Currents* (International Rural Development Centre, Swedish University of Agricultural Sciences) June 1995

Sklair, L. (2001) *The Transnational Capitalist Class*. Oxford: Blackwell

Smith, E. A. and Wishnie, M. (2000) 'Conservation and subsistence in small-scale societies'. *Annual Review of Anthropology* 29: 493–524

Smith, F. D. M., May, R. M., Pellew, R., Johnson, T. H. and Walter, K. S. (1993) 'Estimating extinction rates'. *Nature* 364: 494–496

Smith, M. and Duffy, R. (2003) *The Ethics of Tourism Development*. London: Routledge

Smyth, D. M. (2001) 'Joint management of national parks'. In R. Baker, J. Davies and D. Young (eds) *Working on Country. Contemporary Indigenous Management of Australia's Lands and Coastal Regions*. Oxford: Oxford University Press

Southgate, C. (2006) 'Ecotourism in Kenya: The vulnerability of communities'. *Journal of Ecotourism* 5(1, 2): 80–96

Spence, M. D. (1999) *Dispossessing the Wilderness: Indian Removal and the Making of National Parks*. Oxford: Oxford University Press

Spinage, C. (1998) 'Social change and conservation misrepresentation in Africa'. *Oryx* 32: 265–76

Stattersfield, A. J., Crosby, M. J., Long, A. J. and Wege, D. C. (1998) *Endemic Bird Areas of the World*. Cambridge: Birdlife International

Steadman, D. W. (1995) 'Prehistoric extinctions of Pacific island birds: Biodiversity meets zooarchaeology'. *Science* 267: 1123–1131

Stegeborn, W. (1996) 'Sri Lanka's forests: Conservation of nature versus people'. *Cultural Survival Quarterly* 20(1)

Steinhart, E. I. (2006) *Black Poachers, White Hunters. A Social History of Hunting in Colonial Kenya*. Oxford: James Currey

Stephenson, M. and Chaves, E. (2006) 'The nature conservancy: The press and accountability'. *Nonprofit and Voluntary Sector Quarterly* 35(3): 345–366

Stepp, R. (2005) 'Documenting Garifuna traditional ecological knowledge for park co-management in southern Belize'. Paper presented to the meetings of the Society for Applied Anthropology, Santa Fe, NM

Stepp, R., Servone, S., Castaneda, J., Lasseter, H., Stock, A. and Gichon, Y. (2004) 'Development of a GIS for biocultural diversity'. *Policy Matters* 14: 256–266

Stern, N. (2007) *The Economics of Climate Change*. London: The Cabinet Office – HM Treasury

Stevens, B. (2005) *Disney's Commitment to Conservation*. Lake Buena Vista, FL: Walt Disney World Conservation Initiatives

Stoner, K. E., Vulinec, K., Wright, S. J. and Peres, C. A. (2007) 'Hunting and plant community dynamics in tropical forests: A synthesis and future directions'. *Biotropica* 39(3): 385–392

Stork, N. E. (1997) 'Measuring global biodiversity and its decline'. In M. L. Reaka-Kudla, D. E. Wilson and E. O. Wilson (eds) *Biodiversity II. Understanding and Protecting Our Biological Resources*. pp41–68. Washington DC: Joseph Henry Press

Stuart, S. N., Chanson, J. S., Cox, N. A., Young, B. E., Rodrigues, A. S. L., Fischman, D. L. and Waller, R. T. (2004) 'Status and trends of amphibian declines and extinctions worldwide'. *Science* 306: 1783–1786

Stuart, S. N., Chanson, J. S., Cox, N. A., Young, B. E., Rodrigues, A. S. L., Fischman, D. L. and Waller, R. T. (2005) 'Response to comment on "Status and trends of amphibian declines and extinctions worldwide"'. *Science* 309: 1999c

Sulayem, M., Saleh, M., Dean, F. and Drucker, G. (1994) 'North Africa and the Middle East'. In J. A. McNeely, J. Harrison and P. Dingwall (eds) *Protecting Nature: Regional Reviews of Protected Areas*. Gland: IUCN

Sullivan, S. (2000) 'Gender, ethnographic myths and community-based conservation in a former Namibian "homeland"'. In D. Hodgson (ed) *Rethinking Pastoralism in Africa: Gender, Culture and the Myth of the Patriarchal Pastoralist*. pp142–164. Oxford: James Currey

Sullivan, S. (2003) 'Protest, conflict and litigation. Dissent or libel in resistance to a conservancy in north-west Namibia'. In D. G. Anderson and E. Berglund (eds) *Ethnographies of Conservation. Environmentalism and the Distribution of Privilege*. New York: Berghahn

Sullivan, S. (2006) 'The elephant in the room? Problematising "new" (neoliberal) biodiversity conservation'. *NUPI Forum for Development Studies* 2006(1): 105–135

Sundar, N. (2000) 'Unpacking the "joint" in joint forest management'. *Development and Change* 31: 255–279

Sunseri, T. (2005) '"Something else to burn": Forest squatters, conservationists, and the state in modern Tanzania'. *Journal of Modern African Studies* 43(4): 609–640

Suzman, J. (2002/3) 'Response from James Suzman to Stephen Corry'. *Before Farming* 4(14): 4–10

Swatuk, L. A. (2005) 'From "project" to "context": Community-based natural resource management in Botswana'. *Global Environmental Politics* 5(3): 95–124

Sylvaine, R. (2002) 'Land, water, and truth: San identity and global indigenism'. *American Anthropologist* 104(4): 1074–1085

Taiepa, T., Lyver, P., Horsley, P., Davis, J., Bragg, M. and Moller, H. (1997) 'Co-management of New-Zealand's conservation estate by Maori and Pakeha: A review'. *Environmental Conservation* 24(3): 236–250

Tapia, C. (2005) 'Neoliberalism, security agendas, and parks with people: Implications for community-based conservation'. Paper presented to the meetings of the Society for Applied Anthropology, Santa Fe, NM

Taskforce, Alpine Grazing (2005) *Report of the Investigation into the Future of Cattle Grazing in the Alpine National Park*. Melbourne: Victorian Government. Department of Sustainability and the Environment

Taylor, P. (2005) *Beyond Conservation. A Wildland Strategy*. London: Earthscan

Terborgh, J. (1972) 'Preservation of natural diversity: The problem of extinction prone species'. *Bioscience* 24(12): 715–722

Terborgh, J. (1999) *Requiem for Nature*. Washington DC: Island Press

Tilman, D., May, R. M., Lehman, C. L. and Nowak, M. A. (1994) 'Habitat destruction and the extinction debt'. *Nature* 371: 65–66

Tofa, M. (2007) 'Justice in collaboration? Indigenous peoples and postcolonial conservation management'. Master of Arts, University of Aukland

Toogood, M. (2003) 'Decolonizing Highland conservation'. In W. M. Adams and M. Mulligan (eds) *Decolonizing Nature. Strategies for Conservation in a Post-colonial Era.* London: Earthscan

Topp-Jorgensen, E., Poulsen, M. K., Lund, J. F. and Massao, J. F. (2005) 'Community-based monitoring of natural resource use and forest quality in montane forests and miombo woodlands of Tanzania'. *Biodiversity and Conservation* 14(11): 2653–2677

Townsend, J. G. and Townsend, A. R. (2004) 'Accountability, motivation and practice: NGOs North and South'. *Social and Cultural Geography* 5(2): 271–284

Tsing, A. L. (2004) *Friction: An Ethnography of Global Connection.* Princeton: Princeton University Press

Turner, I. M., Tan, H. T. W., Wee, Y. C., Ibrahim, A. B., Chew, P. T. and Corlett, R. T. (1994) 'A study of plant-species-extinction in Singapore: Lessons for the conservation of tropical biodiversity'. *Conservation Biology* 8(3): 705–712

Turner, T. (1993) 'The role of indigenous peoples in the environmental crisis'. *Perspective in Biology and Medicine* 36(3): 526–545

UN High Commissioner for Human Rights (1989) Convention (no. 169) Concerning Indigenous and Tribal Peoples in Independent Countries. Geneva: Office for the United Nations High Commissioner for Human Rights

Upton, C., Ladle, R., Hulme, D., Jiang, T., Brockington, D. and Adams, W. M. (2008) 'Protected areas, poverty & biodiversity: A national scale analysis'. *Oryx* 42: 19–25

Urry, J. (1990) *The Tourist Gaze: Leisure and Travel in Contemporary Societies.* London: Sage

Urry, J. and Lash, S. (1987) *The End of Organized Capitalism.* Madison, WI: University of Wisconsin Press

Van-Amerom, M. and Büscher, B. (2005) 'Peace parks in southern Africa: Bringers of an African renaissance?'. *Journal of Modern African Studies* 43(2): 159–182

Vanclay, F. (2002) 'Conceptualising social impacts'. *Environmental Impact Assessment Review* 22: 183–211

Vandergeest, P. and Peluso, N. (1995) 'Territorialization and state power in Thailand'. *Theory and Society* 24: 385–426

Vayda, A. P. and Walters, B. B. (1999) 'Against political ecology'. *Human Ecology* 27(1): 167–179

Verschuuren, B., Mallarach, J. M. and Oviedo, G. (2007) 'Sacred sites and protected areas'. Paper produced for the IUCN Categories Summit, Andalusia, Spain, 7–11 May 2007

Villa Boas, O. and Villa Boas, C. (1968) 'Saving Brazil's stone age tribes from extinction'. *National Geographic* 134(3): 424–444

Wade, R. (1988) *Village Republics: Economic Conditions for Collective Action in South India.* Oakland: ICS Press

Waitangi Tribunal (1996) *The Taranaki Report* – Kaupapa Tuatahi. Wellington

Walley, C. J. (2004) *Rough Waters: Nature and Development in an East African Marine Park.* Princeton: Princeton University Press

Walsh, M. (1997) 'Mammals in Mtanga'. Notes on Ha and Bembe ethnomammalogy in a village bordering Gombe Streams National Park, Western Tanzania

Walsh, P. D., Abernethy, K. A., Bermejo, M., Beyersk, R., De Wachter, P., Akou, M. E., Huljbregis, B., Mambounga, D. I., Toham, A. K., Kilbourn, A. M., Lahm, S. A., Latour, S., Maisels, F., Mbina, C., Mihindou, Y., Obiang, S. N., Effa, E. N., Starkey, M. P., Telfer, P., Thibault, M., Tutin, C. E. G., White, L. J. T. and Wilkie, D. S. (2003) 'Catastrophic ape decline in western equatorial Africa'. *Nature* 422: 611–614

Waters, K. (2006) Discussion Paper on Wellbeing and Co-management. Earlwood: Waters Consultancy

Weiner, D. R. (1988) *Models of Nature. Ecology, Conservation, and Cultural Revolution in Soviet Russia*. Bloomington: Indiana University Press

Weiner, D. R. (1999) *A Little Corner of Freedom. Russian Nature Protection from Stalin to Gorbachev*. Berkeley: University of California Press

Wells, M., Brandon, K. and Hannah, L. (1992) *People and Parks: Linking Protected Area Management with Local Communities*. Washington DC: The World Bank

Wells, M., Guggenheim, S., Khan, A., Wardojo, W. and Jepson, P. (1999) *Investing in Biodiversity. A Review of Indonesia's Integrated Conservation and Development Projects*. Washington DC: The World Bank

Wels, H. (2003) *Private Wildlife Conservation in Zimbabwe: Joint Ventures and Reciprocity*. Leiden: Brill Academic Publishers

West, P. (2006) *Conservation is Our Government Now: The Politics of Ecology in Papua New Guinea*. Durham: Duke University Press

West, P. and Brockington, D. (2006) 'Some unexpected consequences of protected areas: An anthropological perspective'. *Conservation Biology* 20(3): 609–616

West, P. and Carrier, J. G. (2004) 'Ecotourism and authenticity. Getting away from it all?'. *Current Anthropology* 45(4): 483–498

West, P., Igoe, J. and Brockington, D. (2006) 'Parks and people: The social impacts of protected areas'. *Annual Review of Anthropology* 35: 251–277

West, P. C. and Brechin, S. R. (1991) *Resident Peoples and National Parks*. Tuscon: University of Arizona Press

Western, D. (1994) 'Ecosystem conservation and rural development: The case of Amboseli'. In D. Western and R. M. Wright (eds) *Natural Connections. Perspectives in Community-based Conservation*. Washington DC: Island Press

Western, D. (2001) 'Taking the broad view of conservation: A response to Adams and Hulme'. *Oryx* 35: 201–203

Western, D. and Wright, R. M. (1994) *Natural Connections: Perspectives in Community-based Conservation*. Washington DC: Island Press

Westing, A. H. (1993) *Transfrontier Reserves for Peace and Nature: A Contribution to Human Security*. Nairobi: UNEP

Wijnstekers, W. (2001) *The Evolution of CITES*, 6th edition. Geneva: CITES Secretariat

Wiles, G. J. W., Bart, J., Beck, R. E. and Aguon, C. F. (2003) 'Impacts of the brown tree snake: Patterns of decline and species persistence in Guam's avifauna'. *Conservation Biology* 17(5): 1350–1360

Wilkie, D. S. and Carpenter, J. F. (1999) 'Bushmeat hunting in the Congo Basin: An assessment of impacts and options for mitigation'. *Biodiversity and Conservation* 8(7): 927–955

Wilkie, D. S., Morelli, G. A., Demmer, J., Starkey, M., Telfer, P. and Steil, M. (2006)) 'Parks and people: Assessing the human welfare effects of establishing protected areas for biodiversity conservation'. *Conservation Biology* 20(1): 247–249

Williams, R. (1973) *The Country and the City*. London: The Hogarth Press

Willis, K. J. and Birks, H. J. (2006) 'What is natural? The need for a long-term perspective in biodiversity conservation'. *Science* 314: 1261–1265

Willis, K. J., Gillson, L. and Brncic, T. M. (2004) 'How "virgin" is virgin rainforest?'. *Science* 304: 402–403

Wilson, A. (1992) *The Culture of Nature: North American Landscapes from Disney to the Exxon Valdez*. Cambridge, MA: Blackwell Publishers

Wilson, G. A. and Memon, P. A. (2005) 'Indigenous forest management in 21st-century New Zealand: Towards a "postproductivist" indigenous forest–farmland interface?'. *Environment and Planning A* 37(8): 1493–1517

Wilson, K. A., McBride, M. F., Bode, M. and Possingham, H. P. (2006) 'Prioritizing global conservation efforts'. *Nature* 440: 337–340

Wilson, K. A., Underwood, E. C., Morrison, S. A., Klausmeyer, K. R., Murdoch, W. W., Reyers, B., Wardell-Johnson, G., Marquet, P. A., Rundel, P. W., McBride, M. F., Pressey, R. L., Bode, M., Hoekstra, J. M., Andelman, S., Looker, M., Rondinini, C., Kareiva, P., Shaw, M. R. and Possingham, H. P. (2007) 'Conserving biodiversity efficiently: What to do, where, and when'. *PLoS Biology* 5(9): 1850–1861

Wily, L. and Haule, O. (1995) 'Good news from Tanzania: Village forest reserves in the making – the story of Duru-Haitemba'. *Forest, Trees and People Newsletter* 29: 28–37

Wily, L. A. (2001) 'Forest Laws. Tanzania gets it right'. *Ecoforum Long Rains* 2001: 35–38.

Wily, L. A. (2002) 'The political economy of community forestry in Africa: Getting the power relations right'. *Forest, Trees and People Newsletter* 46: 4–12

Wily, L. A. and Dewees P. A. (2001) 'From users to custodians: Changing relations between people and the state in forest management in Tanzania'. World Bank Policy Research Paper 2569

Winer, N., Turton, D. and Brockington, D. (2007) 'Conservation principles and humanitarian practice'. *Policy Matters* 15: 232–240

Wolf, E. R. (1982) *Europe and the People Without History*. Berkeley: University of California Press

Wolmer, W. (2003) 'Transboundary conservation: The politics of ecological integrity in the Great Limpopo Transfrontier Park'. *Journal of Southern African Studies* 29(1): 261–278

Wolmer, W. (2007) *From Wilderness Visions to Farm Invasions: Conservation and Development in Zimbabwe's South East Lowveld*. Oxford: James Currey

Woodruff, D. S. (2001) 'Declines of biomes and biotas and the future of evolution'. *Proceedings of the National Academy of Sciences of the United States of America* 98(10): 5471–5476

Wroe, S. and Field, J. (2006) 'A review of the evidence for a human role in the extinction of Australian megafauna and an alternative interpretation'. *Quaternary Science Reviews* 25(21, 22): 2692–2703

Wroe, S. and Field, J. (2007) 'A reply to comment by Brook et al "Would the Australian megafauna have become extinct if humans had never colonized the continent?"'. *Quaternary Science Reviews* 26(3, 4): 565–567

WWF (1997) *Indigenous and Traditional Peoples of the World and Ecoregion Conservation*. Gland: WWF International, Terralingua

WWF and IUCN (1997) *Centres of Plant Diversity*. Gland: WWF, IUCN

Xu, J. and Melick, D. R. (2007) 'Rethinking the effectiveness of public protected areas in southwestern China'. *Conservation Biology* 21(2): 318–328

Young, D. (2004) *Our Islands, Our Selves. A History of Conservation in New Zealand*. Otago: Otago University Press

Young, I. (1990) *Justice and the Politics of Difference*. Princeton, NJ: Princeton University Press

Young, O. R. (1989) 'The politics of international regime formation: Managing natural resources and the environment'. *International Organisation* 43: 349–375

Zaradic, P. and Pergams, O. R. W. (2007) 'Videophilia: Implications for childhood development and conservation'. *The Journal of Development Processes* 2(1): 130–147

Zimmerer, K. S. (2006) 'Cultural ecology at the interface with political ecology: The new geographies of environmental conservation and globalisation'. *Progress in Human Geography* 30(1): 63–78

Index